Arthur Flemming:
Crusader at Large
A Memoir

Arthur Flemming:
Crusader at Large

Bernice Flemming

CARING
PUBLISHING

519 C Street, NE, Stanton Park, Washington, DC 20002-5809

Printed in the
United States of America.

Library of Congress Catalog Card Number 91-076347

ISBN 0-9628363-2-X

To Arthur,

who has made my life an exciting adventure,
and to our children and grandchildren
this book is lovingly dedicated.

Arthur Flemming:
Crusader at Large
A Memoir

CONTENTS

Illustrations follow page 168.

FOREWORD

by Elliot L. Richardson

This is a fascinating account of an extraordinary life. It can be—should be—read on two quite distinct planes, one literal, the other metaphorical. On the first plane is the story of a marriage, a family, and two careers—the subject's and the author's. On the second is a life so completely and unswervingly dedicated to fundamental American values and so uniquely the product of those same values as to make it speak for them.

You think I exaggerate? Let me, then, try to establish my warrant for making this statement. It is based partly on the breadth of my own exposure to the American political scene and partly on long and close association with Arthur Flemming. The latter began in President Eisenhower's second term, when Arthur was secretary of Health, Education, and Welfare, and I was his assistant secretary for legislation. We worked together again in the Nixon administration when I had Arthur's old job at HEW and he was the White House consultant on aging. In more recent years we have been associated through the Citizens' Commission on Civil Rights, which he founded and chairs, and through such shared concerns as health care financing and Social Security, in which he has continued to take leading roles and for which he has occasionally called on my support. We also have a chance from time to time to start off the day by comparing notes on matters of mutual interest at the Hay-Adams, where Arthur has breakfast with one or two friends almost every day when he's in town.

Not that the subject of Bernice Flemming's book is ever in town for long. Its title is perfect: Her husband of fifty-some years *is* a "Crusader at Large," and an extremely effective one. Since 1981, when his forthright criticism of the Reagan administration's foot-dragging on civil rights led to his ouster as chairman of the Civil Rights Commission, he has constantly been on the road, reaching out to audiences beyond the Beltway on behalf of one or another of his causes. In the strong, emphatic style developed in his college debating years, he speaks with simplicity, force, and deep conviction. No one who hears him can mistake the fact that it is the cause, and not himself, that Arthur is promoting.

And that brings me to the first plane of my thesis, the literal one. On that plane the author writes with candor and wry humor toward both her spouse and herself. Bernice Flemming leaves no trace of doubt that Arthur has always been a thoughtful, caring husband and a devoted father. She also tells us that his work has invariably come first—that it has often, in fact, been virtually all-consuming. She makes no bones about the problems thereby created for her, and she treats her sometimes heroic adjustments to them matter-of-factly. She also gives the reader some appealing examples of Arthur's involvement in family events. Her description, indeed, of his annual last-minute Christmas shopping forays with the children is a delightful vignette of "quality time."

Although acknowledging the downside of Arthur's dedication, Bernice never implies that she or the children ever felt inclined to challenge his priorities. On the contrary, the reader gathers that Arthur's family has always accepted and supported his sense of obligation to tackle the large concerns of the society around him. The children seem to have understood that he felt called, as a minister is called, to a life of service. This, surely, can only have been a result of Bernice's teaching as well as his own.

Teaching, in fact, became an important part of Bernice's life. Having at Arthur's urging obtained an MA in American government at American University, she taught a course in the subject there while he was heading the School of Public Affairs. Later, during his college presidencies, she taught at neighboring community colleges, and was not in the least put off by the local ladies who sniffed disapprovingly that "the wife of our president has *never* worked."

We now come to the metaphorical plane. Arthur Flemming is a symbol. His whole life speaks to the conviction that intractable social, economic, and educational problems will yield to the right combination of energy, ingenuity, and good will. He believes that public opinion matters and that leaders in the private and public sectors alike share responsibility for building public consensus. He takes it as given that public office is a public trust. To him, every individual, rich or poor, weak or powerful, is of equal worth.

Arthur Flemming does not shrink from reliance on government but, like others who in the 1950s called ourselves "modern Republicans," embraces Abraham Lincoln's wise precept: "The purpose of government is to do for people what they cannot do at all or do so well for themselves." If Alexis de Tocqueville could meet Arthur Flemming now, he would instantly recognize him as belonging to that unique breed so perceptively described in *Democracy in America.*

Arthur Flemming's religious faith is also deeply ingrained. He does not parade his religion; he works at it. He has taught Sunday school all his life and, when his children were little, took them there by the hand. He has been chairman of the National Council of Churches, the American Council on Education, and the National Conference on Social Welfare. His beliefs emerge in his actions. He has never been drawn to the pursuit of money. Although Bernice cites an episode from his student days when he became totally exasperated with his fraternity brothers, I never saw him angry. Indeed, I shall never forget the occasion when, after receiving a flat turndown by the White House of a proposal he cared deeply about, he put down the phone and said quietly, "Damn." That is the strongest expression I ever heard him use.

But Arthur is no wimp. To the contrary. And yet, although he is a resourceful and tenacious fighter, he readily forgives and forgets personal attacks.

It is to be expected, of course, that the values embodied in the Declaration of Independence and the Constitution of the United States would have a large place in Arthur Flemming's scheme of things. He identifies with the universal aspirations sanctified by the Bill of Rights. He insists that people are entitled to equality before the law. The right to be let alone, the right to be heard, the right to have a voice in shaping policies that directly affect our lives are quite literally fundamental. They are rooted in the human condition. That is why Arthur Flemming sees democracy as the noblest as well as the most practical means to their fulfillment.

These are the facts that give the life recorded by Bernice Flemming its metaphorical dimension. Arthur Flemming's qualities, although extraordinary in the aggregate, have been—and are—shared in varying degrees by countless others who throughout the history of the United States have made our government and voluntary institutions work. The people who manifest these qualities are a living reproach to the cynic. Are they a vanishing breed? The greedy self-seekers, like the poor, will always be with us, but I am confident that they will not prevail. Largeness of mind and spirit will continue to be renewed so long as Arthur Flemming's example is remembered. To that end, his wife has made an enduring and endearing contribution.

Elliot L. Richardson
September 4, 1991

INTRODUCTION

The first week of May, 1984, found Arthur Sherwood Flemming on the campus of the University of California at Santa Cruz. He had been invited to be the Adlai Stevenson Fellow at Stevenson College there. He was seventy-nine years old.

The Adlai Stevenson Fellow is selected each year, and is invited to spend a week on the campus, with a daily schedule of lectures and meetings with students, faculty, and interested townspeople.

I was invited too, and was happily anticipating this break from normal routine. We stayed at the home of the provost of Stevenson College, Doctor David Kaun. The first night David explained the schedule to Arthur, and the following morning, Monday, we had breakfast with the student Host Committee, a carefully selected group of two men and two women students. From then on we were watched over by these students from breakfast until bedtime, so that by the time we left Santa Cruz we felt as if we had acquired four more grandchildren.

About the second day David found out that Arthur was not going to stick to the planned script. He kept adding meetings and speeches as additional requests were made. A couple of people whom Arthur had known previously wanted a share of his time, and Arthur willingly granted each request.

About the third day David had a clear picture of the mode of operation of his Stevenson Fellow, and he didn't know what to make of it. Here was this seventy-nine-year-old man running everybody ragged to keep up with him, and David was clearly worried.

One day David and I were chatting alone at his home, and he expressed his concern to me. Changes and additions in the schedule were something he had not counted on. In exasperation, he said, "He ought to be spanked," while at the same time marveling at the fact that this was apparently very ordinary, daily activity for Arthur.

I told David I was quite accustomed to it since I had been married to Arthur for fifty years. David shook his head in disbelief, and asked, "How have you managed to stay married to this man for fifty years?"

"Easily," I replied. "You see, David, it's just more fun this way."

David's reaction to Arthur's compulsive, round-the-clock, you've-got-to-keep-moving lifestyle is shared by many people who have known Arthur through the years. He has always kept up a pace that wears many younger people out, and being older hasn't resulted in any change.

Just look at his schedule for one week in 1984, which I copied from his calendar:

September 14: Pittsburgh, PA. Hearing for Senior Citizen's Health Care for National Council of Senior Citizens

September 15: Ft. Lauderdale, FL. Hearings for Citizen's Board of Inquiry Into Health in America

September 17: Kansas City, KS. Speech before Kansas City Regional Home Health Association

September 18: Germantown, MD. Chair, Commission on Education and Action for the Interfaith Conference of Metropolitan Washington

September 19: Greensboro, NC. Speech before Statewide Training Conference on Aging

September 20: Speech at breakfast for Congressional Caucus for Women's Issues

12 NOON: Chair, District of Columbia Health Hearing for the National Citizens' Board for Inquiry Into Health in America

2 PM: Press Conference on Capitol Hill on Civil Rights Act of 1984

4 PM: Chair, Advisory Conference of District of Columbia Office of Local Initiatives Support Corporation

7:30 PM: Emmaus Board Meeting

September 21: Board of Directors Meeting of National Council on Aging

September 22: Albany, NY. Speech at Conference of Management Employees of New York State

September 24: Speech at American Health Planning Association and Veterans' Administration on "Future Dimensions: Shifting Societal Obligations"; Executive Meeting of Community Foundation of Greater Washington

September 25: 7:30 AM: Breakfast with Steering Committee of Villers Foundation

Afternoon: Zion, IL. National Symposium of Church and Aging of the Lutheran Church; spoke on "The Role of the Church as an Educator and Advocate in Aging Issues"

Whew! Doesn't this man *ever*, like Ferdinand the Bull, just "sit down and smell the flowers?"

The answer is, "No, he doesn't."

What manner of man is this Arthur Flemming, and why did I think his life one worth writing about? And why have I kept at it right down to the present moment when he is now eighty-six years old?

The reason is simple: he has had a most astonishing career,

see-sawing between high-level appointments in the federal government, three college presidencies, and through the years carrying on all kinds of other responsibilities in wide-ranging fields.

When I first conceived the idea, over thirty years ago, of
writing about Arthur's life, I thought in terms of a story for our
children. But it was also a way of amusing myself. Moreover, I
was at a very difficult period in my life, with a husband carrying
two jobs and commuting between Washington, DC, and Delaware, Ohio.

There were five children to care for, with three of them in the
difficult teen years; a huge house to manage with only occasional
help; and many outside demands because of the children's
activities and Arthur's absentee presidency of Ohio Wesleyan
University. I was often tired, frustrated, bogged down with
problems attending growing children, and lonely. Hence, my
spasmodic writing relieved tension, tedium, and even sometimes
boredom.

Of course, I had no way of knowing when I began this in 1953
what was ahead. No idea that life with Arthur up to that time was
just the "tip of the iceberg."

Now, with a fiftieth wedding anniversary here, and with all
of the children grown and long since dispersed to lead their own
lives, I have plenty of time to get my thoughts and the facts
together. I am pursuing my project with determination to air the
full story of Arthur's unusually productive life.

His first big struggle came when he was seeking a career
direction: law? the ministry? public service? teaching? His
ultimate decision was to go to law school, but he never took a bar
examination, and hence, never practiced law. Opportunities
tended to come to him, entirely unsolicited, from other areas.

His path crossed mine when he was twenty-three years old.
Already he was a college teacher and debate coach, with a
master's degree in international law, and headed for George

Washington University's Night Law School. Even then he was sought after as a speaker in various civic clubs and churches. The big reason for his popularity was that he never said "No," and he never charged an honorarium. He still doesn't.

David Lawrence, founder of the old *United States Daily* (now the *U.S. News and World Report*) persuaded him to leave teaching and try journalism. Arthur agreed, and he spent the ensuing five years doing various reporting assignments for "D.L." Under D.L.'s direction, he also undertook editing a high school current events publication called *Uncle Sam's Diary*.

After law school graduation, The American University offered him his first educational administrative job as director of their brand new School of Public Affairs. Franklin Delano Roosevelt spoke at the launching ceremony for this new venture. Wide public attention followed the development of Arthur's In-Service Training Program for government employees. Within a few years thousands of these young bureaucrats were flocking to the new school, hoping to improve their chances for promotion in the public service.

An opening occurred on the United States Civil Service Commission in the spring of 1939, when the then-Republican member of this bipartisan, three-member commission resigned. Arthur was appointed by President Roosevelt to this vacancy. He was thirty-four years old, the youngest Civil Service commissioner since Theodore Roosevelt, who was appointed at thirty. Later, when Arthur was a member of the Theodore Roosevelt Memorial Association, he and Mrs. Edith Kermit Roosevelt enjoyed reminiscing about Civil Service experiences.

World War II came along soon after Arthur was sworn in as a member of the commission. Arthur was asked by his colleagues to head up the commission's wartime program. He was responsible for the development and implementation of a system of war service appointments designed to get the best qualified persons on the job in the shortest possible time. Later he served as a member of the War Manpower Commission and as chairman of its strategic Labor-Management Policy Committee.

Arthur left the Civil Service Commission in 1948 to take his first job as a college president. His alma mater, Ohio Wesleyan University, asked him to come to Delaware, Ohio, and assume the presidency of that institution.

Just before leaving Washington, seven hundred people came to a testimonial dinner in his honor at the Mayflower Hotel. Frances Perkins, then a member of the Civil Service Commission, was one of the speakers. She crooked her little finger in the air and said, "Arthur, you can handle Ohio Wesleyan with your little finger. I predict you'll be back in Washington."

She was right. In 1950, he began a commuting schedule between Washington and Delaware, holding a full-time job as deputy to Charles Wilson (General Electric "Charlie") at the Office of Defense Mobilization and flying back to Delaware Fridays for almost round-the-clock meetings with Ohio Wesleyan faculty, administrative officers, trustees, and students. Sunday nights he would fly back to Washington. This went on for two years.

President Eisenhower named a new director of the Office of Defense Mobilization, Arthur Flemming, who was to serve as a member of the cabinet and the National Security Council. Arthur served four years in that capacity while on leave from Ohio Wesleyan. The children and I moved back to Washington and lived in rented, furnished houses.

When the four on-leave years from Ohio Wesleyan were over, I was loath to return to life in middle America.

But return we did, and the familiar Delaware way of life was soon our normal routine. Arthur resumed the college administrator's life of meetings, speeches, and trips away from home. Soon the local papers were speculating about what was ahead for

Arthur, even suggesting that he run for governor of Ohio. It was not to be.

Marion Folsom, secretary of Health, Education, and Welfare, asked President Eisenhower to relieve him of his duties in that department for health reasons. Our lives picked up considerable momentum when the president asked Arthur to become Mr. Folsom's replacement. Arthur describes this period of soulsearching and decision making as the most difficult quandary he ever faced.

How could he leave Ohio Wesleyan again after the trustees had been so generous in granting him a four-year leave of absence for his service in the Office of Defense Mobilization? How he struggled with that decision! He actually told President Eisenhower that he felt he could not leave Ohio Wesleyan again, but the president came back and said, "Arthur, think about it some more. Talk again with your friends on the board of trustees. Then talk with me again."

Finally Arthur, still with misgivings, decided to accept the appointment. Arthur was sworn in as secretary of Health, Education, and Welfare on August 1, 1958. This ceremony took place in the president's office and followed Senate confirmation without a dissenting vote.

The curtain fell on the cabinet experience on January 20, 1961. We rode to the Kennedy inauguration in the government limousine assigned to the secretary of HEW, went to a farewell luncheon for the Eisenhowers at the F Street Club, and were driven home in the limousine. We had had our last ride with our wonderful friend and driver, John Wood.

Arthur went through a difficult period deciding what to do next. Several weeks before the end of the Eisenhower administration, Arthur announced at dinner one evening, "How would you like to go to Oregon?"

"Doing what?" I asked.

"The University of Oregon is looking for a new president."

"Fine," said I. "Since we're forced to make a change, let's have a real adventure."

Thus, our see-saw swung in the academic direction again, and we had seven golden years in Oregon. We loved the Pacific Northwest from the moment we arrived there.

A third college presidency was a three-year stint at Macalester College, in St. Paul, Minnesota. Arthur had been promised a free hand in developing a program for disadvantaged students, and he obtained real satisfaction from opening up opportunities for minority students. The fact, however, that some of the support that had been promised for this and other innovations was not forthcoming led to tensions, which, in turn, led to Arthur's resignation in January, 1971.

Arthur left Macalester to become the full-time chairman of the upcoming White House Conference on Aging, scheduled to begin in late November, 1971. Later President Nixon appointed him a consultant to the president on aging, later United States commissioner on aging, and still later, chairman of the United States Commission on Civil Rights.

I have a conviction that Arthur's eight years of public service on the Civil Rights Commission brought him more satisfaction than any of his other appointments, primarily because it gave his crusading instincts full play. The commission's investigations disclosed many areas of discrimination, and Arthur insisted on continuing the watchdog approach. This placed him in positions contrary to those of the Reagan administration, and President Reagan summarily dismissed him in November of 1981, appointing in Arthur's place a more congenial type of Republican, Clarence Pendleton, from California, to be chairman.

Throughout his entire lifetime Arthur was active in his local church, most of the time teaching a Sunday school class, being on the official board, superintendent of the church school, or wherever else he could be useful. From 1948 on he was active in the Federal and then the National Council of Churches, and served a three-year term as president from 1955–1958.

Additional services, voluntary, included the presidency of three other national organizations: The Conference on Social Welfare, the American Council on Education, and the National Council on Aging.

A continuing feature of Arthur's life since his Civil Service Commission days has been his frequent appointment to various special government study commissions. The first of these was his selection by President Truman to be a member of the Commission on the Organization of the Executive Branch of the Government, known as the Hoover Commission, since Herbert Hoover was the chairman. This provided an exceptional opportunity to get to know Mr. Hoover personally, and we were several times his guests at private dinners in his Wardman Park Hotel apartment. Mr. Hoover was a great storyteller, and I suspect he invited us mainly to provide an audience for him to talk to.

In November of 1952, President-elect Eisenhower asked Arthur to serve on a commission to make recommendations for change in the executive branch. His fellow members were Nelson Rockefeller and Milton Eisenhower, and these three met regularly throughout the Eisenhower terms. President Eisenhower also appointed him to the second Hoover Commission.

More recently, President Carter appointed him to serve on the Commission on the Wartime Relocation and Internment of Civilians in World War II. This commission held extensive hearings to determine just what the reasons for this internment were and what kind of treatment these Japanese-Americans (most of them U.S. citizens) had received. The commission's report containing recommendations for redress of the wrongs was accepted by the Congress.

Among the committees he chaired were: a study of the

operation of the Hatch Act and a study of proposals for health insurance for older people. The report of this committee was presented to President Kennedy just one week prior to his assassination.

The single thread running through virtually all of these activities is Arthur's concern for justice for *all* people.

Numerous national awards and honors have come his way, as well as forty-seven honorary doctorate degrees. They are all stashed away in cartons in our storage area.

At eighty-six he is as busy and involved as ever, making speeches and going to meetings all over the country. All of his current activities, however, are carried out on a voluntary basis. "Can't" and "tired" are words he doesn't know how to say.

1

R O O T S

Every time I dust the chess set hanging in its own small cabinet on the wall of our living room, I am reminded of Arthur's grandfather who purchased it many years ago in Hong Kong. Just why he was attracted to it is not known, for he was not a chess player, nor was his son Harry, nor his grandson Arthur.

Perhaps it was simply its beauty that caught his eye. It is truly lovely—the pieces all hand-carved ivory, and all perfect examples of the skill of meticulous craftsmen. Buying it is the sort of thing a lonely sailor, thousands of miles from home, might be expected to do, that is, if he had the price in his pocket.

The chess set came to us when Arthur's father died. It was carefully packed between layers of cotton in an old cigar box. Apparently it had been stowed away for over a hundred years, with no mention of it ever being made so far as we know. For it is at least that long since the young English sailor spied it in the shop window in Hong Kong as he explored the ancient city while the *H.M.S. Snake* was docked there.

Robert William Flemming had signed on the *H.M.S. Snake* when "it got up steam and put to sea" on October 12, 1859, at Spithead, England. His chief duties were that of ward room steward. He was nineteen years old, the son of another Robert Flemming of Chatham, County Kent, England. The senior Robert was a tailor.

The *H.M.S. Snake* was a dispatch boat bound for China commanded by Commander Moresby. It was badly fitted for sea duty, with nothing on the upper decks prepared for sea, and with the lower decks in consequence very, very wet. Much of Robert's time was spent bailing out water, and then bailing out more water.

But he had time for other pursuits, too. When he left home, in addition to his personal effects, he took along two notebooks— a large one and a small one about the size of an autograph book. I have them before me now. The covers are crumbling with age. They both tell a story.

In the large one, in a tiny, spidery script, so tightly written that it is hard to decipher, is the log Robert kept of each day's happenings. There are profuse illustrations of islands he saw, birds he observed, and faces of people—all done in pencil or ink, and all signed with a simple "R.F." in the right-hand corner. The smaller book is full of his drawings, too, but much more elaborate in detail. There are some of birds, horses, buildings, bridges, and people, probably drawn from memory during long, lonely evenings. All are executed with painstaking regard for detail and perspective.

Three years and two months spent on the *H.M.S. Snake* gave Robert his dreamed-of opportunity to see the world. Lisbon, Nanking, Peking, and Hong Kong all became familiar places to him.

Much of the time all hands on the *H.M.S. Snake* were fighting to keep it in shape to continue on the voyage. Bailing out water, and helping with a virtually continuous need for repairs of one kind or another were daily duties for Robert. When it finally reached Portsmouth and was declared "unfit to put to sea again" he felt he was taking leave of a good friend. He said of the years on that ship, "I feel happy to say she really was a happy ship during the whole of that time, and a very remarkable thing is that there was no corporal punishment during the whole of that time."

On leaving, Commander Moresby gave Robert a letter of commendation in which he said, "Robert Flemming, having served as ward room steward under my command, I have much pleasure in stating that I have always observed him to be strictly sober, intelligent, respectful, and an exceedingly well-conducted man."

After six months of doing nothing much but "to enjoy himself," Robert's urge to return to the sea reasserted itself. He learned that the *H.M.S. Salamander* was to be put in commission, so on December 4, 1863, he joined her crew as a ward room steward. This time he was bound for Australia.

In the spring of 1865, he left the *H.M.S. Salamander* at his own request because of his dislike of the first officer, whom he described as "a beast of a man."

He was in Sydney at the time. He got a job as a waiter in the Royal Hotel, and after a couple of years became the hotel's night watchman. He "moonlighted" by doing the marketing for the hotel and supplying it with vegetables.

But he became restless to see "Old England" again, and in August, 1867, bought passage for home on the *Great Britain*. He sailed around Cape Horn and landed in Liverpool in October.

Back home he went into the tea business with his brother, but abandoned it after a couple of months when it proved unprofitable.

Meanwhile he was busy in another area, though taciturn about telling of it. He, who could describe a storm at sea, or an island he saw, devoted a single sentence in his diary to the most important event of that year: "I married on December 3, 1867." At times when Arthur shows this trait of being taciturn, I think back on that sentence in his grandfather's log book.

Robert didn't even include the name of his bride, nor had there been any mention of his interest in girls at all. Other records reveal her to be Elizabeth Margaret O'Brien, also of Chatham.

He spent the next several months in a fruitless search for work, and then one day in April, 1868, he went to Liverpool and bought passage for two for America on the ship *The Isaac Webb*. After forty-two miserable days, Robert and Elizabeth arrived in

3

New York on June 10, 1868.

One day in New York convinced him that he was unlikely to find a job that appealed to him. So they started up the Hudson, and he began his search for work again in Rondout. There he found work as a dock builder for the Delaware and Hudson Company.

The place Robert and Elizabeth chose for their home borders the Rondout Creek and is one of New York's principal cities and first capital, Kingston. Its location on the Hudson River was its chief asset.

Its history dated back to 1610 when a group of Amsterdam merchants established trading posts on Manhattan Island and then sailed up the river to establish trading connections at two other points—one where Kingston later developed, and one which became Albany.

There were fine forests along the river hills, and trade in lumber and shipbuilding became flourishing enterprises. Fur trading was another of the Dutch interests.

When a dispute arose with the English as to who was to control the river, the result was a change from Dutch to English domination. A significant political effect of the change was the resulting territorial solidarity of the English colonies on the American coast, which made possible a united front of revolution many years later.

Names changed, too. New Amsterdam became New York, Beverwyck became Albany, and Rondout became King's Town, later Kingston.

The river itself was given the name of the discoverer, and became known as the Hudson.

From its beginning as a base for traders with the Indians, Kingston became a thriving civic and commercial center.

And so it seemed to Robert to offer a good opportunity to begin a new life there. His job on the docks was hard work, but he was used to that. There was apparently no thought of returning to England, though Robert did not take the final step toward American citizenship until seventeen years later. He was naturalized on February 29, 1884.

Robert and Elizabeth became the parents of four children: Robert, Harry, Thomas, and Anna. All of them lived out their lives in Kingston.

One of these sons, Harry Hardwick Flemming, became a leading lawyer of the New York State Bar and a judge of the Surrogate's Court in Kingston. In 1928 he was a candidate for the New York Supreme Court.

Harry, at the age of nineteen, entered into an interesting agreement with two friends. Couched in strictly legal terminology, and duly signed and sealed, these three identified themselves as The Bachelors' Club. The agreement bound them "not to marry or become engaged until we have, respectively, reached the mature and sensible age of thirty years."

"In witness whereof we have . . . " and then the three signatures follow, with seals attached.

We know that Harry Flemming waited until he was thirty years old before marrying pretty, blue-eyed Harriet Sherwood. These two became the parents of Arthur Sherwood Flemming.

We don't know whether the other two members of The Bachelors' Club waited to marry until they were thirty or not.

Harry, as well as his two brothers and his sister, lived his entire life in Kingston. After graduation from high school he, the second child of the four, went to work for the old Ulster and Delaware Railroad and assumed the responsibility for the support of his family upon his father's death. Robert, the oldest, was married. Harry was a good student in high school, and was valedictorian of his graduating class. On the occasion of his commencement, the principal speaker was the minister of the Wurts Street Baptist Church, the Reverend Henry Sherwood.

Henry Sherwood returned home that night singing the praises of the young graduate whose address he had heard and predicted a successful future for him. But his daughter Harriet did not meet Harry until ten years later.

Harry had dreams of becoming a lawyer. But this was not an easy dream to realize with a mother and brother and sister to support.

A sympathetic employer made it possible for him to read law at night, and his diligence and perseverance enabled him to pursue his goal. In a couple of years he took examinations for placement in a class at the Albany Law School, and he emerged from these tests with senior rank. His employer granted him six months' leave from his job at the Ulster and Delaware so that he could live in Albany and pursue his law studies in the regular way. He managed to graduate from the Albany Law School with only six months' actual work in residence.

His admission to the bar of the State of New York followed, and he returned to Kingston to begin the practice of law. He opened his office in the downtown section of the city instead of the more impressive uptown area. He soon built a prosperous practice and extended his activities into civic and political organizations. He was also a devout and active member of the downtown Trinity Methodist Church.

Harry paid off the mortgage on his mother's house and by this time was receiving help with the family's support from his brother Tom. He also began paying serious court to his friend Reverend Sherwood's daughter Harriet. He was twenty-nine years old when he gave her a diamond ring, but even then Reverend Sherwood had a hard time giving consent to his daughter's leaving home. So Harriet, sensitive to her father's feeling of possessiveness, wore her diamond ring around her neck on a ribbon and slept with it at night for many months before wearing it openly on her left hand.

She was twenty-three, and Harry was thirty, when they were

married in the Wurts Street Baptist Church, with her father performing the ceremony. Over thirty years later, Grampa Sherwood, then ninety, married Arthur's sister Betty and her husband in a ceremony in the same church.

Harry and Harriet settled down in a two-story red brick house at the end of West Chestnut Street. They first rented the house, and then bought it two years later after Arthur was born. The birth of Arthur was the occasion for Harry to present Harriet with a beautiful Chickering grand piano. Six years later Betty was born. Both Arthur and Betty pounded out their music lessons on that Chickering piano. Arthur's musical education lasted only until his first recital, when he suddenly became aware that he was the only boy performing on that occasion. "No more music lessons for me," he announced.

No amount of persuasion on his mother's part changed his decision, and his musical training stopped right there. Perhaps his expertise in winning debates began at that time as well.

Harry and Harriet lived in the West Chestnut Street house for forty-five years, making improvements and additions as the years went by, and also accumulating a large tract on the west side of the house toward the Catskill Mountains. They lived in comfort, but not luxury. I have heard Betty say she never wanted anything she couldn't have as soon as she vocalized her desires in her mother's or father's hearing.

The privations of his early years left their mark on Harry Flemming, and he was never extravagant in his tastes. For example, he never owned a car in his life. He managed to be satisfied with taxicab service for all of his comings and goings, though he could well have afforded a Cadillac and a driver if he had desired one. He always referred to himself as a "working man," and he liked to ride on public conveyances part of the time. Usually he walked to his office, and continued to walk as much as four or five miles a day right up to his death at age eighty-four.

He was not only an ambitious lawyer, he was also a service-driven citizen of Kingston. He was constantly engaged in civic pursuits of one kind or another to make his city a better place to live in. He served as president of the Water Board; president of the Kingston City Hospital and its treasurer for sixteen years; president of the Young Men's Christian Association and chiefly responsible for the building that houses the activities of that organization. A few years ago Arthur was invited back to Kingston to speak at the dedication of a new addition to the YMCA building his father had helped to build fifty years earlier. It was a nostalgic occasion for Arthur. Also, Harry was president of the Board of Education in Kingston for fifteen years, and during this period he handed high school diplomas to both Arthur and Betty.

In addition, during his entire adult life Harry was an active churchman and participant in the political affairs of his local and state Republican organizations. He loved a good political fight and was active in many campaigns. He and Arthur's mother both looked a little askance at their Democrat daughter-in-law and wondered why Arthur couldn't, or wouldn't, influence me to become a proper Republican. Once, in commenting on this, Harry, then eighty, said, "All my life I've always tried to vote for the best man, but he has never happened to be a Democrat."

Harry found his greatest professional satisfaction as a trial lawyer, and he was a formidable opponent to meet in the court-room. He was shorter than Arthur, actually standing only about five feet three inches tall, and he had a quiet, almost gentle, voice most of the time. He went straight to the heart of a case. He never went into the courtroom without thorough and painstaking preparation for the argument of his client's case. And most of the time he won.

He became a judge of the Surrogate's Court in Kingston, and also president of the Rondout Savings Bank. In his last years he would spend the mornings in his law office or in court, and the afternoons at his bank.

Arthur's iron constitution came from both sides of his family—from his father and from his maternal grandfather, his beloved Grampa Sherwood.

Henry Sherwood was born in Upstate New York, but his family moved to Pennsylvania when he was quite young. He early became interested in entering the Baptist ministry and graduated from Crozier Theological Seminary. He served pastorates in New York State, with his longest service being at the Wurts Street Baptist Church in Kingston.

Grampa's first wife lived only a short time, and he then married her sister, Anna Goss. They were the parents of six children: Steward, Arthur (for whom Arthur was named), Lawrence, Clarence, Harriet, and Gertrude. A third marriage when he was about seventy was to an older woman named Cora.

Grampa lived to be ninety-two years old and never really retired from activity in his chosen profession. He served churches in Syracuse, Hudson Falls, and Kingston, and was formally retired at seventy. He then moved to Rhinebeck, New York, across the Hudson River from Kingston, and there he supplied a Lutheran congregation in what was called the Old Stone Church. This church had been inactive for some time. After the Reverend Henry Sherwood arrived in Rhinebeck, he continued to supply the Old Stone Church, and every Sunday morning found him in the pulpit conducting religious services for a congregation made up of people of all faiths.

During the week he spent his time reading and gardening. He raised a variety of beautiful flowers, as well as vegetables and fruits. He provided most of the fresh food for their table, and was particularly proud of his luscious red raspberries.

Often he journeyed across the Hudson River by ferry boat to Kingston to visit his daughter Harriet and her family, sometimes bringing some of his prize raspberries if they were in season. He delighted in playing with his grandson Arthur, and later these two found constant pleasure in exploring the wonders of nature, the fascinating problems of philosophy and religion, and the ever-changing political scene.

Grampa occupied the pulpit of the Old Stone Church in Rhinebeck for over twenty years. One of his neighbors a few miles south on the Hudson was the squire of Hyde Park, Franklin Delano Roosevelt. In Arthur's strongly partisan Republican family, I learned the truth of the Biblical injunction that, "The prophet is not without honor save in his own country." None of these New York relatives of Arthur's thought very highly of Mr. Roosevelt.

Arthur not only loved his Grampa dearly; but he also admired him and looked up to him. The first letter Arthur ever wrote to me was on a visit back to his home in November of 1928. His grandfather lay ill in the hospital in Poughkeepsie, New York, and Arthur had been summoned to see him for, he thought, the last time. At that time Grampa was eighty-four years old. Arthur's deep love and genuine admiration are expressed in a letter, a portion of which follows:

> I'm going home to spend a part of the last days one who is very dear to me is going to spend on earth. His whole life has been one of service to his fellowmen—a service which has been given efficiently and ungrudgingly. There are thousands of people who would rise up and call him blessed if they could. I know of no one who has given more to, or received more from, life. His ministry was never of the "other world" type, but has always been designed to inspire people to give everything they have to this life that they might receive from it all that it holds for them.

Grampa recovered, however, and lived eight years after this letter was written. He even resumed his work in the Old Stone Church. He was ninety-two years old when he died, and he preached his last sermon the Sunday before his death on a

Tuesday.

His father Harry and his grandfather Henry were the really potent influences in Arthur Flemming's life. In fact, I think it entirely accurate to say that Harry Flemming exerted tremendous influence on Arthur as long as he lived. Arthur always regarded his father as his number-one counselor and friend. Sunday afternoon telephone conversations, begun when Arthur first went to Washington after his college graduation, continued as long as his father lived, and for the eight years that remained of his mother's life. If Arthur was away from home on Sunday, as he frequently was, he still managed to put through his weekly call to Kingston. I can remember many times when we were driving to some engagement on Sunday afternoon that Arthur would stop at a drug store or a roadside booth and telephone his mother and father.

On occasions when we were trying to arrive at an important decision, whether it was to buy a house, or to undertake a new job opportunity, the telephone conversations increased in number and time consumed. Arthur used to say that our telephone bill was the best barometer of how things were going in the family. He *never* made an important decision without talking it over with his father. His father didn't make the decisions, nor did he exert undue pressure to follow one course or another. He simply listened attentively and sympathetically and gave Arthur the benefit of his judgments.

He passed on to Arthur his own standard for making decisions involving his personal future, and this standard I have seen Arthur revert to many times. It was *never* the economic yardstick of where he could make the most money; it was always what course would enable him to serve his fellow man best. I have saved letters written to Arthur by his father in which this standard as a basis for making decisions was stressed.

From his father Arthur also inherited a driving, never-let-up

11

kind of energy, plus an equally strong civic conscience. Arthur carried this notion of driving himself physically to the point of absurdity. Once when he was really sick with a bad case of intestinal flu, and I insisted on his going to bed, he insisted even more vehemently that he wasn't going to bed. "The minute you give up and get in bed, you're really sick," he maintained. "I can fight this germ better on my feet."

Admitting illness was a blow to Arthur's pride, and this idea he got from both his mother and father. I remember one time his father was visiting us and obviously was suffering from a bad cold, but when asked, he'd insist he was fine. Arthur's Uncle Tom, who was present, said, "Harry has what anybody else would call a cold."

Arthur inherited both his religious affiliation—Methodist—and his political affiliation—Republican—from his father. His father, however, although ideologically conservative, was a strong supporter of Theodore Roosevelt and Charles Evans Hughes. In fact, when the regular Republican organization refused to support Justice Hughes for the presidency in 1916, he broke with them and ran the Hughes campaign in Ulster and nearby counties. As Arthur moved through life he became one of the country's leading Republican liberals.

2

G R O W I N G U P

Arthur's mother loved to talk about his babyhood and took delight in showing her big, leather-bound album filled with snapshots of Arthur and Betty. He had come bouncing into the world on June 12, 1905—a lusty nine-pound boy, starting out with a strong, healthy body that was to make it possible for him always to do the work of three men, with seldom a sign of fatigue. Arthur Sherwood Flemming was the name decided on—Arthur for a favorite brother of his mother, and Sherwood, of course, being her family name.

His arrival into the family caused great rejoicing, partly because he was the first grandchild on the Sherwood side. His mother described him as strenuous from the moment of his birth. According to her, he could cry louder and be more demanding for his small baby needs than any other baby that ever lived.

He spent his early years developing happily in the warm family atmosphere in and around Kingston. Holidays, with the lot of them assembled together, were Arthur's favorite occasions. When he was six, his sister Betty was born.

It was at this point that Harry Flemming, completely oblivious to the hardships his wife would have to suffer in the process, decided that an addition should be built on the back of the house to provide more room for the needs of the family. For months during the summer while the carpenters were busily sawing and hammering, Arthur's mother had to wash the daily supply of diapers in the wash bowl in the bathroom, in addition to washing all of the dishes and kitchen utensils. Caring for her family was accomplished under great difficulty during the long weeks of adding the additional space to the house. She often spoke of the inconveniences of that period.

As he prospered, Harry acquired considerable additional land on the west side of the house, which guaranteed that the inspiring view of the creek and the mountains would remain as it was for their enjoyment. To the rear of the house was a cemetery, and as a youngster Arthur roamed over this area. His first job, when he was twelve years old, was driving a horse-drawn cart around the cemetery lanes to pick up the accumulation of dead flowers and other rubbish.

His first venture into the outside world alone was down the hill to the Grade School Number Two, the same school attended years earlier by his father and his uncles and aunt. The family went together each Sunday morning down a couple of long hills to the Trinity Methodist Church where Harry Flemming was an active layman and member of the board of trustees. There were no babysitting services provided in that day for parents of young children, so early on Arthur began the practice of attending the morning service sitting between his mother and father. Discipline was stern on these occasions, and he had to sit quietly while the minister exhorted from the pulpit.

In the summers the family took brief vacations up to Prout's Neck in Maine where "Grampa" Sherwood also went for respite from his parish duties.

Another influence in Arthur's early life was Captain Haber, master of a boat that made regular runs up and down the Rondout Creek. Captain Haber frequently took Arthur out on the boat with him, letting him pretend he was steering the craft. Arthur loved these expeditions and regularly announced to his parents and other relatives that he intended to be a captain of a boat during the week and a preacher on Sundays. To this day Arthur simply cannot pass any boat dock without inquiring whether or not rides are available.

High school was a period of special development for Arthur. In his junior year he joined the high-school debating society, and he found this extracurricular activity exactly to his liking and suited to his talents. He began spending afternoons in the library, digging out material to use in developing arguments on both sides of such subjects as disarmament, should the United States join the League of Nations, the open versus the closed shop, and so on. He took many trips around Ulster County, visiting other high schools and tasting the satisfaction of matching wits with his peers.

He was also an avid sports fan and a regular reporter of sports events for his high school paper.

In his senior year, the selection of a college began to occupy his thoughts. He was fairly certain he wanted to go to a liberal arts college, though not at all certain what his vocational objective might be.

During this period he was active in the youth work of his church, and, in fact, thought of the possibility of becoming a minister. He secured a local preacher's license, and on several occasions tested his oratorical skill in the little Methodist church across the Rondout Creek from Kingston.

He also felt a strong pull toward his father's profession of law, and his success as a debater gave him a taste of the thrill a lawyer feels in winning an argument in court. Sometimes he went along to court with his father and listened with fascination as his father argued his cases. He felt a tremendous excitement when his father won his case. He also suffered acutely when he lost.

He decided on Wesleyan University, in Middletown, Connecticut, as the most appealing place to go to college. That institution, he decided, would give him an excellent background in liberal arts and would provide him with the broad general training he would need if he later decided to enter a theological seminary, or if he decided to follow his dad in the legal profession. Life looked good to Arthur when he marched up to get his high-school diploma one hot evening in June, 1922. This bit of parchment paper, tied with ribbons of the school colors, was handed to him by his father.

Dreams were pleasant that night. He had a summer job on *The Kingston Daily Freeman*, and college loomed ahead as an exciting adventure.

The following Monday morning Arthur reported for work at the office of *The Freeman*. The managing editor, Abe Hoffman, took him in hand from the start and gave him the usual assignments cub reporters get, mostly sand lot games, fires, police court cases, and so on. Arthur plunged into his job enthusiastically, often staying after hours to chat with Mr. Hoffman about his work, or about life in general. Mr. Hoffman had been a newspaperman all of his life, and he had a kindly tolerant view of the business of living.

The smell of printer's ink proved to have the same fascination for Arthur that it does for most people who are ever placed in a position to be influenced by it—that is, once exposed, enslavement for life ensues.

As the time for carrying out his college entrance plans drew near, he found himself wishing he could stay right on working for *The Freeman*. He liked Mr. Hoffman and his other associates immensely, and he enjoyed his work, finding it stimulating and challenging. College was an unknown factor.

That was the summer that Warren Harding died, and Calvin Coolidge was sworn in to the office of president of the United States. Even at that age, Arthur took a vital interest in what was going on in the national scene. Without saying anything to Mr. Hoffman or anybody else, he wrote an unsolicited editorial in which he pointed out some of Mr. Coolidge's qualifications to assume the office of president. Mr. Hoffman was duly impressed when Arthur showed him what he had done and decided to run the editorial. A short time later he began to talk to Arthur about staying on at *The Freeman* instead of going to college in the fall. "I can teach you all you need to know about the newspaper business. You don't need to go to college," Mr. Hoffman argued.

One night at the dinner table, only a couple of weeks before he was to leave for Wesleyan, he suddenly blurted out the thought that had been twirling around in his head since Mr. Hoffman had suggested he stay with *The Freeman*.

"Dad, what would you think if I stayed here at home and worked for *The Freeman* for a year, and then started to college in the fall of next year?"

Harry Flemming was taken by complete surprise. He knew Arthur had been troubled about something, but he didn't expect this. He was a good listener, however, and that night he listened to Arthur explain why he wanted to keep on with his job during the coming year. They talked the matter over thoroughly. Their combined decision was that there was little to lose by postponing college entrance for a year, and much to be gained from the newspaper experience. Besides, his parents were in no hurry to have him leave home, and they were quite willing to postpone that break in the family unity that comes with the departure of the first child from home.

It was a happy and profitable year for Arthur. The interesting assortment of characters to be found working on any city newspaper had their counterparts on the staff of *The Freeman*. Arthur enjoyed them all, as well as the variety of assignments Mr. Hoffman gave him to carry out. These two formed an attachment of mutual respect and affection that lasted many years. Every visit home thereafter included a trip down to *The Freeman* building and a conversation with Mr. Hoffman.

During that year Arthur made the acquaintance of a young teacher of mathematics at the high school, a recent graduate of Ohio Wesleyan University, in Delaware, Ohio. Her name was Laura Baily.

17

Each time he talked with Laura, Ohio Wesleyan crept into the conversation. She talked about the professors; the buildings, especially the Gray Chapel in University Hall; the athletic program; the emphasis on debating; the traditions of the college, and Delaware, Ohio, itself. She made the college "come alive" for Arthur. It wasn't long before Arthur was transferring his dreams of college from Middletown, Connecticut, to Delaware, Ohio. Of course, it was a lot farther from home, but Arthur reasoned it wouldn't cost his father any more because Harry Flemming was an attorney for the Ulster and Delaware Railroad. Arthur could therefore ride on passes on the long trips from Kingston to the college.

The name Ohio Wesleyan began to enter the dinner table conversations at the West Chestnut Street home. Arthur's mother and father were aware that another time of decision was at hand.

There was some resistance at first to his going five hundred miles away to college when there were so many really good educational institutions all around the Kingston area. But Arthur was, after all, a convincing debater, and his parents finally consented to his applying for admission to Ohio Wesleyan. He was admitted for the fall term in September, 1923.

3

OHIO WESLEYAN: STUDENT

Arthur's father went with him out to Delaware. Neither of them had visited Delaware before, and both had a great deal of curiosity to see the institution Arthur had selected to pursue his education.

They planned their arrival several days before the college year opened in order to locate suitable living quarters for Arthur. At that time all men students entering Ohio Wesleyan lived in private homes in Delaware.

They found a comfortable room in a house on Washington Street, not far from the Alpha Sigma Phi house which was later to loom large in Arthur's college experience.

With this matter settled, Arthur suggested to his father that they visit the office of the local newspaper, *The Delaware Gazette*. He wanted to see if there was an opening on the staff which he might fill. He was sure he could handle a part-time job along with his college courses. With his year's experience as a cub reporter on *The Freeman* as his opening wedge, he emerged from *The Gazette* office a member of the staff of the paper. His assignment was to cover the college athletic events; his salary, the impressive sum of five dollars a week.

Arthur was well satisfied with the way things were going when he said goodbye to his father a short while later at the railroad station. He was all set to pursue his two loves: newspaper reporting and debating. Another love was just around the corner, but he didn't know that.

Soon after registration he hunted up the debate coach and made known his wish to join the debate club at Ohio Wesleyan.

The coach saw in Arthur a first-class prospect for his debating team. Rivalry was keen among colleges on Ohio Wesleyan's debating schedule.

The head of debate work at that time was Doctor J.T. Marshman, and students who studied debate under his instruction were taught to take this activity very seriously. To begin with, intercollegiate debates at the college were always judged, with a decision as to the winning team at the conclusion. As much emphasis was placed on winning debates as on winning football or basketball games.

Doctor Marshman was a thorough and diligent trainer of young minds, and he insisted on complete preparation before going into any collegiate encounter. He taught his students to explore every possible avenue of argument on whatever proposition was under discussion. Moreover, each debater was trained to handle both the affirmative and negative sides, to support arguments with authoritative source material, and to make a clear and understandable presentation before an audience.

Arthur's strong voice, authoritative poise on the platform, and willingness to spend many hours digging out material for the team to use, soon led the coach to depend on him. During his college years Arthur traveled all over the middle west, the east coast, and to California representing Ohio Wesleyan as a member of the debate team.

He also developed some firm friendships during those years with fellow students in debate. Among these were Lawrence Appley, who later enjoyed a distinguished career in the field of business, and for twenty years was president of the American Management Association, the educational and training arm of American business; Gerald Ensley and Francis Kearns, who later became Methodist bishops; and Hurst and Paul Anderson, brothers who became successful college presidents.

Arthur's new life at Ohio Wesleyan provided him with an

opportunity for development in another area, hitherto unexplored—the field of boy-girl relationships. The freedom of the college campus in this particular respect was in sharp contrast to his sheltered West Chestnut Street existence where activity in the field of dating, if not actually forbidden, was certainly frowned on.

So it is not surprising that he soon found himself completely under the spell of a pretty, blue-eyed student named Claora Bell. Claora was the daughter of a Methodist minister, and this gave them a common background of interest in the church. Both were tasting their first bit of real independence from family domination. Many an hour was spent roaming around Delaware with Claora, and they often paused at the sulphur spring on the campus where legend has it that Rutherford Hayes pressed his suit for the hand of another Ohio Wesleyan co-ed, Lucy Webb.

Arthur transmitted his enthusiasm for debate to Claora, and soon she was knocking at Doctor Marshman's door and asking for an opportunity to prove herself in this field. This shared interest gave them an excuse to spend endless hours together— in the classroom, in the library, and during the weekend respite from classes. It was a serious mutual attraction almost from the beginning, and Claora and Arthur remained sweethearts and "pinmates" after their graduation.

In addition to cultivating the joys of feminine companionship, Arthur's years at Ohio Wesleyan were educational ones as far as learning to live with "the boys" was concerned. He joined the Alpha Sigma Phi fraternity, and at the end of his first year in Delaware he moved from his upstairs room in a private home to the fraternity house a few doors away.

Living with the brothers in Alpha Sig was another new adventure. It was vastly different from his sedate and orderly Kingston home, surrounded by aunts, uncles, and grandparents, and under the expert management of his mother.

21

He had considerable adjusting to do. Instead of his quiet room at home, or in the house down Washington Street in Delaware, he found at the Alpha Sig house that he was constantly surrounded by noisy fraternity brothers, many of whom weren't at all interested in spending long hours over their books. The "brothers" were always coming in when he was studying and interrupting him as he struggled over his arguments for his debate team. The intricacies of French grammar were particularly troublesome for him, and constant interruptions added to his difficulties with irregular verbs.

Many times he was annoyed to the point of exasperation. His fraternity brothers delight in recalling one such occasion. Tired to the point of exhaustion, and harassed by his "brothers" who kept breaking in while he studied, he could stand it no longer.

Getting up from his desk, he stormed out of the room, slammed the door, and shouted at the top of his voice, "Go to hell every damned body!" This story makes the rounds whenever Alpha Sigs of Arthur's vintage get together.

When the time came to declare a major field of study, Arthur had no hesitancy in deciding to concentrate on political science. He quickly came under the influence of Doctor Ben A. Arneson, one of Ohio Wesleyan's best-loved and inspiring professors, and a nationally recognized authority on constitutional law. Doctor Arneson made the study of government come to life in his classroom. He awakened in Arthur an intense interest in public service as a possible career.

Doctor Arneson went far beyond the textbook material in his teaching. He encouraged his students, starting with their college years, to participate actively in the political party of their choice. He urged them to offer their services in whatever menial jobs needed to be done for candidates in political campaigns, whether it was ringing doorbells, distributing campaign literature, doing office filing, or stuffing envelopes. They conducted house-to-house surveys to gather material on political questions—and this was a long time before Messrs. Gallup, Harris, and others began to do this sort of poll-taking on a national scale.

Doctor Arneson's example to his students of active participation in the political process even included running for public office himself. Years later, when Arthur became president of Ohio Wesleyan, an Institute of Practical Politics at the college got considerable impetus from Arthur and was named the Ben Arneson Institute of Practical Politics. And, later still, Arthur delivered the eulogy at the funeral of his beloved professor of political science. A few years after that Arthur was asked to assume the role of father of the bride at the marriage of the Arneson's daughter Esther.

Ohio Wesleyan for many years held a mock political convention in the spring of presidential election years, with the students going through all of the procedures of an actual convention. Candidates for the two major national offices were selected for both political parties. Arthur's heritage of keen interest in Republican party activities handed down from his father made him a natural participant in the mock conventions. He worked himself up to a fever pitch on behalf of his candidates, who were always Republicans, of course, at this stage of his life. As he grew older, he often found himself more in harmony with Democratic party platforms, and even announced publicly his support of Democratic candidates.

Doctor Arneson encouraged him to make political activity a necessary part of his life pattern, no matter what career he eventually chose to follow. In later years, I heard Doctor Arneson on several occasions proclaim Arthur as his number-one exhibit of the value of urging students to become active participants in public affairs.

Arthur also continued his interest in journalism throughout his college years. He joined the staff of the student newspaper,

23

a weekly called *The Transcript*, and served in both writing and editorial capacities.

In addition to training his mind along many avenues, Arthur also had an opportunity to develop qualities of leadership. His willingness always to do a little more than was expected of him led his contemporaries to entrust him with all sorts of elective offices. He was president of his fraternity; president of the Young Men's Christian Association, which was a very influential organization in Arthur's time; and president of his senior class.

His love of the church did not lessen during these years. He joined the William Street Methodist Church in Delaware, where many of Ohio Wesleyan's faculty and students affiliated, and he became active there too. He helped with the youth program and did some pulpit supply work in and around Delaware.

There were lasting friendships with members of the faculty. Some of these dedicated and inspiring teachers, well-trained specialists in their fields, had chosen to spend their productive years on the faculty of Ohio Wesleyan, and they made important contributions to the lives of the constant procession of students that came and went out of their classrooms.

Arthur took time to get to know many of these men and women personally. They became fast friends whom he was to keep in touch with throughout their lives. One of these was Doctor Rollin Walker, a bachelor, a teacher of Bible, and a writer of several well-known books in the field of religion. He lived to be eighty-seven years old, and was still living in Delaware when Arthur returned to Ohio as president in 1948. We were living in Washington when Doctor Walker died. His next of kin immediately notified Arthur and asked him to come to Delaware to conduct the funeral service. This relative stated that she made this request at Doctor Walker's expressed desire. This is the only time Arthur was asked to conduct a funeral service, but those who were present testify that it was a memorable occasion.

Another firm friendship was developed with Doctor John W. Hoffman, who was then president of Ohio Wesleyan. "Prexy" Hoffman was a popular and well-loved college administrator. He did not stand aloof from the students, and they did not stand in awe of him. He was their friend, and they all knew it. Arthur often dropped into his office to talk matters over with him, and they remained good friends until "Prexy" Hoffman's death about twenty-five years later.

In short, Arthur's years at Ohio Wesleyan were years of development of the whole man—not just the mind alone.

And when, in June of 1927, he was handed his bachelor of arts degree, he left Ohio Wesleyan fired with an ideal of service to his God, his government, and his fellow man that was to characterize every activity of his later life.

4

ON TO
WASHINGTON

Arthur was hard to live with that summer of 1927. Indecision is always a most difficult bedfellow, and Arthur was tortured with indecision.

To begin with, he missed his friends of the college years, and the incessant activity of the college campus. He missed his Alpha Sig "brothers" and he missed Claora. Kingston was downright dull by comparison.

The summers between the college years are entirely different from the summer following graduation, when suddenly there is the realization that it is all over. He had lost contact with his Kingston contemporaries. He was lonely, even in the midst of his well-loved family.

Worst of all, he had no really clear-cut objective for the future.

Should he go to law school, spend three years completing the requirements for a bachelor of laws degree, and then go into his father's office and stay in Kingston, as his father had done? This would have pleased his father very much indeed. And Arthur was a devoted son and admirer of his father and the pattern of living he followed.

Or, should he enter a theological seminary and follow the example of his beloved Grampa? He knew something of the satisfactions to be found there too.

Or should he head toward Washington and take a really close look at the field of government, perhaps with the idea of some sort of public service career? Doctor Arneson's teachings and example had left their mark on him, and government service had a distinct appeal.

With all of those possibilities running through his mind, day after day passed with no valid signpost to point the way. And, day after day, he would sit on the porch, feet propped up on the rail, deep in thought as he struggled to come to a decision as to which way to turn next.

He did take two positive steps: he inquired about admission to Harvard Law School and to Union Theological Seminary. He was encouraged to apply to both, so at least he had the satisfaction of knowing he could take either the law or the ministry route.

Then, in his moments of reflection, he toyed with still another idea. While traveling with his college debate team on their spring tour during his senior year, he had become acquainted with The American University, in Washington. He wrote the dean of the College of Liberal Arts, Doctor George B. Woods, who had suggested the possibility of Arthur's joining the teaching staff there as the coach of debate, with perhaps a couple of classes in speech and political science. This plan offered another advantage: he could work toward a master's degree in political science at The American University Graduate School at the same time. Doctor Woods had told Arthur to get in touch with him if this opportunity appealed to him.

Each day his mind made the circuit: law school? theological school? government service? or graduate school and teaching? It was like a treadmill, going round and round, and never getting anywhere. Each course had its appeal, its advantages. Arthur learned that summer that the difficult decisions an individual has to make are not decisions between right and wrong. Such decisions are simple. But rightness or wrongness was not his problem at that time.

His family sat by watching helplessly as he tried to work his way through his difficult decision making process. Much of the time he was moody and ill-tempered. He saw the summer slipping away, week after week, with indecision still his daily companion.

Finally, like a flash of lightning, the road ahead suddenly became clear. He would go to Washington, spend a year coaching debate and teaching at The American University, get a master's degree, and above all, take another year to think through this matter of a life career.

And that's exactly what he did.

What blessed relief surged through him as he stepped aboard that southbound train on that crisp autumn day in September, 1927. True, it was a play for time to examine further the question of whether to train for the law or ministry. But the time certainly would not be wasted, because if Dean Woods still wanted him to coach debate at The American University, he could get the master's degree too. And perhaps after that, the decision as to the ultimate goal would come more easily.

At any rate, as the train sped along carrying him toward the capital city, he felt a great excitement and anticipation.

Doctor Woods welcomed him enthusiastically and outlined a year's program of teaching and coaching debate. Then he took a bus downtown to The American University Graduate School and registered for some courses leading to a master's degree in international law. This meant carrying twelve hours of classroom work in the evenings and writing a master's thesis the second semester—a heavy schedule, indeed, but one he was sure he could handle. Even at twenty-two, there was no such word as "can't" in his vocabulary.

The American University's undergraduate College of Liberal Arts was beginning its third year of operation when Arthur arrived there. It was a miniature Ohio Wesleyan, though with fewer than three hundred students, and Arthur was completely at home there from the moment he arrived. It had been founded by a Methodist bishop named Hurst, and it was on its way to the cultivation of traditions similar to those that had made Ohio

Wesleyan an important institution in the field of higher education.

Arthur found his contacts with the students satisfying and his faculty associations friendly and inspiring. One of his debaters that first year was a sophomore from Harrisburg, Pennsylvania, named Pauline Frederick. Pauline was an exceptionally well-disciplined, intelligent, and hard-working student, and he considered her one of his "star" debaters. She was also a political science major. A couple of years later I shared an apartment with Pauline while she worked for her master's degree in international law. It was during that year that Pauline got her first foothold in the field of journalism by doing a series of short feature stories on diplomatic wives for *The Evening Star*. Her fascinating career later in journalism and as a leading political commentator at the United Nations was a source of pride to both Arthur and me, as were her frequent appearances on "Meet the Press" and the "Today" show.

Arthur's graduate work in political science gave him further insight into the workings of government, and he enjoyed exploring the houses of Congress, the Supreme Court, attending congressional hearings, and getting acquainted with the capital city itself.

And, of course, every Sunday morning he went to Foundry Methodist Church, where he developed a fast friendship with the minister, Doctor Frederic Brown Harris. Later we were married by Doctor Harris, and subsequently he officiated at the baptism of all of our children. Doctor Harris's long service as chaplain of the Senate gave him and Arthur an additional bond during the years that followed.

One of his faculty associates, Doctor Paul Kaufman, planted the idea of Arthur's applying for a traveling scholarship that the Washington branch of the English Speaking Union planned to establish in the summer of 1928. The recipient was to be chosen from candidates who were to take an examination on English

30

history. This examination, together with a personal interview, was the basis on which the selecting committee made its choice. The winner was to spend six weeks traveling in England and being entertained in the homes of high-ranking government officials.

The idea had instant appeal for Arthur. Since his heritage on the Flemming side was English, he had great interest in and curiosity about England and its people.

He provided himself with Guizot's *History of England* and Montgomery's *Leading Facts of English History*, and set to work to prepare himself for a try at the English Speaking Union's traveling scholarship. When Arthur prepared for anything, he was thorough and painstaking, never resorting to short-cuts. When he presented himself before the examining committee, he knew a lot about English history. And he won the scholarship.

He completed the work for the master's degree, too, and was awarded an MA degree in June of 1928. Dean Woods was entirely satisfied with his youngest instructor and invited Arthur to continue for the next year.

Arthur agreed to return. His tentative plan was to enroll in the George Washington University Law School and take a couple of courses in the evening division while teaching at The American University during the day. So the next year's program was pretty well crystallized in his mind when he sailed for England in July.

The only real cloud on the horizon was a letter he had just received from Claora telling him that her interest and affection had shifted to another young man. He was deeply hurt by this news, but by the time he reached Liverpool he had recovered his emotional equilibrium. He was happily anticipating his summer of travel and observation of the English way of life, especially as it pertained to her government.

After reporting to the London office of the English Speaking Union, he started out on his schedule of visits in the homes of government officials. Though he spent all of his time that summer in the homes of people much older than he, he was just as comfortable with them as he always was with his father and grandfather. It was a very stimulating six weeks for one with Arthur's interests.

In an interview in *The Christian Science Monitor* after his return, he spoke of his experience in this way:

> "I was privileged to be taken to the inside.... Everywhere I was impressed with the frankness of both men and women in the discussion both of England and international problems. No one seemed to be a propagandist except for the cause of understanding. And everyone seemed to be anxious to remove the cause of misunderstanding. I suppose that is why they were so willing to talk to me and why they were so friendly. . . ."
>
> When asked if he did not think provision for such exceptional opportunities to make these intimate contacts should be greatly enlarged, Mr. Flemming replied emphatically in the affirmative.
>
> "But what is needed far more," he said, "is systematic study by qualified persons in each country of the various fields of cultural, governmental, humanitarian, and industrial activity. In other words, we need trained observers who can spend enough time really to study these various expressions of the English and American way of life and then, what is just as important, the results of their observations need to be broadcast in popular form to reach the people of each country. All suspicion of propaganda could thus be removed, and this is vital for mutual understanding. Moreover, only in this way can we learn from each other, as at present we appear to be loath to do. To know each other's achievements is to desire to emulate them. And in emulation will come respect and sympathy."

Here, in Arthur's own words, at the age of twenty-three, are mirrored the traits of tolerance and understanding that were his trademarks in all of his future human contacts. Arthur spent a couple of weeks in Kingston before returning to The American University to resume his second year of teaching and coaching debate.

His first day back on the campus included his meeting the new registrar at the university, Bernice Moler.

5

MORE ROOTS

The same week that Arthur sailed for England, I sailed for Europe on another steamship, the *Leviathan*. I returned early in August to begin my new job at The American University, and since it turned out that I was destined to play a major role in Arthur's life, perhaps a bit about my background is appropriate.

I was born in a small crossroads town in West Virginia—Junction—where the Norfolk and Western and Baltimore and Ohio Railroads come together. I was the third child in the family. Two more followed, thus labeling me "the unfortunate middle child."

My father was Harry Hamilton Moler, and he was at that time the station agent in the town. His family were all West Virginians.

I knew little about my father's family until recently, when two nephews undertook a study of our Moler forebears. They uncovered the fact that we were direct descendants of one Ludwig Mohler, who came to America on the ship, *Thistle of Glasgow,* on August 29, 1730.

Ludwig settled in Ephrata, Pennsylvania, and became a prosperous farmer and a devout member of a sect called Dunkers, or Dunkards. He actually gave the land for a church there, known now as Mohler Church of the Brethren. It is still an active church and is located on Mohler Church Road in Ephrata.

Not long ago Arthur, my sister Ruth, our daughter Lib, and her husband George, went with me to Ephrata to look into our Mohler roots. We visited the Mohler Church and attended a service there.

We spent an afternoon wandering around the cemetery adjacent to the church and easily located the grave of Ludwig Mohler. About half of the tombstones in that Mohler Church cemetery bear the name of Mohler, and we felt a strong emotional kinship with all of them. The connection was accentuated by noting the many familiar family names on the tombstones, such as Daniel, George, Oscar, Edna, William, Edwin, and Harry.

We visited the Mohler homestead in Ephrata and spent an hour listening to the present owner tell what she knew of the history of the Mohler family.

We also confirmed the fact that Ludwig's third son, George Adam, migrated to Frederick County, Virginia, and changed the spelling to M-O-L-E-R. My father was a direct descendant of George Adam. This part of Virginia later became Jefferson County, West Virginia.

Another interesting sidelight uncovered in our genealogical pilgrimage is the fact that there is no record of my birth in the Charles Town, West Virginia, court house records. Instead there is a record of a female child named Bessie born to my parents on August 26, 1907. I never heard of a Bessie in my family, and to this day I don't really know whether I am Bessie or Bernice. My birthday has always been celebrated on August 22, and the birth year 1906. This has been the occasion for much mirth in the family, with children and grandchildren sometimes referring to me as "Bessie."

My mother was named Annie. She was the eldest of eight children of a Methodist minister, Henry Slicer Coe, usually called Harry. He was the son of another Methodist minister, William Gwynn Coe, whose family had been Catholic. The Methodist influence came into William's life with a chum of his sister Emily, one Annie M. Armstrong. Dropping in at the Armstrong home on New Year's Eve, 1852, he found the whole family about to depart for a watch night service at the Eutaw

36

Street Methodist Church, Baltimore.

Discipline was strict in the Armstrong household, and Annie knew she must go with the family. She suggested to William that, as he had never seen a "watch meeting," he might like to satisfy his curiosity and go along. He had never been to a Methodist church—his father was a strong Catholic—so when urged to go by a young woman he greatly admired, he went. On entering the church, he entered a new world.

William Gwynn Coe was a very thoughtful young man. His diplomas from St. Mary's College—AB and AM—both read *magna cum laude*. On that evening at the Methodist church, with Annie Armstrong beside him, he listened attentively to everything that was said. The congregational singing, the extempore prayers, and the related experiences of sincere men and women produced an atmosphere that was exhilarating to him. He decided to seek out the minister and discuss the experience with him.

Accordingly, on the morning of January 1, 1852, the young man appeared at the parsonage of the Reverend Henry Slicer (the gentleman that my grandfather was named for). Mr. Slicer spent the entire morning talking with young William Coe about the experience of the previous evening at the watch night service, answering his questions and so on. On his way home, detouring to a book store, William purchased a Bible, a Methodist Discipline, and a hymn book—three books that opened up a new world to him and that he kept all his life.

The next step was his affiliation with the Eutaw Street Methodist Church as a member, and shortly thereafter he received from the quarterly conference a license to preach.

Prior to that fateful New Year's Eve when he went to church with Annie Armstrong, he had been his father's assistant in the County Clerk's Office. Then, on the death of his father at forty-five, he was appointed by the court to fill the unexpired term. He was studying law at this time, and his teacher was an old and honored lawyer whom William admired and loved. When William told the lawyer of his decision to forsake the law in favor of the Methodist ministry, the older man refused to believe what he was hearing. He first tried to laugh it off, then he took to pleading, and finally offered William a bribe.

He said, "I am expecting to retire from practice in a few years. I will give you this guarantee—$5,000 a year for five years—after which I will retire and turn over to you my entire practice, $25,000 a year." The older lawyer looked on William's change of heart as a bit of foolish sentimentalism, from which the younger man would recover.

But William had made up his mind, and when he left the Baltimore Court House, and entered the Baltimore Conference of the Methodist Church, he was regarded by his friends as the outstanding fool of the city. Their verdict about him never changed.

On May 4, 1853, he married Annie Harris Armstrong, daughter of James and Mary Jane Armstrong. My grandfather was the second child of this union. He and one of his brothers, Conway, followed their father into the Methodist ministry. I believe about seven of my Coe relatives have been Methodist ministers.

I'd like to tell this about my grandfather. He is the only man I know who lived to celebrate two separate silver wedding anniversaries. There were eight children from his first marriage to Cornelia Pettigrew, of Lexington, Virginia. My mother was the oldest. There were three children of his second marriage to Frances Wierman. Hence, I have two aunts and one uncle younger than I am, as Frances was just my mother's age when she became the wife of my grandfather.

Another story I like to tell about my grandfather is that as a young teenager he ran away from home with one of his brothers. After two days of wandering, they returned. This episode became material for a beautiful, allegorical sort of poem, which my grandfather wrote years later called, "Two Heroes."

I was in my early twenties when I happened on this poem, and I found it completely delightful. I immediately wrote to my grandfather telling him how much I enjoyed it and urged him to investigate the possibility of having it published. I still have his reply. He thanked me, but made light of the matter. He cautioned me not to think too highly of his abilities as he never managed to get his college degree because he couldn't pass the math exams. His letter has sentences written in Greek—in fact, my grandfather said he was fluent in four languages. But that math kept him from graduating from college.

Still another story comes to me that involves my grandfather. After my father's death, there came into my possession two letters that were written to my father by my grandfather. They were written in his careful script, and they bear the same date— September 24, 1901. Both refer to a letter my father had written him asking for the hand of his daughter Annie (my mother) in marriage. The first letter says that my grandfather gives "reluctant consent, as he had hoped for better things for Annie." The second says that my grandfather "imposes no objection to the marriage." We still are not sure whether this was my grandfather's idea of humor, or if he really was reluctant to give his daughter to my father. At any rate, there was certainly no indication to me or my brothers or sisters of anything but a completely amicable relationship between my father and his father-in-law.

I have happy memories of my mother's Coe relations. The Coes were a prolific family, with a fine feeling of loyalty and kinship among the members. Brothers and sisters enjoyed each other's company. So did the cousins. Whenever my aunts and uncles were assembled there was always a lot of fun and laughter. Coe family reunions were a regular feature of my life, right down to the present time.

I was four years old when my family moved to the suburbs of Washington, DC. My father's new job was with the accounting department of the Southern Railway. The first twelve years of my life were almost a complete blank. I can recall nothing of the move from West Virginia, though a vague recollection of an event that took place soon thereafter does remain.

That was the night my younger sister was born. To get the rest of us out of the way, my aunt herded us together on the front porch where she regaled us with endless stories and recitations of poetry. The one I recall quite vividly was her rendition of "Little Orphan Annie" and its wonderful build-up to: "And the goblins will git you if you don't watch out!"

My first day at school is immortalized chiefly because it was the occasion of my first kiss. This momentous event took place in the cloak room and was tendered by a boy named Bennet King. This, and a mental picture of my teacher, Miss Snyder, are all I can recall of that day.

At the age of twelve my life began to take shape. For some reason that I do not know, my family sent me to visit my aunt and uncle in Roanoke, Virginia, for the entire summer. This particular aunt and uncle had no children of their own, so I basked in the glorious light of being an "only child." I didn't have to share with anyone; I didn't have to take a quick look at the cookie plate to be sure I chose the biggest one; nobody teased me; and nobody fought with me or took my possessions from me, and I loved every blessed moment of it!

It was a special summer in many ways.

I hadn't been in Roanoke more than a day or two when I had playmates to while away the daytime hours with. I am not one single bit athletic and have developed no skills whatever in sports. But that summer I did become an expert in the only game I ever excelled in.

I learned to play a really good game of jacks. I could throw those little metal crosses up in the air and quickly spread the back of my hand to catch all twelve of them. Then, up again they went into the air, and my open palm would catch them as they fell, with rarely a miss. Then, through oneseys, twoseys, threeseys, and so on, until the game was over.

Many years later, when Arthur was president of the University of Oregon, one of the co-eds was telling me of her prowess at the game of jacks. "That was my favorite game, too," I told her. One afternoon the following week, Carolyn, the co-ed, appeared at our front door. She held her hand behind her and said, "Guess what I have." Then she showed me a small rubber ball and a handful of jacks. "How about a game?" she asked.

So we went out on the patio and sat on the floor and had a wonderful time trying to outdo each other. She won, by the way.

The summer in Roanoke was notable in other ways.

One day my pals and I must have gotten bored with jacks because one of them decided to enlighten me on what we used to call euphemistically "the facts of life." I was so impressed with my new knowledge and apparently anxious to share it with my aunt, thinking, I suppose, she would be as interested as I was. The shushing I got for that is something I can still remember.

I grew about three inches that summer, and was also fitted for glasses and changed my hairstyle. The combination caused such a transformation in my appearance that when I returned home some of my friends didn't even recognize me. By then I was a gangling teenager, with an attractive, fun-loving older sister and a beautiful blonde doll of a younger sister. The contrast was a truly painful one for me. I remember coming out of church in front of my father and a friend of his one Sunday morning and hearing the man say: "Brother Harry, I hope you can get rid of that one (meaning get me married off) before that pretty little one comes along." I was devastated.

But the fact of the matter is that I did suffer by comparison to my sisters. In addition to the glasses and rapid growth, I was incredibly awkward, a condition neither of my sisters seemed to have. Besides, I was sensitive, bookish, and inclined to introversion. This period of my life is really painful to remember.

One incident that occurred when I was about fifteen, almost sixteen, is still vivid. It concerns my attachment for a seventeen-year-old boy who paid me attention occasionally by inviting me to go to the movies with him.

I might interpolate here that whenever any boy did notice me it usually only lasted until he met my sister. She was so cute and so much fun to be around that she effortlessly succeeded in attracting all the males of any age in her vicinity.

On this particular night I had a movie date with my young swain. He arrived on time, we went to the movie, and he took me home. What I didn't know was that on the way to our house to get me (everybody walked in those days) he had met my sister on her way to a girl friend's house for a meeting. In their chance sidewalk conversation, he made arrangements to pick her up after he'd taken me home and then to walk her home after that.

Well! I heard them come in together, and believe me, there is absolutely no depression quite equal to a fifteen-year-old's realization that her sister can take her boyfriend away from her, for this is the way I interpreted the situation. I exaggerated the incident all out of proportion to its importance. I felt my life was over—at least it wasn't worth living if I had to live under the same roof with my sister who greedily appropriated my boyfriends, even though she had plenty of her own.

I wouldn't eat. I wouldn't talk. I went moping about the house for days, nursing my hurt. I was the woman scorned, and I played it to the hilt.

Finally I decided to tell my mother and father I just couldn't go on living in the same house with her and implored them to send me away. And they did! They hastily arranged for me to visit an aunt and uncle in West Virginia for a couple of weeks. And off I went, nursing my injured air along.

A transformation took place almost overnight in the small West Virginia town. My uncle sang in the church choir, and he took me along with him to choir practice the night I arrived. There I met the young bachelor minister of the church, and he invited me to play tennis the following day. My tennis playing ability was virtually nonexistent, but I was transported with delight at the opportunity anyway. After two weeks I returned home completely cured and restored to my normal fairly happy self.

My sister died very young. One of the regrets of my life is that she did not survive long enough for me to know her in an adult relationship. I am sure we would have gotten along much better.

Going to college was another step in growing up. My family couldn't afford to send me away to college, so I matriculated at the University of Maryland where I believe the tuition at that time was only $37.50 a semester. I could live at home and commute to the campus daily. I do not recall any feeling that I was deprived of an important part of college life because I couldn't live in the dormitory. Rather, it seemed a normal thing to do to live at home because most of my high-school friends who went to college were also living at home and commuting. Besides, I was so happy and excited about going to college under any terms instead of working full-time at a job, that I felt very fortunate indeed.

After my freshman year, which I completed very successfully from a scholastic point of view, I began to look around for a part-time job at the university to help with my expenses. I had taken a course in typing in high school, and this helped make me "employable."

I was able to get a job in the office of the dean of the College of Liberal Arts. So I began working a few hours each week for which I was paid thirty-five cents an hour. Later my work experience was extended to include regular duties on Saturdays in the registrar's office. This in turn led me to regular employment in that office during the summers, where I learned the routine of admissions, handling of grades and grade reports, typing transcripts, and other details. This experience was later to prove more valuable to me than anything I learned in my classes.

Falling in love was also a prime development of my college years. The young man I fixed my affection on reciprocated fully. Though my love affair took a great deal of time, and my grades suffered as a result, I considered it all immensely worthwhile. I still do. It was good for me to find out that when my sister wasn't around for competition I got along quite nicely with the boys.

This period on the whole is a very happy four years to remember, with a normal share of dates, sorority associations, and my two part-time jobs, which gave me unusual contacts with faculty and administrative officials I would have missed completely had I not worked.

The two people who had the greatest impact on me during these years were sisters—Margaret and Alma Preinkert. Margaret, or Margie, was the secretary to the dean of the College of Liberal Arts and Sciences. I did filing and typing chores under her direction for three years. Alma was the registrar, for whom I worked on Saturdays and during the summers. Both of them were patient, helpful, generous, kind, lovable people, and both possessed a great gift for fun and friendship. Their influence far outweighed that of my peers or my faculty contacts. I developed a great affection and admiration for them both. No greenhorn ever had more sympathetic or helpful guidance than they gave me. In later years, whenever I heard any girl or woman say she'd rather work for a man than a woman, my thoughts reverted to Margie and "Miss Preink," and I was ready to "do battle."

Twenty-five years later I returned to the Maryland campus with Arthur one February evening for an American Association

44

of University Professors' banquet at which he was to speak. My old friend and mentor, "Miss Preink," was there. In a conversation with her after the dinner I asked her to tell me the shortest way back to northwest Washington. "It's too complicated to explain," she said, "but you just follow me and I'll guide you home."

Those were the last words I ever heard my beloved "Miss Preink" speak. The next night, on returning to her home after a late evening of playing bridge with Margie and some friends she drove into the garage, and on the short walk from the garage to her house she was accosted by a man who stabbed her many times. She died minutes later as a result of these wounds. Her murderer was never apprehended.

In my senior year Margie was married, and I was offered the opportunity of replacing her when I graduated. Having a definite offer of a job after graduation took much of the pain out of that occasion. Besides, it enabled me to live at home another year and to save enough money to take a long-dreamed-of trip to Europe. A friend in the registrar's office joined me in these plans, and we selected a tour of France, Italy, and Switzerland. It best suited our interests and our pocketbooks.

About a week before our sailing date one of those completely unexpected and wonderful surprises occurred that was to change my life. A faculty friend told me that the new American University, then just three years old, was looking for a registrar. He thought my student work experience qualified me to apply for the job. So an appointment was set up, and I took the one-and-a-half-hour street car and bus ride from my house to The American University campus to see the dean. At that time The American University was a small, struggling institution, with few patterns or traditions to follow, and with limited financial support, buildings, and equipment. But I emerged from my interview as the new registrar. I was ecstatic over this turn of events. I reasoned that the dean couldn't afford to hire a really well-qualified, experienced registrar, so he took a chance on me. My salary was $1,650 a year, with room and board in the women's dormitory as part of my compensation. I was to begin the middle of August after my return from Europe.

It was time for a new adventure, and The American University offered it. I had no way of knowing then just how great an adventure it would lead me into.

The first of July my friend Lisette and I sailed for Cherbourg on the *Leviathan*. My college sweetheart, albeit a somewhat off again, on again, one, came to New York to see me off. That was the next to the last time I saw him.

Our trip to Europe was a complete, unmitigated success. It was my first venture out on my own, and what an eye-opening, soul-satisfying experience it turned out to be. We had people of all ages on our tour, with enough young people to make it a socially exciting group, which provided fun for the evening hours when there were no tours planned. It was an immensely stimulating experience for a girl whose life experience had consisted of a circumscribed area around Washington and its suburbs, with occasional trips into Virginia and West Virginia, and one trip to Chicago.

And then, when I got home, I had my new job to look forward to, and to provide interest and challenge.

6

L I G H T N I N G
S T R I K E S

I reported for my new job at The American University around the middle of August. On a small college campus everything seems to come to a dead standstill ten minutes after commencement is over and remains in its quiescent state until college reopens in September. Only a skeleton crew of administrative officials and secretaries remain to keep the wheels in motion.

Even the dean was on vacation, so my initial weeks at the College of Liberal Arts campus were spent entirely on my own getting acquainted with the office, handling the mail, and conferring with an occasional new student, often accompanied by parents. On such occasions, I would simply close the office door and take the group on a sightseeing tour of the campus, show them the dormitories, and try my level best to create a desire to enroll. In those days there was not so much pressure for college admission. Just about any high-school graduate with fifteen units of academic credit and the price of tuition could gain admission.

Each day brought some unexpected situation to deal with, and I quickly developed the ability to make whatever decision was necessary at the moment. There was no one to advise or help me. I was the registrar's office.

The secretary to the chancellor—now called the president—took me under her wing at the lunch hour and helped me a great deal in getting oriented. She told me about the various faculty personalities and the idiosyncrasies of the other administrative officers she thought I should know about. It was a short, but intensive, period of indoctrination. And within a couple of weeks I felt quite able to tackle the opening registration rush, which was really the crucial part of the entire college program.

My new friend's name was Phyllis. She had been the chancellor's secretary since the College of Liberal Arts had opened three years earlier. Now it had three hundred students. She was a veritable fountain of information.

One name kept recurring in our lunch hour conversations—Arthur Flemming. She described Arthur as being just about the only unattached male faculty member at the time. She told me a lot about him—about his appearance, how smart he was, and especially about his having won the previous spring the competitive traveling scholarship to England. Phyllis's big brown eyes grew wide with excitement in describing this to me. She herself professed no romantic interest in him, as she had plenty of young men friends off campus to provide her a busy social life. But she obviously intended to whet my interest, and she succeeded admirably.

One morning toward the middle of September the professor of English, Doctor Paul Kaufman, came into my office and tossed a letter on my desk. "Put this in Flemming's file," he said.

Doctor Kaufman had been instrumental in getting Arthur to apply for the English Speaking Union scholarship. What he threw in my direction was a copy of a letter written by the secretary of the English Speaking Union in London to the secretary of the Washington branch. Before filing it, I read it, and was particularly caught by one paragraph. It read:

> It is really a little difficult not to be too enthusiastic about him. He is, I should say, the finest young American who has ever come to us. His intelligence made him a most interesting guest, and his modesty, simplicity, and sense of fun endeared him to everybody.

Small wonder, then, that even before I met Arthur, I had developed considerable curiosity about him.

It was a couple of days later, on a Saturday morning, just

before closing time, that the young man I had been hearing about walked into the office, laid his gray fedora hat on the counter, and announced, "My name's Flemming."

"Oh," I replied inanely, "I've heard a lot about you."

I took him all in at a glance. Slightly over six feet tall, slender, with black hair brushed tightly down and parted on the left side, and dressed in a dark blue suit. He was then, as now, strictly a blue suit, white shirt, black shoes sort of person. Of late years, he has taken to wearing blue shirts sometimes; otherwise the picture is the same. Often he has chided me for not noticing that he had a new suit on, but from my point of view, it is difficult to make this observation when the new suit nearly always looks exactly like the old one!

His brown eyes brightened immediately when I said, "I've heard a lot about you." There was no one else in the office at the time, so I went on to tell him that I'd heard of his successful year as the debate coach at the college and of his winning the traveling scholarship to England. I also mentioned the letter Doctor Kaufman had brought in to me earlier.

My first really distinct impression, and one that is written in indelible ink on my memory, was his reply to all this. He smiled his detached, tolerant sort of smile, almost as if I had been talking about somebody else, and said, "But one cannot live on the honors of the past. We must go on to the next job."

Apparently our conversation was not displeasing to him, however, because before he left the office he had asked me to go out with him on the weekend. I declined the first invitation as it was to be my last weekend at home before moving into the dormitory, and I really needed the time to get clothes mended and cleaned and to pack. Moreover, my family was at that time in the throes of moving to Atlanta, where my father had been transferred, and the confusion and disorder were not something I wished him to be a part of.

I accepted his next invitation, and in a very short time had completely cut myself off from other male companionship. He asked me to marry him about ten days after our first date.

Getting to know him was an absorbing project. He was different!

To begin with, he was underfoot at all hours of the day, and many evenings, too. I saw him the first thing in the morning when he stopped in the office on his way to his first class, then we'd have lunch in the college cafeteria and maybe take a walk if there was time.

Later in the afternoon he would drop in again before I left the office, and often he would suggest that we have dinner together. We soon fell into the habit of eating dinner together nearly every evening. It was difficult to find time to wash my underwear, shampoo my hair, or any of those other little chores girls have to take care of.

One thing I became aware of quite early was his devotion to his family and to his home in Kingston, New York. He would talk about them all—his mother, his father, his younger sister Betty, his bachelor Uncle Tom and spinster Aunt Anna, who lived across the street and a few houses down from his own home; his grandfather Sherwood and his wife Cora and his unmarried daughter Aunt Gertrude, who lived across the Hudson river in Rhinebeck, New York. These people all became very real to me long before I laid eyes on any of them.

One evening Arthur got out a sheet of paper and began making marks on it to describe the way his home looked—from the front door on through the hall, the library, the dining room, and the kitchen. He told me where the grand piano stood, where the book cases were, the colors of the carpet and draperies, the stairway, and on upstairs. It was perfectly obvious that this young man loved his home and everybody connected with it, and he wanted to share these people and their surroundings with me.

Another bit of information he made quite clear to me at the very beginning of our acquaintance was that his father expected him to complete his law education (he was enrolled that fall in two evening classes at the George Washington University Law School) and to "get established" before he was to entertain any thought of taking on a wife. It was clear to me that whatever his father said was *law*. This was of course years before I found out about his father's membership in the Bachelor's Club and his own vow not to marry until he was thirty.

Always on Sunday afternoon Arthur would telephone his family. Often I was with him when he called. He would talk to each of them—first Betty, who usually answered the phone, and he would ask her what was going on in the high school (she was a senior); then his mother, and he would ask her about the weather, how she felt, and how the minister's sermon was on that particular morning; and finally, his father. It was not hard to tell that when it was Dad's turn, these two got to the real meat of things. They would explore current political developments—there was a presidential campaign that fall between Herbert Hoover and Alfred Smith—his law school courses, the developments at the college, and the law cases his father was involved in.

Of even greater significance to Arthur that fall was an election being held in New York where his father was a candidate for the New York Supreme Court. So, that first fall of my acquaintance with Arthur, checking up on his father's personal political activities and finding out the details of how the campaign was going was the business of highest priority in those Sunday afternoon conversations.

Harry Flemming had been nominated by the Republican Judicial Convention of the Third Judicial District in a speech made by The Honorable G. D. B. Hasbrouck, a former justice of the Supreme Court of New York. He cited Harry's record as an ex-president of the bar of the Ulster County and treasurer of the

Federation of Bar Associations of the Third Judicial district. He said that "Harry Flemming prepares and argues with rare success in the Appellate Division and the Court of Appeals. Ulster County has no better lawyer. . . . He is a man of high character. . . . His candidature means the satisfaction of every reasonable expectation of a people deserving the services of an excellently qualified man for a judge."

When the election day came around, however, Arthur's father was defeated by a narrow margin and this was truly a major disappointment for Arthur. It is the only occasion I can remember when he actually cried.

One further observation I made as a result of listening to those Sunday afternoon telephone conversations was that when he was questioned by his parents about the state of his own health, Arthur always said, "I'm just fine," even if he was sick with a cold, was running a fever, had a violent headache (he was a migraine sufferer), or anything else.

If I had any of these, or other ailments, I didn't see any reason for keeping it a secret from my family. If questioned, I'd say I felt terrible. But not Arthur. Even to this day, he seems incapable of admitting that he feels anything but perfectly well—as if it were somehow too great a blow to his pride to admit otherwise. But I soon learned, and joined in the conspiracy, that in talking to Arthur's parents, one's health is always excellent, even though one really feels just awful. That way nobody worries.

Truly, life was never the same for me after that September morning when Arthur laid his hat on the counter in my office at The American University. I have no hesitancy whatsoever in saying that, from the very beginning he was the dominating partner in our association. His influence was on me in many ways.

Right off, I became aware that he was an extremely ambitious young man. It was my first close brush with this sort of drive. My father was a quiet, gentle person, the kind who lived a completely routine existence, and who came home with dependable regularity at five o'clock each evening. Then he stayed home instead of running around to meetings, making speeches, or whatever. The only occasions he ventured out at night were to attend church affairs. He was a member of the board of trustees of our church, and he was the church treasurer for twenty-five years. Helping him count and record the church collections was one of my regular Monday evening chores. Neither did my two brothers appear to be afflicted with great ambitions to change the world.

So, when lightning struck me in the form of Arthur Flemming, his driving ambition was about the first quality I noticed. He was not interested in was making a lot of money, but he was fired with a desire to make the world a better place to live in. To him, work was the most important thing in life; work to accomplish a goal, to be sure, but work just the same. Anything bearing the label pleasure or recreation always had to be fitted in after the work was completed, and this meant that very little time was set aside for relaxation of any kind. Now, at eighty-six, this is still true.

Though Arthur wanted us to spend as much time as we possibly could together, such time had to be found along with work. Teaching and coaching debate teams took all day, and law courses took the evenings. Then, study to get ready for the next day took over. I have never known a time when a regular nine-to-five daily work routine was a part of Arthur's plan of existence.

Even on weekends many hours were spent working. I soon found out that, though I never questioned his deep affection for me, I always came after his work—never before, or alongside it.

This is a considerable adjustment for any woman to make, particularly one as young as I was at the time. But since I was in love, I settled for second place. This is not to say I was satisfied to be in second place; it is simply that that was the way it had to be. The alternative was to cut off the relationship at the start. Fifty years of marriage to Arthur have not changed my second-place status one bit.

This meant that during the years Arthur was in law school, I had to be content with brief times of relaxation in between the demands of teaching and studying. On rare occasions we went to the theater, but not often. The result is that over the past fifty years I have become pretty expert at amusing myself. I am almost never lonely—that is if I have a good book handy and some needlework. I also need a deck of cards for solitaire when my eyes are tired. And after the demands of child care were over, I built up a thriving social life with my lady friends for luncheon, antique shopping, visiting museums, or going to an occasional movie, theatrical performance, or the opera.

There was another aspect of Arthur's attitude toward me that I had been unaccustomed to. He wanted me around as much as possible. He might be outlining his class lectures, briefing his cases, grading papers, preparing a speech, judging debate—no matter what—he wanted me around or nearby. He liked me to be within calling distance. In those early days, he did not like the idea of my running off to sorority meetings, playing bridge or other such diversions. It was not that he was jealous of my former associations. It was simply that he was happier if I was in the same vicinity where he was. If, for instance, I was in my room at the dormitory, and if he was studying in his office, he could call me when he was through, and we'd go for a walk, maybe up to the drugstore for a milkshake, or something innocuous like that. Anyway, again, I was in love, and I usually stayed within calling distance.

My habits along this line were the subject of a long tirade delivered by the mother of one of my friends. She telephoned me one day and took me severely to task for spending so much time with Arthur, and so little time with my old friends. It is probably superfluous for me to add that I kept right on staying around with Arthur whenever I could.

Besides, Arthur was prodding me to continue my own education by enrolling for some graduate courses at night. As my undergraduate major had been English, the natural area for me to explore was a master's degree in that department.

The professor at George Washington University who helped me make out my program showed considerable surprise when I told him I had not as an undergraduate completed courses in Anglo Saxon and Neo-Classicism. I did not confess to him that I had successfully avoided these two reputedly difficult courses by the simple expedient of changing from the College of Arts and Sciences to the College of Education where these two courses were not required for a major in English. So this evasion caught up with me when I attempted to enroll for a master's in English at GW. The professor went blithely ahead and made out a schedule for me including these two deadly courses, and I was anything but an enthusiastic prospective graduate student when I left his office.

I met Arthur later for dinner, and I explained to him my disappointment over being required my first semester in graduate school to struggle with Anglo Saxon and Neo-Classicism. As usual he had an alternative suggestion.

"Why don't you get a master's degree in political science instead of English?"

This was a brand new idea to me. "But I can't," I protested. "I've never had a course in political science in my whole life, and I'm sure no graduate school would let me enroll for a master's in it."

"Try it anyway," Arthur advised. "Tomorrow evening go down to The American University and see if they will let you do it."

The only thing to commend this fantastic idea was that it was the field of absorbing interest to him, so it appealed to me only as a means of being better able to understand him. Otherwise, it was completely senseless.

Anyway, I did as he suggested. (I've been doing this ever since; I get along better that way.) It worked out as he predicted. I did enroll as a master's candidate in political science, and in due course I did complete the requirements for the MA degree, including writing a thesis.

The fall following the completion of my graduate studies, the instructor in the course in American Government at The American University College of Liberal Arts left unexpectedly, and Arthur urged me to ask Dean Woods if I could teach it, along with my duties as registrar. He was sure Dean Woods could arrange the schedule so that the course could meet at 8 AM, and hence my office duties wouldn't suffer. He paid no attention to my protestations that I was not qualified to teach political science. According to him, all you had to do was say "I can," and get to work. He was trying his level best to eliminate that word "can't" from my vocabulary too.

He breathed confidence in me so successfully that I actually did ask Dean Woods if I could teach the course, and the dean agreed to let me try it. Apparently I handled it to his satisfaction because I taught courses in both American Government and Constitutional Law for three years thereafter.

Probably this background of study and teaching in political science has served me better than any other part of my educational experience. So much of our life together has been spent in Washington, with Arthur serving in various government capacities. My training in political science has contributed greatly to my understanding of his public service responsibilities.

Another area in which Arthur's influence on me was particularly dramatic is in the area of human relationships. Both my mother and father came from Southern families. I had never had any important friendships that had provided me with an opportu-

56

nity to question the set of inherited attitudes about, for example, race relations and politics.

Then Arthur walked into my life, and the "Yankee" influence made itself felt. But, if Arthur was a new experience for me, I think it is safe to say I was also a new experience for him. He'd never known any Southerners before.

The first departure from family pattern was that I moved my church membership from a Southern Methodist church to Foundry Methodist church, a so-called Northern congregation. This was, of course, some years before the two branches of the Methodist church, separated since Civil War days, united. My grandfather was a minister in the Southern church, and I had in addition to my immediate family, numerous aunts, uncles, and cousins who were members of the Southern church. Nary a one of them, to my knowledge, had ever affiliated with a Northern church. But I did. It was hard for my family to understand.

From the first, Arthur found my attitudes toward Black people somewhat puzzling. It was not that I was the least bit antagonistic toward them; rather it was simply that I had grown up in a framework of living that did not include them. I had never been in a school where there were Black students. I didn't have a speaking acquaintance with a single Black person, and neither had I ever questioned the tenuous basis on which my inherited attitudes rested.

The status quo of that day, that is, that state laws requiring segregation of the races were entirely constitutional as long as equal accommodations were provided for members of the Black race, suited me just fine. In fact, I wrote my master's thesis on Supreme Court decisions upholding state laws requiring segregation of the races. I would deny our Black citizens nothing; but then, at the same time, I wanted to continue living in my little White world surrounded by White people—in schools, theaters, restaurants, or wherever I happened to be.

Growing up, as I had, in suburban Washington, my entire life experience had been in segregated situations. So when Arthur walked into my life in 1928, it was the very first time I even seriously thought about or questioned the status quo as it pertained to segregation. Arthur certainly never overtly set out on a campaign to change my habits of thinking along racial lines, but he did make a point of questioning me. Since he had never had any experience with Southern people, he was curious.

I remember in particular his admiration for Doctor Mordecai Johnson, who was then president of Howard University in Washington. He even suggested that for me to meet Doctor Johnson would give me an opportunity to broaden my perspective about Black persons.

I have a special recollection about Doctor Johnson I'd like to add here. Many years later, before we left the Department of Health, Education, and Welfare for the University of Oregon, we entertained in our home the various division heads at dinner. As secretary of HEW, Arthur was responsible for presenting Howard's budget to the president and Congress. We several times went over to Howard for various activities. Doctor Johnson was among those invited, and I was just as sorry as Arthur that he was unable to attend because of a conflict.

I did, however, have the privilege of being seated next to Doctor Johnson at a dinner in his honor. The occasion was his retirement, after thirty-five years as president of Howard. The dinner was held in the ballroom of the old Sheraton Park Hotel. The huge room, seating well over a thousand people, was full. All of Washington's prominent citizens, including the mayor, the editors of the daily newspapers, and leading educators and ministers. Arthur was among those making testimonial speeches.

I have seldom had a more entertaining or delightful evening than that particular occasion as Doctor Johnson's seatmate. The incident I remember most vividly was when he suddenly turned to me and said, "Mrs. Flemming, do you know what the most exciting moment of my life has been?"

I replied, "I've no idea what it was. Do tell me."

And then, to my complete surprise, Doctor Johnson said, "It was the first time a White man ever addressed me as *Mr. Johnson.*"

I shall never forget the shame I felt at that moment—shame for all of us White people.

Arthur's influence on my thinking in this area was not by insistence or persuasion. It was simply that by going along with him, and watching how he handled all of his human relationships, that is, by treating each individual on his own merits, I found it became quite painless for me to follow suit. I was to have many such opportunities for growth in my thinking and in my actions in the years that followed. And I can add, unequivocally, that Arthur is the only person I've ever known who could look at a person of any color, and see only a human being. He didn't *see* the color.

In the field of politics, too, Arthur pursued a course of peaceful coexistence as far as I am concerned. He was a Republican, and his father was a politically active citizen all of his life. Arthur followed his pattern, though as the years went on he was definitely aligned with the liberal wing of the party. His father was much more conservative. Both sides of his family were Republicans, and mine entirely Democrats. I think he had never been close to a Democrat before.

But Arthur accepted the fact that I was a Democrat, though I am sure his family never understood why he permitted such a situation to continue without taking steps to correct it. His view of this peculiarity of mine was tolerant, and he never tried to influence me to change. Neither did he ever question me as to how I voted. We discussed the candidates and the issues, but when the curtain went down in the voting booth, our votes were secret!

In other subtle ways his influence was constantly felt. I recall one occasion early in our acquaintance when I was being extremely critical of the actions of one of my contemporaries. Arthur listened until I had finished my tirade, and then he said simply, "Judge not." That was all, but it was certainly effective.

And, then, in the bank crisis of 1933, with banks all over the country closed, I had a perpetually worried look on my face for days over the loss of the amount I had in the bank at that time. But not Arthur. Money has simply never been important to him (except that he really likes the comforts and services it can buy!), and he began then to try to change my perspective regarding money. He tried, but I still worry about money.

After we were married I was always the one to worry whenever things didn't go right. One time I was expressing concern about a situation involving one of the children. "Aren't you worried about . . .?" I asked him. "No, indeed. Why should I worry? You do such a good job of it."

It all adds up to the fact that his influence on me was tremendous, whether or not he intended it to be.

Two years later when Arthur's mother invited me to spend Christmas with the Flemmings in Kingston, I journeyed up on the train with Arthur and had the opportunity to experience how the holiday was celebrated at his home. We started out for Union Station in a cab, but Arthur directed the driver to stop at Brentano's book store on F Street so he could jump out and get some books for his father's gift. That was the way he always shopped—on the run. He never questioned prices; he never shopped around to see if he could get an article cheaper somewhere else; and he never bought a gift until the actual moment the occasion rolled around. But neither did he settle for anything less than what he felt was sure to please the recipient.

I had previously met his mother and father and Betty, who was by that time a student at The American University. But this was my first opportunity to become acquainted with the other New York relatives who were so important to Arthur.

Perhaps I should interpolate here that my own family background, being strictly Southern, practiced a much more relaxed approach to living than was the rule in the Flemming family. The mixture of discipline, restraint, and formality that marked Arthur's home was a new experience for me. My own upbringing in a do-it-yourself, do-as-you-please atmosphere was certainly not adequate preparation for the kind of daily living I found in that Kingston home.

I first noticed the difference when the train pulled into the station at Kingston, and there was nobody from the family to meet us. My occasional comings and goings in my own family circle always included being "met" on returning from a trip; or, if guests were expected at our house, someone always met them when they arrived at the station. Arthur apparently was not expecting anybody, however, so we took a taxicab and started winding our way through the streets of Kingston and finally arrived at the long hill which is West Chestnut Street. At the very end of it, Arthur proudly announced, "That's our home."

It was a large red brick house aglow with lights, with a wide porch all across the front of it. The light from the porch fell on two giant blue spruce trees, covered with snow, which flanked the steps. Arthur explained that these spruces had been planted when he was a little boy, and they had long since outgrown him. On the west side was a sun porch, which had recently been added to the house, and which he was curious to see. Through the windows we could see the lights and trimmings of the Christmas tree.

Strangely enough, as soon as we were in the house, I felt as if I had been there before, so complete and graphic had been Arthur's description of it. I knew exactly where the grand piano was, the bookcases, the stairways, and so on. His mother's loftiest ambition was to create a lovely setting for her husband and children, and she succeeded admirably.

Blue was the basic color everywhere—in the draperies, in the huge velour sofa in the library, in several chairs, and in the lovely Chinese rugs scattered about on top of the carpet.

Being a guest in Arthur's home was an experience that "kept me on my toes," as far as both appearance and deportment were concerned. His mother was a lady, from the top of her meticulously groomed head to her slender, well-shod feet, and all points in between. When she made an appearance, either in the morning or at any time throughout the day, she was carefully and completely dressed—every hair in place, tastefully and expensively attired, and perfectly groomed. It was impossible for her to descend to anything slipshod or careless, whether it be her own appearance, a meal she prepared, or any portion of her house. Every drawer, every closet was in order. Her home was the place she expressed herself. Her imagination began and ended there. But what a place of beauty she created. Arthur took me all over it. Believe me, there was no "letting down" in that household.

On later visits, and in the summer time, I found out that she expressed herself equally eloquently in the area immediately surrounding the house. She developed large flower beds of exquisite beauty, kept them weeded and cultivated, and always had an abundant supply of cut flowers all over the house. She also superintended the care of the lawn and shrubbery. Each tree and bush was carefully edged and trimmed. She was an authority on unusual varieties of flowers and rock garden plants, and each different specimen was carefully chosen for the spot it occupied. The total effect was highly professional, and she took great pride in keeping it so.

Arthur and Betty were her creations, too. As children they were always perfectly dressed. Betty's black curls were her special delight, and she would spend hours brushing and training and arranging them. I've seen many snapshots of both of them as children, and in all of them they were dressed as if going to a party.

Even after the children were grown, she always took a keen interest in what they wore and how they looked. If Arthur, on a visit home, seemed to have delayed getting a hair cut, she would notice it at once and tell him he must go to the barber and get this matter attended to. Or, if his hat seemed to be a bit past its original freshness, she would insist that he get a new one immediately. When she insisted on anything, it was usually a great deal easier just to do what she wanted rather than subject one's self to more insisting. She kept right on until she succeeded. She never let go of any subject until she had won her point. I've never known anyone who was her equal in this respect. She put great price on proper appearance and proper behavior and had no tolerance for a more casual approach in either area.

Arthur's mother watched over all of them. If it was raining, she wanted them to be sure to wear rubbers. "Your feet are your chest protectors" was one of her favorite maxims.

Like most normal girls, Betty developed an aversion to rubbers and galoshes, and this distressed her mother greatly. Sometimes departures from the house would be delayed many minutes while the advantages and disadvantages of wearing rubbers would be argued by Betty and her mother.

She watched over the diet of all of them, too. And she insisted that they get proper rest at night. The emphasis on all of these aspects of daily life was new to me. In my casual upbringing I couldn't remember anything quite like it. My mother never lectured me about anything. Her method was strictly of the "teaching by example" school. Both of my parents did expect a high standard of behavior, albeit without accompanying lectures. Arthur's mother, however, left nothing to chance. Arthur and

Betty were carefully instructed. And years later, on her visits to our home, she would lecture me on many areas.

On this first visit to Kingston, I noticed that all of them appeared for breakfast completely dressed and on time. No careless lounging robe attire was ever tolerated around that table. They all said "Good morning" to each other, inquired about each other's night's rest, made observations about the weather, and so on.

All of this made a deep impression on me. My own metabolism is of a different sort. I never want to say anything to anybody in the morning. In fact, it is a major effort for me just to get out of bed. These early morning pleasantries had always seemed to me to be unnecessary. To this day, I depend on Arthur to wake me up, and once awake, I don't care to be bothered for a while.

The orderliness of everything and everybody that I observed in Arthur's home and the attention to minute details to dress, food, rest, rubbers, speech, and behavior were all evidence of the kind of disciplined behavior and living that I had never been exposed to before. It was a far cry indeed from my own upbringing, and there were many times that I seriously doubted my ability to live up to the standard set in that house.

After we were married I strove unsuccessfully to achieve the standard of performance Arthur's mother had attained. When expecting a visit from his parents, I'd literally wear myself out trying to order our household as efficiently as she did. Telling myself that Arthur's mother had the same live-in housekeeper for fifteen years while Arthur and Betty were growing up, and moreover, that she had only two children six years apart in age (instead of five in seven years as we did) did not keep me from trying to compete with her in orderliness and efficiency in the household department.

We didn't have a guestroom, so we always gave Arthur's parents our bedroom when they came to visit; and when they arrived, it bore little resemblance to its customary state when we occupied it. I'd remove everything from the closet, just about everything from bureau and chest drawers and from the medicine chest in the adjoining bathroom. I'd also remove my sewing machine and other impedimenta so that the bedroom was sterile and devoid of its usual "lived in" look, and resembled a hotel room.

But still I felt I always fell short in this area, though it took me many years before I finally decided I'd just be myself and not keep kicking myself around to be like her.

But, on my first visit to Arthur's home, I realized I was on display as Arthur's "girl," and I wanted very much to please them all. Still, all the while, I felt a bit gauche, as if my slip were showing all the time.

The usual flurry of preparations took place the day before Christmas. Arthur's mother was a perfectionist in all things and would insist on getting exactly the right thing to get the effect desired, whether it was the flowers, the turkey, the molded ice cream, or whatever, and she ended up with a Christmas dinner setting that was absolutely beautiful.

The day started off with breakfast, just like any other day. Not a single gift was opened by anybody until the meal was over. At the table there was much talk of the weather and whether the ferry from Rhinebeck would be able to get through the ice to Kingston. Leaving gifts untouched was another evidence of restraint that I truly marveled at, as in my home anybody could open anything anytime he wanted to. But the gift-opening ceremony in Kingston was as fixed as the laws of the Medes and Persians. Arthur's mother and father and Betty and Arthur and I opened our gifts in turn amid much mutual admiration. Betty always had a veritable mountain of gifts from her mother and father, as it was her custom to provide them with a long list of things she wanted. Always she got everything on the list.

Shortly thereafter Uncle Tom and Aunt Anna arrived from their home down the street. And at about ten o'clock the Sherwood relatives from across the river were safely delivered at the front door. After greeting them all, Arthur's mother disappeared toward the kitchen and was not seen again until dinnertime.

The women gravitated to the new sun porch where we could look out over the snow-covered hills on the west side of the house. Not far down below was the Rondout Creek, a branch of the Hudson, and in the distance, the Catskill Mountains. Arthur had told me earlier that it was this view of the creek and the mountains that Theodore Roosevelt had once described as "the finest view he had ever seen."

Arthur's father and Uncle Tom settled down in the library, and Arthur sought out his Grandfather Sherwood. This was a time these two looked forward to from one Christmas to the next. Some years they didn't see each other in the months between, but Christmas they could count on having a few hours together to discuss the political situation, the developments in Granpa's church, the books they had read, and anything else that came into their heads. They were completely compatible and comfortable in each other's company.

Grampa was, at the time I first met him, eighty-six years old and still an active minister holding weekly services in the Old Stone Church in Rhinebeck. He was a very handsome man still, with full ruddy cheeks and bright blue eyes that sparkled with interest in every situation. He could easily have passed for sixty-five years old, and loved to be told that.

I enjoyed getting acquainted with them all—but, again, feeling as if I already knew them because of Arthur's frequent mention of them all.

In due time, Arthur's mother announced dinner, and ten of us came from all directions to the dining room. What a picture that Christmas dinner table was! In the center was a huge bouquet of brilliant American beauty roses. Arthur's mother had let me arrange them the day before in a special container, a sort of three-in-one affair of green crystal mounted on a mirror base. The big oval table, set with beautiful linen, crystal, silver, and china was, I thought, the prettiest dinner table I had ever seen.

First, the blessing by Grampa, with the rest joining in. Then, Arthur's father began the carving ritual while the family conversed about what a pretty "bird" it was, how perfectly browned, and estimates of its weight. I had never heard a turkey called a "bird" before, but this term was always used by Arthur's mother in referring to the holiday fowl.

I could feel Arthur watching me to see what my reactions were. He was so completely happy in the family circle and wanted me to be, too.

After the main course was finished, and the dishes had been removed, the woman who helped in the kitchen brought in an enormous pink ice cream mold, rectangular in shape, and served on a lovely oblong painted china dish. Arthur's mother handled the ice cream serving ceremony, and it was every bit as carefully and expertly performed as had been the turkey serving ceremony by Arthur's father earlier. We watched her count out the pieces with the serving knife before she cut into the mold. Then she slowly forced the knife through the end piece, and so on until each person around the table was served a generous slice of the tasty dessert. Fruit cake accompanied each serving.

Nuts and raisins on the stem were piled high in crystal dishes on either side of the red centerpiece. And two silver compotes held mints. These were passed after dessert, and we sat at the table a long time nibbling at them and drinking coffee and lazily talking together.

Afterward I helped with the cleaning up chores. In wiping one of the goblets it slipped from my fingers and shattered in a hundred pieces as it hit the floor. With typical restraint Arthur's mother passed it off as "just one of those things." But I was acutely unhappy about it. It made me literally sick inside. That was certainly no way for me to impress my future mother-in-law.

Later, relieved of the responsibility of the dinner, Arthur's mother joined the group of women who again gravitated to the sun porch. Betty disappeared upstairs where she telephoned all her friends and compared notes on gifts received.

Uncle Tom retired to a corner of the library with his cigar, lost in meditative comfort, with only an occasional word to the other men. Arthur, his father, and Grampa had a lively political discussion.

About four o'clock everybody's attention began shifting to the weather, with each evaluating the prospects of the ferry's being able to get across the Hudson on the return trip for the Rhinebeck relatives.

There were other Christmases too, and brief summer visits with Arthur and his family in Kingston. These helped me to understand as nothing else could the part that each of them had played in the making of the man I had fallen in love with: his father, the ambitious, hard-driving, energetic, civic-minded lawyer who called most of the plays for all of them; his mother, whose sole mission in life was to minister to the needs of her family, and whose constant daily emphasis on good food, keeping busy, and getting a good night's rest seemed to be her answer to all of life's difficulties; his pretty, friendly, fun-loving sister Betty, who could never make ends meet on the allowance her father provided, and who could always count on the gap being taken up by her indulgent brother; his gentle, humorous, low-keyed Uncle Tom, whose love of dogs, bridge, and fishing formed an entirely different emphasis from his father's; his Aunt Anna, who was always ready with a cookie and an understanding heart whenever Arthur or Betty dropped in at the house down the street; his preacher grandfather, whose life of service for his fellowman provided direction and single-mindedness of purpose; Grampa's wife Cora, who usually just listened, but who had taken good care of Grampa since her marriage to him when he was nearly seventy; and his spinster Aunt Gertrude, an intelligent, well-educated woman who had never quite mustered the courage to go out and attack life on her own but who, instead, retreated into a world of illness, living vicariously on the activities of those around her.

These visits also helped me to understand and appreciate the part that the physical surroundings he had grown up in had played in the shaping of Arthur. Space, physical comfort, financial stability, and love were all fused together in his West Chestnut Street world. I drank in every single scrap of information about all of these factors that had contributed to making Arthur who he was.

There came a time a couple of years after I met Arthur when he became convinced that The American University lacked imaginative leadership. He had an opportunity to join the staff of David Lawrence's *United States Daily*, now the *U.S. News and World Report*. He had become acquainted with Mr. Lawrence through his debate work, and he admired him greatly. So Arthur decided to give up teaching and try journalism again.

He hadn't been working for "D.L.," as Arthur affectionately called him, very long before Mr. Lawrence began to talk about the establishment of a sort of junior *U.S. Daily*. His plan was to prepare government news geared to high-school readers and to distribute it to classes in civics. For this purpose an organization named the United States Society came into existence.

Arthur was asked to head up the editorial side of this new venture. He had had a year's experience editing *The Weekly Observer,* which the owner, Doctor Walter Myers, asked him to edit while he was recuperating from an illness. When the United States Society was organized, David Lawrence became chairman of it; Mary Roberts Rinehart, vice-chairman; Breckinridge Long, secretary and treasurer; and Arthur Flemming, executive director. Publication of a high-school current-events paper, *Uncle Sam's Diary*, was begun. Pauline Frederick and Benjamin Brodinsky were the original staff members.

With his background as a teacher of government, and with this new experience on the paper, Arthur was getting many invitations to speak, both in and out of Washington. Civic, church, and educational groups invited him to talk before them. Always, when I questioned him about what he was going to talk about, he would reply, "The government." (Our son, Harry, gave me precisely the same answer a short time ago when I queried him about what he was going to talk about to a college group he was scheduled to address.)

Moreover, whenever it was humanly possible for him to do so, his answer was always "Yes" to those invitations. So it follows that he received an increasing number of such requests, especially when he still didn't demand an honorarium. Incidentally, I had even then a strong conviction that Arthur is never happier than when he is on a platform making a speech. This, too, is still true.

The years of activity in the publications field followed the pattern I had grown accustomed to. The demands of work always took precedence over me. It was during this period that I developed the habit of carrying a book with me whenever I was to meet Arthur for dinner. There was never any certainty that he would appear at the designated place at the time agreed on. Particularly on the days when *Uncle Sam's Diary* had to be "put to bed," he might be anywhere from a half-hour to a couple of hours late. I was saved many hours of frustration and annoyance by having a good book to keep me company. I never did really enjoy my second-place role, but the books did help!

It was during this period, and not during my undergraduate

English major days, that I learned to be a discriminating reader. I can still remember vividly many of the books I read: *The Romance of Leonardo Da Vinci, Kristin Lavransdatter, The Outline of History, Wuthering Heights* (I don't know how I missed this one in college, but I did), biographies of Anne Boleyn, Florence Nightingale, Napoleon Bonaparte, and that exquisitely lovely story in the realm of fancy, *Green Mansions.* Whether this is labeled reading for escape, or a defense mechanism to ward off frustration, the end result is the same. Arthur forced this development on me by his own pattern of living. It has served me well over the years.

Besides, there was usually just enough fun and stimulation and unexpected excitement to keep me going. Knowing Arthur convinced me that "All work and no play makes Jack a dull boy" is a silly generalization. Arthur has always been the least dull person I've ever known.

The depression years were on us then, and Arthur found that launching a new publication was an exceedingly difficult task. Even with the help of an expert in the field of direct mail advertising, *Uncle Sam's Diary* never succeeded in "leaving the ground," much less to achieve the heights envisioned by David Lawrence and Arthur when they boldly started this new adventure.

There was an opportunity to sell *Uncle Sam's Diary* to the American Education Press, in Columbus, Ohio. And so, The United States Society passed out of existence.

Meanwhile, there were other important developments about to materialize that offered another experience in the field of education.

But I should first record two events of significance that occurred. Arthur got his bachelor of laws degree, and we got married.

Even after the years of going to school at night and taking summer courses in law school and finally completing the requirements for a degree, I do not recall that Arthur had any real urge to take the bar of the District of Columbia, or of the State of New York. In fact, he seemed less sure that he wanted to practice law at that time than when he entered law school.

But one thing we were both sure about was that we would make a date with Doctor Frederic Brown Harris, of Foundry Church, to get married. We were married on December 14, 1934.

That day I prepared an hour-long mid-term examination for my class. At four o'clock that afternoon, we were married. Both of our families were present, as well as a few close friends.

If this sounds like our wedding was a casual affair, I must explain that it wasn't. It was carefully planned and executed in every detail. To help me, I secured a copy of Emily Post's treatise on proper wedding procedure months in advance and pored over it by the hour. Everything had to be perfect.

For weeks beforehand, I spent several hours every evening sewing on my wedding dress and my "going away" dress. Every single stitch in both dresses was done by hand. I loved doing this all by myself, dreaming all the while of the new life ahead. Both garments turned out to be beautiful. At least I thought so!

Since my family was seven hundred miles away in Georgia, and Arthur's family was in Kingston, New York, all of the details had to be planned, supervised, and carried out by me. And all the while I was doing a full day's work as registrar and teacher at The American University. I worked right up to the evening of December thirteenth, the day before the wedding.

Sometimes on Saturday afternoons and Sundays we would look for a place to live. Arthur's idea of a proper setting was a house overlooking a river, with a view of mountains beyond. His Kingston home was his ideal, and he wanted us to have one as much like it as possible, an obviously impossible standard to achieve in Washington, DC. He couldn't bring himself to consider an apartment, with the confinements such living imposed, though we did look at a couple.

On one Sunday we went down to Alexandria, Virginia, to look at possible places along the Potomac River. Even if we had succeeded in locating a house we could afford with a view of the river, the specifications fell far short as far as a mountain view was concerned.

Eventually we decided on a new house on an ordinary city block, just a half-mile north of The American University campus. The first story was brick, and the upper story clapboard, painted white. It had six rooms and two bathrooms. Our plan was for me to continue in my job until the end of the school year. By that time we hoped to have the furniture paid for.

Our house cost $12,500. Fifty years later, I drove past it on my way to a friend's home and noticed a "For Sale" sign in the front yard. I told my friend our old house was on the market, and she forthwith telephoned the real estate agent to inquire the asking price. The price quoted to her was $260,000.

We spent one evening visiting a furniture store—only one, mind you—and bought all of the items necessary to set up housekeeping. That was great fun, but in retrospect, I can hardly believe that two fairly intelligent people would do such a really stupid thing. We made, I am sure, more than our share of errors in judgment on that occasion, but we didn't have time to approach the matter more cautiously. Besides, neither of us knew what we wanted as far as a decorating plan was concerned. And our choices were a hodge-podge, for sure.

For the record, I should add that this was the only occasion, with one exception, in our entire married life when Arthur went along with me to select furniture. After that he turned the house and its furnishings and maintenance completely over to me. Always thereafter I went alone on buying expeditions, or occasionally helped by one or more of the children. If it was a car that was under consideration, the boys were always happy to help make a choice. Arthur would say. "If you like it, it's all right with me."

In the years since then, I've bought bedroom suites, washers, dryers, refrigerators, deep freezes, sofas and chairs, a piano, tables, cars, houses, well, everything. He always liked them, so we kept them.

This brings up another facet of Arthur's character: he always had implicit confidence in my ability to do anything. He was sure I could do whatever needed doing—in fact, could rise to any emergency. This, I came to realize, is a good trick for any husband to develop. That way he can turn any job over to his wife. He can delegate any amount of responsibility, and she'll turn hand-springs to do it. Of course, there were occasions when he stretched his luck a bit too far, or when he had a belated idea that he tossed out too late for execution. One such time was a luncheon at our house for forty people, all set up for buffet service and ten card tables to sit at, when he appeared with the first guest and insisted I should have a seating arrangement with place cards! I managed to get him to understand it was too late for that idea to be carried out.

Also, he had a habit of appearing in the kitchen just at the time the guests were due to ask what the menu was and whether I was sure there was enough food. Another of his habits was to nibble from nut dishes and cookie and sandwich plates all arranged prettily for a tea or reception. This necessitated rearrangement at the last minute to fill in the holes his nibbling left. But, generally speaking, he took no part at all in household management.

In our family, we call this delegation of authority. And since he had developed into a professional administrator, I, in turn, developed my thumbnail definition of an administrator: a person who does only those things he can't delegate to someone else!

Arthur loved his home, and he was proud of it. But he didn't spend much time in it. He had too many other things to do.

Being married didn't hamper him one single little bit as far as any of his activities were concerned. It did, however, revolutionize mine!

7

THE SCHOOL OF PUBLIC AFFAIRS

An opportunity was presented to him about the time he got his law degree that offered an alternative to taking the bar examination and entering the practice of law. It came about when new blood was infused into The American University through the election of Doctor Joseph M. Gray as chancellor.

Franklin Delano Roosevelt, then president of the United States, was the speaker at Doctor Gray's inauguration in Constitution Hall, in Washington. Doctor Gray, in his inaugural statement, announced that the university intended to establish a new School of Public Affairs, which would offer specialized training in the field of government, both on the graduate and undergraduate levels, with emphasis on what was termed "in-service" training for public employees.

In his remarks following this announcement, President Roosevelt said, "I am especially happy in the announcement of the establishment of the School of Public Affairs. I can assure you of the hearty cooperation of the administration in all its branches."

Arthur was asked by Doctor Gray to become the first director of this new school. The idea had great appeal, not only because it was an opportunity to pioneer in a new field, in a setting natural for such a venture, but also because it gave him a chance to be part of the public service set-up. It fired his imagination tremendously to envision the possibilities inherent in the activities of the new school. So he decided to undertake the direction of it.

Obviously, at that time, returning to academic life was more appealing than going into the practice of law.

He set to work organizing the school, setting up a program of courses, and selecting a faculty. Its first session was advertised as a Summer Institute for a First-Hand Study of the Emergency Agencies of the Government.

To assist him, he obtained the services of Doctor George Graham, of Princeton University, as visiting dean for the session. He also persuaded a group of outstanding political scientists to join him, including Doctor Arnold Bennett Hall, a former president of the University of Oregon and at that time director of the Institute of Government Research of the Brookings Institution; Doctor George Benson, of Harvard University, and later president of Claremont College of California; Doctor William Casey, of Columbia University; Doctor Ernest Griffith, dean of American University's Graduate School; Doctor Howard Piquet, of New York University; and Doctor Richard Schenck, of The American University's department of political science. Some of these men never went back to their jobs outside of Washington after that summer experience. It was an impressive group indeed that Arthur assembled to launch the new School of Public Affairs.

The plan he developed for studying the so-called New Deal Emergency Agencies proved stimulating and attractive to students and faculty alike. In addition to formal lectures by faculty members, the heads of many governmental agencies came out to the campus and talked about their work and answered questions.

In the fall Arthur developed another ambitious program for the School of Public Affairs. He organized what was called the "In-Service Training Program" for government employees in which his faculty cooperated with officials of the federal departments. Courses were given in such subjects as Survey of Personnel Management, Executive Management and Supervision, Introduction to Government Accounting, Changing Relations between Congress and the Executive, and Administrative Statistics of the Federal Government.

The program had instant appeal for a ready-made clientele: the federal employees in the sprawling government buildings all over the capital city, many of whom were anxious to improve their chances for advancement by using the opportunity for further study in the field of government.

Naturally, since this was a pioneering adventure, and Arthur was feeling his way along, he sought the advice and counsel of the best men he could find. Fortunately, at that time there were some exceptionally capable and farsighted men available in Washington who were willing to help.

One of these was Doctor Leonard D. White, who was serving as the Republican member of the United States Civil Service Commission. Doctor White was on leave from the political science department of the University of Chicago. His rich teaching experience, combined with his years in government, made him exactly the kind of imaginative counselor that Arthur needed.

Between these two men a firm and understanding attachment developed. Doctor White listened patiently when Arthur outlined his dreams for the school, and he offered assistance and advice on both organization and operation. He came out to the campus frequently and talked to classes, and generously answered questions raised about various phases of the civil service procedures.

Another extremely devoted public servant also became a friend and consultant. He was Congressman Robert Ramspeck, a member of the United States House of Representatives from Georgia, who was chairman of the House Civil Service Committee. Congressman Ramspeck took a vital interest in the new school and offered encouragement at every turn. He was the speaker at the first annual luncheon sponsored by the school at the Mayflower Hotel, in January, 1937, and had this to say:

> The In-Service Training Program of the School of Public Affairs for government employees would prove to be not only an advantage for the employees themselves, but to the government

service, and hence to the people of the United States.

Another former teacher and former member of the U.S. House of Representatives, Doctor Frederick W. Davenport, was also helpful. He was then chairman of the President's Council on Personnel Administration. His advice was always sound, and his judgment mature. He was considerably older than Arthur, but the difference was no handicap.

Interest in the School of Public Affairs also came from other sources outside of Washington. Arthur made the acquaintance of Robert L. Johnson soon after the school opened. Mr. Johnson was one of the original founders of *Time* magazine. He had a strong civic conscience, and at the time Arthur met him he was the president of the National Civil Service Reform League, a private organization that worked to improve policies affecting government employees. He was particularly helpful to Arthur in presenting the viewpoint from outside the actual government circle. Later he became president of Temple University and asked Arthur to become a member of his board there.

To provide professional academic direction for the program, Dean Emery E. Olson, dean of the School of Government of the University of Southern California, joined the staff at The American University for a two-year period.

All of these men were significant as far as setting up the program of the new School of Public Affairs was concerned. Arthur realized that he needed help from experienced and imaginative people who were not afraid of an innovative program, and he sought this assistance in the top people in the field of public administration. All of this group became firm, lasting friends of Arthur's, whose paths were to cross his for many years to come. When Doctor White resigned from the Civil Service Commission to return to the University of Chicago, a New York attorney, Samuel H. Ordway, succeeded him. Arthur immediately sought him out and enlisted his aid and advice for the school.

Close contacts with men such as these, who believed firmly in the merit system of selecting employees for government service, had far-reaching impact on Arthur. The speeches he made at that time reflected his own growing conviction that government service demanded trained personnel. He became outspoken in denunciation of the so-called "spoils system." In a speech made in August, 1937, his feelings on the matter were expressed in colorful language. *The Evening Star* headlined the story, "Doctor Flemming Hits Spoils System." The story includes: . . . Doctor Flemming insisted that 'the present Congress is going straight to hell' [Imagine!] in its attitude toward the spoils system versus the merit system issue."

And later, in a speech delivered before the Loyal Knights of the Round Table: "Concentration of power in the hands of the government, and the practice of giving jobs to those who 'rang the most doorbells during the last campaign,' rather than to qualified civil service applicants, combines to undermine democracy."

Arthur also began writing magazine articles on the subject of training for public service. He appeared on programs of conventions of organizations in this field. In *Public Administration* (the journal of the Institute of Public Administration) for July, 1938, there is an article entitled, "Problems of Training for the Public Service," which was based on a speech he delivered at the Summer Conference of the Institute in July of that year.

He joined the Civil Service Assembly of the United States and Canada and became a member of its executive council.

He also spoke out forcefully in another direction. In a speech delivered before the Eastern States Conference of the Civil Service Assembly, he promoted the idea of a lobby for civil service legislation. He urged the assembly to join with other organizations interested in the merit system to pool their resources for an effective lobby to work for beneficial legislation.

Arthur had a strong conviction that the merit system should not be used as protection for inefficiency. He had an equally strong feeling that completion of in-service training courses should be only one of the factors to be considered in determining promotion in government service.

Arthur's voice was growing in influence among the men in Washington who were concentrating their energies in the public service field. He was fearless in his championship of the merit system, and even the president of the United States was soon to take notice of it.

That his activity was pleasing to the administration of The American University is indicated by the fact that he was named executive officer of the university. Doctor Gray wrote him a Christmas letter in 1937 to express his appreciation of Arthur's service to the university during the year just closing. "For your industry and the cooperation you have shown, for your loyalty to the University as a whole, while at the same time you have developed the School of Public Affairs into a splendid institution, I am very grateful," he said.

I have kept one letter from a faculty colleague expressing similar feelings. This letter, however, included another idea. He said, "The institution itself needs your demonstrated ability as a realistic and skillful administrator. The fact that you are taking on these added duties—while onerous to you—is going to make us all more confident as to the future of the Graduate School. . . . While you would undoubtedly make an excellent university or college president, I hope you will resist temptation . . . and that you will find adequate gratification of any personal ambition in Washington."

Such a possibility was even then being tossed about by decisionmakers out in Delaware, Ohio. That same spring, 1938, Arthur's alma mater was looking for a new president. Arthur was then thirty-two years old.

A trustee of Ohio Wesleyan, Mr. Edward D. Jones, for some reason not entirely clear to us, became an ardent advocate of Arthur for the job. He came to Washington to propose this possibility to Arthur and to get Arthur's permission to have his name presented to the board of trustees. He also made arrangements for Arthur to speak to the students at the regular chapel service at Ohio Wesleyan as a sort of "trial balloon." Our good friend, Doctor Arneson, was also behind this movement.

From his old friend Fannie Koontz, "Prexy" Hoffman's secretary, Arthur received this note:

> Methinks you are the one to rejuvenate the old school! Like the school boy, I am keeping my fingers crossed until it is all over, for that board has made mistakes before, and bad ones, but I surely hope they will see the light in this instance. I shall be scanning the headlines hoping to learn for certain that you are elected.
>
> My best wishes to you, and I do hope you are elected! Nothing would please "Prexy" Hoffman more than to know that you were in his chair on the O.W.U. campus!

The possibility caused considerable excitement in our lives. We both wanted to go to Delaware if the opportunity to be president of Ohio Wesleyan came to Arthur.

A combined faculty-board of trustees committee was working on the selection. There were two strikes against Arthur, both potent factors: one, he was young; and two, he was not a minister. So, when the decision was finally made, Arthur's youth and the fact that he was not a minister mitigated strongly against him.

In a long letter from Mr. Jones, dated June 13, 1938, there is this paragraph:

> It is unnecessary to say the idea of a preacher commands the approval of the ministers on the board. . . . Also, it should be said with reference to the special committee (i.e., the faculty-trustee selecting committee) that the faculty members show to some

83

extent the teacher complex (near relative to the parent complex) in that they cannot realize that a former student has grown up and become a man, and even (and this is probably the most distasteful idea of all) has grown past them.

So the board chose a minister in his fifties, Doctor Herbert Burgstahler, who was then president of Cornell College in Iowa.

Meanwhile, the mills of the gods were grinding slowly in another direction, and another time of decision was near.

Before continuing with the recital of Arthur's vocational activities, perhaps it is appropriate to make a few observations as to what was going on on the home front.

I became a full-time coordinator of domestic affairs at our new home in September of 1935. The furniture was all paid for, and it seemed safe for me to take this step.

From the beginning, I found myself spending many an evening alone. Occasionally, if the situation permitted, I went along with Arthur to whatever he was doing, but not often.

Naturally, at first, setting up a household was an absorbing task, particularly since in the early stages everything in that area had to be taken care of in the evenings and on Saturday afternoons. Saturday mornings were spent in my office. There were curtains to make, and my sole domestic skill at that time was that I was a good seamstress. There were equipment and household supplies to secure, meals to prepare, and laundry to do. The fact that in our case marriage had been delayed a few years did not add one whit to my efficiency in household management. I was awkward, lacked knowledge and expertise, and was ill-prepared to carry out most housekeeping details.

Arthur was patient and understanding and didn't seem to notice that I suffered considerably in comparison to his mother, a real "pro" in this respect. At least, he has never, in all the years of our marriage, ever used his mother as a standard in assessing my own performance.

I found out early, however, that he was not the least bit interested in assuming any responsibility for any part of the household operation. The house and everything about it were mine. His mother had never expected any help from him. In fact, when he was growing up his family had a live-in housekeeper. And over the years he has never deviated from the pattern established in the beginning of being a sort of guest in his home.

He did, the first year, cut the grass a few times, but he soon abandoned this in favor of a regular yard man to take over this demanding chore. Also, he insisted that I have regular help from a cleaning woman after the children came. But he didn't want to be involved in any of it himself. His brief hours at home were not for the purpose of mending anything, installing storm windows, cleaning garages or basements, or running any errands.

When I made the choice of retiring from my job at The American University, it was obviously an adjustment to a new pattern of daily living for me. But I never regretted it and had no yen to return to the so-called more glamorous activities outside my home. Now, with the Women's Liberation Movement blasting away at the underprivileged role of women, I can hardly believe I was so naive as actually to relish my new role. But, anyway, I did.

We furnished one of our upstairs room as a den-study, so that Arthur had a comfortable place to work at home. He seldom used it, but, for a few years, it was there anyway.

When he was away at night, or out of town for a few days, I was lonely—lonelier, by far, than I had been before marriage. The answer to this kind of loneliness was provided on April 1, 1936, when Elizabeth Anne Flemming was born.

Arthur was home the night she was born. In fact, he was home for the births of all of our children. This fact itself is something of a miracle, because none of the children arrived when the doctor said they would. And he was with our daughter when our first grandchild was born.

Once when I remonstrated with him about his being absent for nearly all of the family crises—an emergency operation of mine when he was on his way to Europe; several operations of various kinds on the children; and accidents and fractures suffered by the children—he replied, "But I've never missed a baby!" He was really quite good at the bedside of a woman in labor—quiet, unexcitable, sure everything would be all right.

When I got home from the hospital with our little girl, I had my first object lesson in what life was going to be like for many years to come. At the time Elizabeth Anne was born (or Lib, as we came to call her) it was the rule for new mothers to remain in bed in the hospital for two weeks and then to forego climbing steps for another two weeks. Since we lived in a two-story house, this meant that I was confined to the upstairs and unable to participate in any household activity until the baby was a month old. A wonderful woman named Mary Brown helped me during this period and also when the next two children were born. I consider her one of my best friends.

Lib was the first grandchild in Arthur's family, so she created quite a stir. The day after I returned home with her from the hospital, Arthur's mother and father came to Washington from Kingston to make her acquaintance. Arthur's sister Betty was employed in Washington at the time and was living in our house.

The new grandparents arrived on a Friday night. They were properly enthusiastic about the baby and pronounced her healthy and beautiful. But apparently they didn't see any reason why life for everybody else shouldn't go on as usual.

The next evening, Saturday, they had dinner with us, along with Betty and her fiancé, Donald Sherbondy. After dinner the lot of them left for the theater. I forget what the show was, but the tickets had been obtained beforehand. Remember, I was still confined upstairs in accordance with the doctor's orders.

I watched them go out the front door from the top of the stairs: Arthur, Betty, Donald, and the senior Flemmings. They all waved a merry goodbye to me as they left, but I felt anything but merry. I was well aware that my situation prevented my being a participant in the theater party, but somehow that didn't keep me from feeling very "put upon" at that moment. I shall never forget the feeling of utter desolation that swept over me as I looked longingly after them on that lovely spring evening. The message I got was: life goes on as usual for everybody else, but I had a baby, and from then on my role in life was to take care of her, and whatever I did in the future was to be bound by her needs. Even today, I feel a wave of annoyance when I remember that evening.

It was a hard adjustment to make, and certainly for me it was much more difficult than the transition from career girl to homemaker, full time. But it is just as well that I learned that lesson right off, because the next twenty-five years of my life were lived within the framework of routine baby and child care— a never-ending repetition of washing, ironing, feeding, and cleaning, plus, of course, deliveries to music lessons, play practice, girl and boy scout meetings and camps, and so on. When I read Gail Sheehy's *Passages*, I fell to wondering just how I escaped jumping off a bridge!

I soon got over feeling sorry for myself and settled down into the round-the-clock baby-tending routine. I even managed to get to the theater myself occasionally in the years that followed. And temporary escape between the covers of a good book was always possible.

We lived in our six-room brick and clapboard house for six years. During this time we had three children: a sister for Lib, Susan, arrived three years later, and then a boy, Harry.

One cold January day I went for a walk while the children were napping. There was a lot of building going on in our neighborhood. A whole block of new houses in various stages of construction was just a short walk away. So I amused myself by visiting them all.

One struck my fancy. Right away I had a distinctly warm reaction to it. It was a square, Georgian all-brick house, sitting high on a terrace. It was entirely surrounded by mud, to be sure, but it looked beautiful to me anyway.

I gingerly picked my way through the mud, around the stumps, up the plank steps, and went in. Immediately my imagination went to work. We needed more space, I decided, and here it was. It was a considerably larger house than ours, with four bedrooms, a bath on the first floor, and a library.

It took me a couple of months to sell Arthur on the idea, but eventually I did. We moved into our new house in March. That move taught me something else about Arthur. Here his ability to delegate responsibility was complete. The move was my party. Mine alone. On moving day, he went to his office as usual, and he came home to our new address in the evening, expecting dinner also, as usual.

In the many moves we've made since then—fourteen in all—the pattern has been the same. In fact, I try, if possible, to arrange for the loading and unloading when he is out of town. It's easier that way. He doesn't pack a single thing, nor does he unpack anything. As the children got older, they helped a great deal, but Arthur has never, to this day, varied in his complete detachment from the moving process.

Well, moving is a mess any way you look at it—whether it is three blocks away, as ours was at that time, or hundreds or thousands of miles, as subsequent moves have been. It is a tremendous physical and emotional upheaval, and children did complicate the process somewhat on that first move.

But we did it, and all of us were delighted with our new home. Here, I thought, we can live happily and comfortably for the rest of our lives. How naive I was!

On the next adventure as far as family expansion was concerned, symptoms indicated that something unusual was afoot. On a certain hot afternoon in July, I had an x-ray picture taken which showed beyond a doubt that there was indeed something a bit out of the ordinary going on. The x-ray technician put his arm around me (I think he thought I might faint) as he showed me the picture. "Here they are," he said, "just like shoes in a box."

I hurried to a public telephone and put a nickel in the slot (those were the good old days) and dialed Arthur's office number. When I reached him I gasped excitedly, "Guess what—we're going to have twins!"

"That's wonderful," he replied, "but I have one direction for you. You are not to go out and look for a larger house."

Arthur got as much fun as I did over the anticipation of the arrival of twins. At first we decided to keep the information secret, but after a couple of days the excitement level was so high we shared it with our families. Life, which has been good to us indeed, never tossed us a situation that was more fun than that one was.

Arthur always maintained he didn't want a son named after him. No juniors, he insisted. On the contrary, I had a normal desire to perpetuate his name. I liked it.

I was on the stretcher ready to be wheeled to the delivery room and decided the time was ripe for a decision. Surely he could deny me nothing at that point. As I started rolling down the corridor toward the elevator, I said, "By the way, if we have two boys, I am going to name one of them Arthur."

Two boys it was—Arthur and Thomas—and they were the last additions. We felt we wound up in a blaze of glory.

I have never known a man who enjoyed being a father more than Arthur did. True, he had absolutely nothing to do with their physical care. He may even be the only father of five children in captivity who has never changed a diaper or fed a baby. He delegated everything in the baby department to me, too.

But, from the first, he enjoyed the experience of fatherhood. He didn't care what sex the babies turned out to be. He loved them all, and never mentioned a preference, either in anticipation or afterward.

As each one reached the age of two, he began taking them along with him to Sunday school. He was superintendent of the Foundry Church School, so he always went himself. Usually I followed later for the morning church service. Some of our Washington neighbors have told me that one of their favorite sights was watching Arthur on Sunday morning, in fair weather or foul, making his way to Sunday school with his children.

Being a father was a responsibility he welcomed, joyfully adding this to all the others he assumed.

8

THE UNITED STATES CIVIL SERVICE COMMISSION

N ewspaper reports of the resignation of Samuel Ordway as the Republican member of the Civil Service Commission set in motion a wave of speculation as to who would be his successor. In late May and early June of 1939, "dope" stories began to appear. *The Washington Post* of May 30 carried a story under the headline, "'Dark Horse' Forecast for Ordway's Job" and listed persons being talked about for the appointment. Arthur's name was among those included in the list. That was our first inkling that such a possibility was afoot. Congressman Charles West (D-OH), an old friend from Ohio Wesleyan days, telephoned Arthur and offered to help in any way he could if Arthur was interested in being considered.

When *The Post,* dated June 6, printed a story about the expected appointment, Arthur's name was again there as a "leading favorite in speculation." A period of quiet followed, and then the speculation burst out anew in *The Post* on June 23. This time the story indicated that "the vacancy on the Civil Service Commission is due to be filled this week. The appointment looms as a big surprise." A day later, June 24, *The Daily News* carried this: "Known to have been recommended to the President to replace Samuel H. Ordway, Jr., are three of the leading college professors in the field of public administration. They are Doctor Arthur S. Flemming, Director of American University's School of Public Affairs; Dean Emery W. Olson, of the University of Southern California's School of Government, and who is a former American University instructor; and Doctor Floyd W. Reeves, who formerly was personnel director of the Tennessee

Valley Authority. Doctor Reeves has been on two of the president's committees that studied Federal personnel problems." The Civil Service Commission was a three-man body, bipartisan, which meant that by law two members were of the president's political party (then Democratic, of course) and the third member of the opposition party, or the "outs," the Republicans.

(Actually, Arthur was not at that time entitled to the prefix "Doctor." He still does not have an earned doctorate, though forty-seven American colleges and universities have conferred honorary degrees on him. Some years after he received his LLB from George Washington University, the university changed its bachelor of laws degrees to doctor of jurisprudence and made this retroactive for all degree holders in law.)

Up to this time, Arthur had not been an active participant in party politics, except for student activity in mock conventions, and in political science department projects at Ohio Wesleyan University. The reason was that he had been living in Washington, where citizens at that time had no voice in government, ever since his college graduation. The Twenty-third Amendment, giving limited voting privileges to residents of the District of Columbia, was not ratified until many years later.

Therefore, when the speculation about the upcoming appointment to the Civil Service Commission became so lively, Arthur took the precaution of writing back to Kingston for an affidavit testifying to the fact that he was on the list of enrolled electors in the City of Kingston, Ulster County, New York, for the year 1928, as a Republican. Thus armed, he was ready in case any question was raised as to his political qualifications.

We really began to take the speculation seriously when Arthur was asked by the then-director of the budget, Harold Smith, if he would accept the appointment in case President Roosevelt decided to nominate him for the vacancy on the Civil Service

Commission, and if he could prove he was a Republican.

I have seen Arthur struggle through many times of decision as to which way to turn when a new job opportunity was presented to him, but this was not one of them. He was absolutely sure that a wider field of service was open to him as a member of the Civil Service Commission than as director of The American University's School of Public Affairs. Hence, there was no struggle, no necessity for time to consider whether to accept the appointment if offered. He would do it if the opportunity came his way.

He was going about his business as usual on the afternoon of June 24 when his office telephone rang. It was Gene Wolfe, the university's director of publicity. His excited voice relayed the news that the president had just sent Arthur's name to the Senate as his nomination to succeed Mr. Ordway as the Republican member of the United States Civil Service Commission.

This simple act on the part of the president set in motion a chain of events completely unexpected as far as I was concerned. I found out in a few moments that appointment to public service makes a man and his family newsworthy. The evening and morning papers all carried pictures of Arthur, with stories of his appointment, his experience, his family background, and whatever else enterprising reporters could dig up. All emphasized his youth. Most compared him to Theodore Roosevelt, who had been appointed Civil Service Commission at the age of thirty. *The Times Herald* said:

> When Flemming takes the oath of office when the Senate confirms him, he will be the youngest Civil Service commissioner since Theodore Roosevelt, whose battered desk still stands on display in the patio of the Commission building. Flemming is 34. Roosevelt was 30 when he took office on May 13, 1889, and Commission officials say they know of no other appointee at this level of youth.

There was excitement at home, too. Two reporters called to

ask if they could take pictures of the family. In fact, the telephone began ringing as soon as the afternoon papers were delivered, and it never stopped until late that night. I kept a list of the people who called, so I could report to Arthur. Nearly a hundred friends and well-wishers telephoned to express their pleasure over the appointment. I look back on that particular night as one of the most heart-warming experiences of my life. I found out that after an appointment such as this, and particularly since Arthur served during a critical period of the defense preparation and through World War II, a man and his family never quite get back to the precious world of anonymity. Lib was three years old, and Susan, four months. Such mundane pursuits as dinner preparation and baby care were difficult that night. The appointment met with general approval from all quarters. An editorial in *The Evening Star* had this to say:

> In selecting Professor Arthur S. Flemming, of American University, to be the Republican member of the Civil Service Commission, President Roosevelt has conformed to his policy of filling the minority commissionership from the growing list of those specializing in the field of government.
>
> Professor Flemming, who is but thirty-four years old, could be expected to lack the background of his predecessors, Doctor Lenorad D. White of the University of Chicago, and Samuel B. Ordway, Jr., who had been a member of the New York Civil Service Commission, but he brings to office youth and enthusiasm and a record of accomplishment at the University where he has directed the School of Public Affairs. His nomination, therefore, will be confirmed speedily by the Senate.
>
> Professor Flemming has been particularly interested in the promotion aspect (i.e., building up Government employment as a career service) of civil service, and has been instrumental in developing a course of in-service training at the University which started with a class of eighty-five and now has more than twelve hundred young men and women from Government offices who are

fitting themselves for advancement. With the Government itself preparing to do more in the way of training, Professor Flemming's experience in this field should be particularly helpful to the Commission.

His appointment was also pleasing to the commission employees. This is reflected in a story that appeared in *The News*, a sort of house organ compiled and published by them, which said:

> Mr. Flemming has been on the staff of the American University for a number of years and has always had most cordial relations with the Commission. He has been particularly interested in the problems of the Government service and has taken a leading part in in-service training activities in Washington. He has emphasized that there need be no competition between universities and the Government in training programs, but that by cooperating fully both can move toward a common goal. Mr. Flemming comes to the Commission with one rather unique asset, namely, that he already knows hundreds of Federal employees in all parts of the service. He has discussed with them their problems and ambitions and has a broad view of both the opportunities and the needs of the service.
>
> The new Commissioner has many varied contacts with officials in and out of the service, and he is an effective public speaker. He has presided over numerous important gatherings in Washington in recent years and has impressed all who know him with the fact that he is an energetic individual who has at heart the best interests of the service and of the employees.
>
> It is safe to predict that he will never lose sight of the human element in Government administration and that his judgments and decisions will be tempered with both kindliness and force.

On June 30, 1939, the Senate Civil Service Committee, without a dissenting vote, approved Arthur's nomination, and on July 7, the Senate unanimously confirmed the appointment. The way was then clear for him to be sworn in to his first job as part of the federal bureaucracy. From that time on he served both Republican and Democratic presidents in a variety of capacities. Truman,

Eisenhower, Johnson, Nixon, Ford, Kennedy, and Carter, in addition to Roosevelt, all called him. His appointments under Roosevelt, Truman, Eisenhower, and Nixon were to full-time jobs in the executive branch; the other appointments were part-time.

The actual swearing-in ceremony took place in the rotunda of the commission building, which was then also often referred to as "the old Patent Office Building." Arthur's parents came down from Kingston for the occasion.

Short addresses of welcome to their new colleague were delivered by the two Democratic commissioners, Mr. Harry Mitchell, a former newspaper editor from Great Falls, Montana, and Mrs. Lucille Foster McMillan, widow of a former governor of Tennessee and member of the U.S. House of Representatives, who had been active in Democratic politics in that state ever since her marriage at nineteen to the governor.

Subsequently, a strong friendship developed between Mrs. McMillan and me. She shared with me a liking for spending lonely evenings in bed with a good book for company. Often she would telephone me, or I would call her, and we would talk by the hour over our bedside telephones. She loved to reminisce about the years as the young bride of the governor of Tennessee. She developed her political skills then. At other times she would dwell at length on her beloved only daughter who had met a tragic death years earlier as a result of a fall from a horse. We called these conversations our pillow talks. Though I did not see her often, Mrs. McMillan and I enjoyed a warm, understanding friendship, developed and nurtured largely through our long telephone conversations when we were alone at night.

She was a dear, gracious lady, and I developed a great fondness and respect for her. She was a member of the commission during seven of the nine years Arthur served on that body. When she retired, she was succeeded by former Secretary of

Labor Frances Perkins, appointed to the commission by President Truman.

Arthur's attitude toward his new job and its opportunities is well expressed in his brief response to the welcome of his colleagues at the time he was sworn in.

> It is a privilege and an honor to have the opportunity of becoming associated with this commission. I have had the opportunity of becoming acquainted with many of you, and I know of the splendid service which you have rendered. Great things have happened during the last few years in the field of personnel administration. There are many unsolved problems, and I look forward to the opportunity of grappling with these problems with you.
>
> Everywhere we hear persons talking in terms of the tremendous responsibilities which have been placed on our democracy, and many individuals ask, "Will our democratic machinery work?" The answer to that question of whether or not the Government can meet its responsibilities successfully depends to a considerable degree upon the personnel problems which face us being met and solved in the right way. We are here to serve the departments of the Federal Government, and we must not at any time permit an impasse to develop between these departments and the Civil Service Commission. I like to think of the Civil Service Commission as a great service agency, and it is in that spirit that I assume my new duties. I am looking forward to my association with my new colleagues and with all the personnel of the United States Civil Service Commission.

All presidential appointees to the various independent commissions, or agencies, are presented, on assuming the office, with a commission testifying to that fact. The commission that was presented to Arthur on his induction was a large scroll bearing the great seal of the United States and signed by both the president of the United States, and the secretary of State, Cordell Hull. The wording was interesting and furnished us with many a laugh about the tenuous character of membership on the Civil Service Commission. It read, in part:

Know ye, that reposing special trust and confidence in the integrity

and ability of Arthur S. Flemming, of the District of Columbia, I have nominated, and by and with the advice and consent of the Senate, do appoint him:

A CIVIL SERVICE COMMISSIONER

and do authorize and empower him to execute and fulfill the duties of that office according to law, and to have and to hold the said office, with all the powers, privileges, and emoluments thereunto appertaining unto him, the said Arthur S. Flemming, during the pleasure of the President of the United States for the time being.

It was that last phrase, "for the time being," that we found so amusing.

At that time, all of the other major commissions of the executive branch of the government were set up by Congress with specified terms for the members. The Civil Service Commission was the sole exception, with no specified term of office provided by law. So that wording of Arthur's commission, "during the pleasure of the President of the United States for the time being," made it abundantly clear to us that holding office on the United States Civil Service Commission was a hazardous undertaking. We, of course, had no way of knowing at that time that his nine years on that commission would be his longest tenure of all the various positions that he occupied in both the public and the private sector during his life.

It was an impressive ceremony in which Arthur, with right hand upraised, promised to uphold the Constitution of the United States. I have witnessed five other swearing-ins with Arthur in the stellar role, each time a deeply moved spectator. Those five appointments to follow were: director of the Office of Defense Mobilization;

secretary of Health, Education, and Welfare; White House consultant on aging; the United States commissioner on aging; and chairman
of the United States Civil Rights Commission. All of them provided
ample opportunity for Arthur to use his crusading instincts.

After the induction into office, he went to work. From that day
on he was the champion of the government worker, toiling
ceaselessly for improvement in working conditions and salaries,
for improvement in civil service practices and procedures, and
speaking out courageously whenever the merit system was under
attack.   Years later, when he watched both Democratic and
Republican nominees for president—Jimmy Carter in 1976, and
Ronald Reagan in 1980—campaign for the nation's highest
office by castigating the people who make up the bureaucracy in
speech after speech, he was deeply disturbed.

I learned early that public servants, high and low, are favorite
targets for bricks thrown from all directions by uninformed,
misinformed, and carelessly critical individuals. So Arthur had
many opportunities during his years on the commission to answer
charges of various kinds, and some that came from cabinet
officers.

Arthur was the government workers' friend and defender
from his first day on the job. He believed in their ability and
competence, and he had no patience with persons who habitually
made blanket charges of incompetence and laziness against civil
servants. He did, however, find many points at which the civil
service could be improved, and he dug right in to bring improvement about.

Already, when he was appointed, there was considerable
emphasis on a preparedness program in the event of war. Taking
note of the fact that the commission was far behind in keeping its
recruitment through competitive examinations up to date, he
worked for more efficiency in this area.

He also urged more planning in the commission and in the

various federal departments as far as anticipating their needs for personnel was concerned. He suggested that personnel directors should acquaint themselves with the future plans and policies of their particular organizations and lay their own plans before the commission in time to have their needs met.

He advocated reforms of civil service examinations and urged the commission to keep in touch with learned and professional societies to work out examinations for the more important posts. He pointed out that procedures worked out for lower-bracket jobs would be entirely inadequate for higher-bracket positions.

Arthur took the view early in his career as a civil service commissioner that minorities and disabled persons were a fruitful source of "manpower" for government positions. The preparedness program under way made it necessary to uncover new sources of supply, and he worked to liberalize the government's policies concerning the opportunities available for the physically handicapped. He believed that if the government took the lead in this area, then private employers would follow suit.

When Congressman Ramspeck, chairman of the Civil Service Committee in the House of Representatives, in 1940 sponsored a bill to bring two hundred and fifty thousand federal workers under the civil service, Arthur appeared as the commission's representative before both the House and Senate committees holding hearings on the bill and urged its passage.

Arthur had been on the commission less than six months when the civil service system became the object of a bitter attack by a member of President Roosevelt's cabinet, the secretary of the Interior, Harold Ickes. Secretary Ickes summarily dismissed one of the most competent officials in his department, Doctor John M. Finch, director of the Bureau of Mines. Questioned about this dismissal at a press conference, Secretary Ickes let out a blast against the civil service system and declared that the Bureau of Mines, a subsidiary of the Interior Department, was controlled by a "bureaucratic clique" protected by civil service regulations and that any attempts to "can" them would necessarily result in trials. The secretary further insisted that Doctor Finch did not have enough "iron in his blood" to prevent the "clique" from running the bureau. He pointed out that he was an advocate of civil service and wanted more of it as "the lesser of two evils" in selecting government employees. The secretary said further that "cliques" such as he alleged existed in the Bureau of Mines "happen all the time when people have life-time tenure under civil service."

The "iron in his blood" attack by Secretary Ickes stirred up a storm of protest in many quarters. Arthur drafted a reply to the secretary's charges, and the commission unanimously approved it. He struck back at the secretary with one of the most caustic statements ever hurled at a New Deal cabinet officer by a federal agency, stating that "any administrator who alleges that it is impossible for him to deal with an administrative situation in his own agency because of civil service rules or regulations is attempting to explain his own unwillingness to act by providing the public with misinformation." The commission's statement continued bluntly, "The allegation that persons under civil service have life tenure also has no basis in fact. Such statements by high-ranking administrative officials can have no other effect than to unjustifiably discredit the federal merit system."

Taking issue with the secretary's statement that he was in favor of more civil service as the lesser of two evils, the commission said: "In other words, Secretary Ickes, instead of being an advocate of a strong and vigorous merit system in the federal government, is one who 'damns with faint praise.' The American people are being asked to determine whether the spoilsman is to discharge the tremendous responsibilities that have been placed on government today, or whether persons are to discharge these responsibilities who have been selected by fair, open, practical, competitive tests."

Support for the commission's indignation came from many quarters. Mr. Samuel H. Ordway, at that time president of the National Civil Service Reform League, and White House Member of the Council on Personnel Administration, termed Secretary Ickes "an irresponsible and incompetent reformer." Congressman Ramspeck said he was "astonished at Ickes' apparent lack of knowledge."

The Evening Star published an editorial under the title, "Iron In the Blood," which concluded with this paragraph:

> In this incident (i.e., the Finch dismissal case) the most serious attempt at sabotage has been the iron-blooded attack on the civil service. The Civil Service Commission, having iron in its blood, correctly resents the slurring and inaccurate reference by Mr. Ickes to the protection offered employees by the merit system. As the Commission correctly says, Mr. Ickes has taken the traditional method of the politician to undermine the principles of the merit system by attributing to them inefficiency of government personnel. The taxpayers who support both Mr. Ickes and the merit system would not hesitate in deciding which of the two is more valuable in effecting economy and efficiency in government.

Another verbal clash with a cabinet officer came when the secretary of the Navy, Frank Knox, made a public statement about "thoroughly incompetent government employees."

Questioned about this by the Ramspeck investigating committee in March, 1943, Arthur, representing the commission, replied, "We're spending considerable time and money recruiting people for the Navy; and if these people are thoroughly incompetent, we should be told about it instead of reading it in the newspapers. There is no rhyme or reason to spend time and money to hire people if they are thoroughly incompetent. But, I wonder," he added, "how many people have been discharged. They have no business in government if they are thoroughly incompetent." He went on to say that Secretary Knox's charges damaged morale.

On at least one occasion a blast against the commission came all the way from Columbus, Ohio, when Governor Bricker charged that the commission was trying to "smear" the Ohio Bureau of Unemployment Compensation by investigation tactics. In this instance, Governor Bricker, a Republican, had refused permission to the commission to establish headquarters in the Bureau of Unemployment Compensation building to pursue questioning of its employees about alleged political activity in violation of the federal Hatch Act, which prohibited such activity.

The commission dispatched Arthur to Columbus to talk the matter over with Governor Bricker. It was amicably resolved.

Another occasion in which Arthur spoke out in defense of federal employees was when he appeared before the Senate Civil Service Committee, which was holding hearings on a bill to cover one hundred and fifty thousand employees into civil service. Senator Schwartz (D-WY) opposed the bill and said that "civil service employees weren't worth a thin dime to any political party." Senator Schwartz opposed the inclusion of Tennessee Valley Authority employees under the proposed bill, as this was such a fruitful ground for political favors.

Taking note of the "thin dime" reference, Arthur, in his testimony, said that "Civil Service employees may not be worth much to political parties, but they are worth 100 cents on the dollar to the American people."

A vicious attack on the civil service was printed in *Harper's Magazine* in October, 1954, in an article entitled, "Let's Go Back to the Spoils System," by John Fischer. The explanatory heading by the editors stated that "Mr. Fischer is not an unbiased observer."

Basing his comments on a seven-year experience in govern-

ment work, Mr. Fischer made all manner of fun of the civil
service, its red tape, its inefficiency, its slowness to act, its
ineffective dealings as far as undesirable employees are concerned. He did have a good word to say about Arthur, however.
It reads:

> Paradoxically, the Commission is actually run by its lone Republi-
> can member, Arthur S. Flemming, the youngest, most progressive, and
> best qualified of the three (i.e., the members of the Commission).
> Roosevelt drafted him six years ago from The American University
> School of Public Affairs, which Flemming had directed with marked
> ability. To him belongs the credit for most of the wartime improve-
> ments in the Commission's operation.
>
> His major reform was a temporary relaxation of the regulations
> to give the war agencies considerable freedom in recruiting their
> own staffs, subject to a review of each appointment by the Com-
> mission. He also decentralized a good deal of responsibility to the
> field services, brought in a number of able assistants, and cleaned
> out most of the witch-hunters and hayseed dicks from the investi-
> gating staff.
>
> In these and other efforts to shore up their rickety machine,
> Flemming has won the assent of his Democratic colleagues by the
> exercise of unmeasured patience and tact. They now leave to him
> the day-to-day chores of management, and even permit him to
> speak for the Commission before Congressional committees. He
> has had less success, however, in gaining the support of the
> Commission's permanent staff: the most in-bred, tradition-ridden
> claque in Washington.

Arthur, on reading this, was unimpressed by the bouquet
tossed to him by Mr. Fischer and forthwith proceeded to write to
the editors of *Harper's* pointing out inaccuracies in the article.
He ended with a plea for them to carry an article by a competent
authority presenting the other side of the picture, but I do not
believe this was ever done.

Occasionally even I was acutely aware that those who eat

from the public trough endure all sorts of criticism from unin-formed persons. At a private luncheon attended by young women who were long-time personal friends of mine, a conversation got started over application blanks used by the commission for prospective public employees. A great deal of fun was poked at the entire process of recruitment, with some really unkind and vicious banter about the commission members thrown in for good measure.

It went on and on with most of those present trying to out-do each other with their tales of recruitment experiences heard or encountered. I sat in stony silence, not caring to enter into any argument, but aware that much that was said was of doubtful validity and really malicious. Apparently no one present both-ered to connect me with the onslaught, though I was acutely uncomfortable throughout the luncheon. I made my departure as soon as I decently could.

Later, in relating the incident to Arthur, he smiled in his tolerant way and said simply, "Forget it. You can't be thin-skinned in our business."

So I tried to develop a thick skin. I'm still trying.

When the House Civil Service Committee started an investi-gation of federal personnel practices in March of 1943, Arthur appeared before them to set the record straight on the matter of whether government employees could be fired. Several mem-bers on this occasion declared that federal agencies were alto-gether too lax in firing incompetents. Arthur's testimony in re-ply was very specific. He made it clear that the authority of various agencies of the government is absolute, and that a government administrator could fire an employee with cause, and that there was little the Civil Service Commission could do about it. An employee who feels that he has been unjustly fired can make an appeal to the commission, and although the commis-sion could not reinstate such an employee, they could certify him for a job in another agency. Arthur insisted that the blame for failure to get rid of incompetent employees rested on the agencies and not on the commission.

Once in a while somebody had a kind word to say about the commission. In an appearance before the Ramspeck Committee investigation of the commission, General Breton Somervell, Chief of the Armed Service Forces, was high in his praise of the commission. He testified that, in his opinion, the commission was doing an excellent job.

The Ramspeck Committee also investigated personnel practices in the Office of Price Administration. Committee members contended that the OPA under Leon Henderson flaunted civil service and appointed whomever he wanted. Again Arthur carried the ball for the commission and informed the committee that the commission prevented the appointment of "obviously unqualified employees," and he added that thousands more incompetents would have had war agency jobs if the commission had not stopped the appointments. Arthur assured the committee on this occasion that the commission had "gotten tougher" within recent months and promised the committees that they intended to get "even tougher." This was one of the rare occasions when the committee members warmly applauded Arthur on his testimony.

Whenever Arthur appeared before congressional committees to answer charges of one sort or another against prevailing civil service practices, he always sought to put the blame where it belonged. For example, when he was asked to explain why there were thousands of employees on the federal payroll as the result of nepotism, "vicious office practices," and other methods of favoritism, Arthur emphasized that during the war emergency, when personnel demands increased, the commission could not follow its normal procedure of accepting those who stood at the head of civil service lists as a result of competitive examinations. He insisted that the commission honestly endeavored to get the best qualified persons available, but that existing circumstances of time, resources, and war pressures made it impossible to investigate all cases, in view of the demands for large numbers of employees. Hence, in some cases, the administrative officers took matters in their own hands and indulged in "unauthorized recruitment procedures."

Some of Arthur's problems as a Civil Service commissioner were accompanied by sidelights quite humorous in nature. One such situation developed between the commission and Senator McKellar, of Tennessee, who sponsored a bill in 1944 that would require Senate confirmation of all federal employees making $4,500 or more. Testimony on the proposed bill brought out the fact that the senator was interested in a postmaster in the little Virginia town of Edinburg. This man had been a fourth-class postmaster for ten years, and the senator thought he should be promoted to a third-class postmaster.

The commission thought otherwise because, it came out, the postmaster not only drank heavily, but "he had an affiliation with a lady which he should not have had." In fact, witnesses testified that he was generally regarded as inefficient.

Senator McKellar accused the commission of being "blue-nosed reformers." Much verbal wrangling went on between Senator McKellar and Arthur during the committee hearings over whether or not the postmaster involved was entitled to the raise in status. What Senator McKellar didn't know was that Arthur's parents-in-law were retired and living in Edinburg and were therefore well acquainted with the postmaster in question.

Because the commission refused to approve the promotion of the postmaster to third-class status, Senator McKellar retaliated by persuading the committee to cut the commission's appropriation from $19 million to $14 million or just about 25percent. Such are the human factors at work in this government of ours.

Another tough verbal battle with an influential senator occurred in 1945. This time the antagonist was Senator Harry Byrd, of Virginia, chairman of the Joint Committee on Nonessential Government Expenditures. Arthur again represented the commission at a hearing in which Senator Byrd took exception to the commission's statistics on the number of employees then in the government, and insisted that the data presented to his committee by Arthur was valueless. In defending the commission's figures, Arthur told Senator Byrd that "the federal government has subjected itself to more checks on utilizing its manpower at top efficiency than any other single employer," emphasizing that it should be commended rather than constantly criticized.

Arthur's conflicts at various time with members of the legislative branch of the government did not, however, dilute his generally positive attitude toward his job and the constructive work that could be done. Along with his frequent defense of the civil service system and the public employees selected through its procedures, he was also constantly working toward making Uncle Sam the country's best employer. Pay increases, vacation and sick leave, insurance benefits—all these became matters of interest to him and which he worked constantly toward improving.

I have previously indicated that the nation's defense program was already under way when Arthur took the oath of office in 1939. Within a matter of months after that, the commission began making plans for filling orders for manpower that were expected to come in from defense agencies.

Led by Arthur, at the request of his two colleagues, the commission began making revisions in its practices and procedures in order to gear the government's recruiting of skilled workers for the national defense plants.

In a speech before the Civil Service Assembly of the United States and Canada in September of 1940, Arthur stated that the commission would have to fill more than two hundred thousand defense positions by the following June. He outlined specific plans for accelerating recruitment. *The Times Herald* carried a story about the speech, headlining it, "Flemming's Ideas Should Seep into Every Agency of Government."

When President Roosevelt asked the Congress to approve an overtime pay plan, Arthur again represented the commission in urging its passage. He said that it was vitally needed to maintain morale of government organizations and to halt large-scale turnover, which could disrupt the war effort. This bill was designed to correct inequities in pay between different executive departments.

Another pay raise bill was introduced by Senator Downey of California, in 1946. Arthur represented the Truman administration in backing a program for a 20 percent raise in government workers' pay to cover the increase in cost of living. When the bill was finally passed, Arthur was present when President Truman signed it. The president presented him with the pen he used on this occasion.

On problems involving the fate of federal employees, Arthur worked cooperatively with employees' unions such as the National Federation of Federal Employees, the American Federation of Government Employees, and the National Association of Letter Carriers. He counseled with the officers of the unions and worked with them to improve conditions of employment. He was frequently a speaker at their national conventions.

Just once during these years was he tempted to leave the commission. This was when Governor Thomas Dewey of New York asked him to come to Albany to become chairman of the Civil Service Commission for the state of New York. It was a very attractive opportunity, but his decision was to remain where he was.

Even now I feel tired when I recall the many different assignments Arthur undertook with the national defense program, and later the war effort, all on top of his job as Civil Service commissioner.

Two years after his appointment to the commission, the first of these assignments was given to him. It was when an organization for assuring ample numbers of skilled workers in expanding defense industries, if necessary by transferring them from less important plants on a priority basis, was set up through the Office of Production Management. The idea grew out of a request by President Roosevelt, who wrote to Mr. Sidney Hillman, then associate director general of OPM, that he was "disturbed about the number of defense industries that declared themselves unable to obtain enough skilled workers and supervisors to achieve full complements of labor on the second and third shifts."

Mr. Hillman asked Arthur to assist him in this new labor supply set-up, and in doing so he said that this job "was unquestionably one of the most significant poolings of labor, management, and government resources that has thus far taken place in the national defense program." In the huge task of supplying labor for the entire defense industry, Mr. Hillman announced, Arthur would have a policymaking body to assist him that would consist of the head of the United States Employment Service, the acting commissioner of Labor Statistics, heads of other appropriate agencies in the Labor Department, Federal Security Agency, and Federal Works Agency, as well as chiefs of various OPM labor division sections.

The Knickerbocker News, Albany, on September 20, 1941, described the development in these terms:

> On the broad shoulders of youthful appearing Arthur Sherwood Flemming the Administration has placed the twin tasks of finding skilled workers for defense industries and placing in new jobs those thrown out on the street by that paradox of the defense program—priorities employment. Although faced with two of the worse headaches of the gigantic defense program the 36-year-old former college instructor from Kingston is enjoying his assign-

ment. It makes him the biggest job finder in the nation's history.

The number of workers expected to be thrown out of employment by priorities displacement has been variously estimated between 1,000,000 and 2,000,000. Flemming's task is to get them as quickly as possible into defense jobs before they feel the pinch of privation.

Coincident with this task he must find and guide into defense industries the hundreds of thousands of workers needed for more planes and guns, and tanks, ships, and ammunition. . . .

And so Arthur undertook with this assignment the handling of two tough jobs—one as Civil Service commissioner, and the other as chief of OPM's Labor Supply Division. He then embarked on a twelve- to fifteen-hour work day, which continued until the end of the war in 1945 (only one salary, however). It meant that six days weekly, most evenings, and all holidays he was either in his office or doing something connected with the pursuit of his duties. Christmas Day was absolutely the only day except Sunday (which he devoted to helping run Foundry Methodist Church) that he took off from the steady, grinding routine. Many other officials in the government were doing the same thing.

In his two-fold task—as a Civil Service commissioner charged with the rapidly increasing roster of classified employees and as chairman of the Labor Supply for OPM helping industry to get human forces needed to turn out defense materials, plus trying to take steps that would obviate further problems—Arthur necessarily had to travel over the country holding conferences in strategic areas to speed up defense work and provide for transfer of workers from non-defense to the defense industry.

The first big test of the workability of the OPM's new Labor Supply Division was in meeting the unemployment problems caused by the shut-down in August, 1941, of the Buffalo-area Chevrolet plant while this plant changed over to aircraft engine production. It affected three thousand workers.

Arthur was dispatched to Buffalo to confer with representatives of four big defense plants in that area in an effort to plan effective use of these workers. Plans for training this large pool of manpower and for their absorption in the defense plants were laid at this meeting.

This first "test case" attempt to find new defense jobs for the displaced Chevrolet workers was pronounced a complete success by OPM Chief, Mr. Hillman.

At about the same time, Arthur developed a program to alleviate the problem of twenty-five thousand silk hosiery workers. The Buffalo program provided the pattern to be duplicated in hundreds of other situations, particularly in the automobile, washing machine, refrigerator, and other durable consumer goods factories faced with shutdowns as a result of the diversion of raw materials to defense plants. This, he believed, could be accomplished through cooperative machinery set up by government, labor unions, and management of defense industries.

General Hugh Johnson, former National Recovery Administrator, in his syndicated column of December 5, 1941, took note of Arthur's work in this area. After commenting on the need for insuring of selected and efficient manpower to guarantee skilled labor to defense production efforts, he said:

> It is true that there has been created within the general framework of OPM a labor supply committee operating under the able direction of Arthur S. Flemming, of the Civil Service Commission. This committee has been working for some time, but very little public attention has been given to its activity. It has at least one virtue—in this field the Government seems to have at least partially appreciated the vital necessity of coordinating the efforts of all agencies affected by a single purpose under a single directive hand. This is a basic principle of organization which has been too generally neglected in other phases of our mobilization effort.

Then, after commenting on the confusing element necessarily encountered by the reason of the number of government agencies involved in the Labor Supply Division's work, General Johnson continued:

> Under these handicaps the work of Mr. Flemming and his emergency organization are subject to even more commendation. It is to be hoped that the progress he has made will not be impaired by the petty interdepartmental bickerings likely to be engendered, the rumblings of which are already beginning to be ominously heard from some of the highly perfumed prima donnas who are the titular heads of the organization from which some of the subcommittees are drawn.

That was on December 5, 1941.

On December 7, 1941—a Sunday evening—we heard on the radio that the Japanese had bombed Pearl Harbor. The defense preparedness effort of the United States suddenly became an all-out war effort.

I suppose none of us old enough at the time to realize the tragic implications of the Pearl Harbor bombing will ever forget that moment. First, there was stunned disbelief, to be followed shortly by a clammy kind of fear that gnawed at our hearts for days, and months, and then years.

The news came to us when we had a group of friends in for supper to initiate our newly completed and furnished downstairs recreation room. One guest was a naval officer stationed in Washington. The implications as far as he was concerned were far-reaching indeed.

The next day, I sat glued to the radio to hear President Roosevelt as he appeared before a joint session of the Congress to ask for a declaration of war.

Life suddenly became very serious indeed.

I was luckier than most. Although Arthur was already involved deeply in the country's defense program, and was working day and night, I was spared the tremendous strain that accompanied actual service at the war front.

I did two things to insulate myself: I bought eight canvasses to make needlepoint seat covers for our dining room chairs, and I enrolled in a Red Cross Nurses' Aide course. I called these my "war" projects. The first project took me eleven years to complete. I finished the first chair cover in six weeks, and the last one took two years.

The second project was more immediately concerned with the war itself: the crying need for nurses in hospitals to replace the ones who left for various military, naval, and air assignments both at home and around the world.

After completing my course and getting the coveted certificate, the capping ceremony itself was an inspiring occasion. I remember how big we all felt when the speaker said "we could hold our heads high" because we were helping with the really critical needs of the country in replacing the regular nurses in much routine patient care.

After the training period in a general hospital, I chose to do my volunteer hours in a women's hospital in Washington, which had both surgical and obstetrical wings. For me, the choice added a big dash of glamor to my life because the captain of the nurses' aides in our hospital was Mrs. Louise Macy Hopkins. Louise Macy had married Harry Hopkins, a man who occupied many roles during the Roosevelt administration, including that of secretary of Commerce, in a ceremony at the White House. Actually, the Hopkinses lived in the White House so that the president could have this trusted adviser close at all times during the difficult war period.

Louise Hopkins gave a full day's work every week day as a volunteer nurses' aide, and she worked as hard as any nurse during every hour she was there. She was a really beautiful woman—tall, slender, with dark brown hair and merry brown eyes. At the lunch hour, when we gathered in the nurses' lunch room for a brief respite and nourishment, Louise would regale us with tales of what was going on at the White House on the lighter side. Madame Chiang Kai Chek and Pearl Buck were guests there during this time, and Louise told interesting episodes of their visits. We all loved her. She really spiced up our days in a very special way.

Another incident that occurred during my nurses' aide period was the privilege I had one morning of witnessing a cesarean section being performed. My own obstetrician was on the staff of the hospital, and on that particular morning when I reported for duty I ran into him on my way down the corridor for my day's assignment. His name was Doctor Prentiss Willson.

"Would you like to watch a cesarean?" he asked me.

"I'd love it," I replied. I'm a gory individual.

"If you will promise not to faint, you can come along with me."

So I followed him to the operating room and waited while the scrubbing took place. Then he showed me just where to stand and proceeded to explain to me each step in the process of delivering a baby by cesarean section. When the moment was reached that he drew the baby out and held it up for me to see, I felt a tremendous thrill.

Often during these hectic days I would bathe a dozen or more babies in a morning and then wheel them around to their mothers to be fed. Ultimately, this kind of activity had interesting repercussions. At least, Doctor Willson delighted in telling me that my nurses' aide activity in caring for large numbers of babies in the hospital nursery stimulated my hormones so much that I had to discontinue my volunteer work in favor of caring for the set of twins that arrived in our family in October of 1943. Arthur took time off to come to the hospital for this event.

Before this, however, he had taken another major assignment

in connection with the war effort. This was in the spring of 1942, when the War Manpower Commission was created by President Roosevelt to have charge of mobilizing the nation's manpower and womanpower to carry out the war program.

Under the chairmanship of Federal Security Administrator Paul McNutt, the War Manpower Commission consisted of three cabinet members—Secretary of the Navy James Forrestal, Secretary of Agriculture Claude Wickard, and Secretary of Labor Frances Perkins—and War Production Board Chairman Donald Nelson, Labor Production Chief Wendell Lund, Selective Service Director Louis Hershey, the War Department's representative Goldthwaite Door, and Arthur.

When he created this commission, the president authorized it to provide adequate supplies of industrial and farm labor to assure the success of war production. He also gave it the power to direct all federal agencies on recruiting and training men and women for industrial and agricultural jobs essential to the war program.

In September of 1942, the president and the War Manpower Commission gave to the Civil Service Commission authority to transfer government employees to other jobs in the federal service without their consent and without the approval of the agencies involved. This move was made to place employees in the spot of most use in the war effort, and placed sweeping power over the nation's two million federal employees in the hands of the commission. In explaining this order to a joint press conference held by "Manpower Czar" McNutt and Arthur, representing the commission, Arthur took pains to explain that steps would be taken to protect the basic rights of employees. Briefly, these rights consisted in the same job security that was guaranteed federal workers who entered military service. Seniority, promotion, retirement, and other benefits would not be lost because of the transfers.

Concurrently, Mr. McNutt asked Arthur to be chairman of the Management-Labor Policy Committee of the War Manpower Commission. Its purpose was to study carefully the fundamental questions of policy that are involved in the consideration of national war service legislation. With this in view, the commission conducted a comprehensive review of the national manpower and womanpower problems that had come before the War Manpower Commission since its establishment in May, 1942.

The committee, composed of equal numbers representing management and organized labor, held weekly meetings after it was established. One of their reports to the War Manpower Commission in November included specific recommendations urging government, industry, agriculture, and labor to provide strong leadership, aggressive action, and cooperation to bring about needed changes in existing practices to speed the nation's war effort.

In November, 1943, the secretary of the Navy, Mr. Forrestal, named Arthur a member of the Navy Department's Manpower Survey Board. The purpose of this board was to survey all naval shore establishments to determine whether they were over-manned or under-manned, and whether the Navy's manpower was being used to the best advantage.

As a result of his work on this board, Arthur was awarded the Navy's Distinguished Civilian Service Award.

It was in April of 1945 that we were all stunned by the news of the death of Franklin Roosevelt while on a visit to Warm Springs, Georgia. Mrs. Roosevelt immediately summoned Vice-President Harry Truman from the Senate chamber to come to the White House. She cautioned him to say nothing about where he was going.

On his arrival, Mrs. Roosevelt said simply, "Harry, the president is dead." And then, without further preliminaries, Harry Truman was sworn into the office of president of the United

States.

President Truman immediately took an interest in the personnel problems of the executive branch and took the unusual step of inviting the personnel officers and agency heads to a meeting held in the motion picture room of the White House to discuss their problems.

On this occasion President Truman aired his own views in a new White House order converting the Civil Service system back to peacetime basis. At this meeting Arthur was asked to speak. This was a truly unique occasion—probably the only time a president of the United States has shown enough interest in federal personnel problems to invite the personnel directors of the various executive departments and agencies to the White House.

Included in the new presidential order was a directive to the Civil Service Commission to restore the peacetime system of filling job vacancies through regular Civil Service examinations.

When Harry Truman succeeded to the office of president, Arthur had been on the Civil Service Commission for six years. Since President Truman did not appoint Arthur, he was, of course, free to replace him with a Civil Service commissioner of his own choice. He did, however, ask Arthur to remain as the Republican member. During the three years that he remained on the commission, Arthur found President Truman to be an extremely knowledgeable and effective leader in the federal personnel field.

The war drew to its welcome conclusion in 1946, accelerated by President Truman's difficult decision to drop the atom bomb on Nagasaki and Hiroshima. And then Arthur's attention began to be directed toward the shifting of the high-gear defense production activity to the lower-geared peacetime situation.

About this time an important change in the membership of the Civil Service Commission occurred. The first woman cabinet member, Frances Perkins, who had served as secretary of Labor during all of the Franklin Roosevelt years, resigned from the cabinet on President Roosevelt's death. President Truman then appointed her to replace Mrs. McMillan as a Democratic member of the commission.

Miss Perkins and Arthur enjoyed a good working relationship and a mutually respectful association during Arthur's remaining years on the commission. He felt that she made a really outstanding contribution to the work of that body. And later, after Arthur went to Ohio Wesleyan University as president, Miss Perkins came to the college on the lecture series and was an overnight guest at our house. This occasion is a happy memory for all of us.

Following the close of the war, though our country had been Russia's ally in the conflict with Japan, we entered a period of intensified concentration on the loyalty of federal employees. Attention was focused on this when subcommittee chairman Rees, of the House Civil Service Commission, introduced a bill calling for a full-fledged scrutiny of the loyalty of federal employees. The Rees measure provided for setting up a Federal Loyalty Board which would have absolute power in determining whether employees should be hired or fired. The president also issued a loyalty executive order, calling for a loyalty board to serve in an advisory capacity, with the final decision left up to the individual departments and agencies.

Arthur objected to the Rees bill as being too costly and cumbersome, and he was supported by Commission Chairman Mitchell when he testified before the House committee considering the proposed bill.

Another proposal that attracted widespread interest in the summer of 1947 was a joint congressional resolution authorizing a special study of the organization of the executive branch of the government. The proposed commission was to consist of twelve appointees—four to be named by the president, four by the president *pro tempore* of the Senate, and four by the speaker of

119

the House of Representatives. The twelve were to include six Democrats and six Republicans, and there were to be six government and six nongovernment representatives.

President Truman's choices were announced at a news conference shortly thereafter and included Secretary of the Navy James Forrestal, former Undersecretary of State Dean Atchison, an industrial executive from Dayton, Ohio, George H. Mead, and Arthur.

Ex-President Hoover was one of the appointees of the Speaker of the House, and he became at seventy-eight years of age the chairman of the Commission on the Organization of the Executive Branch of the Government, thereafter referred to as COEBG.

The work of the commission proved to be one of the most challenging assignments ever undertaken by Arthur. He particularly enjoyed the opportunity to get to know Mr. Hoover really well. He admired him greatly.

After the commission made its recommendations for change, it was of course up to the Congress to implement these recommendations. In an effort to muster public support for change, Arthur, even after we moved to Delaware, made many speeches to citizens' groups promoting the suggestions that came out of the commission's study of the operation of the executive branch.

One of Arthur's last presentations for improvement in the federal service was to a subcommittee of the House Civil Service Committee, when he offered a draft of a proposed revision of the Federal Classification Act. The revision would:

1. Simplify the current classification act.
2. Provide rewards for outstanding service in the federal government.
3. Provide for decentralization of the administration of the classification act by making the Civil Service Commission responsible for standards, and departments and agencies responsible for the classification of jobs in line with these standards.

A federal pay increase was also under consideration at the same time. To the last, Arthur worked to improve the lot of the federal worker under the merit system.

One of Arthur's extracurricular activities during his final years on the commission was to work with the Washington Junior Chamber of Commerce on plans to institute annual awards for young bureaucrats who have made outstanding contributions in their jobs as public servants. After he left the commission the Junior Chamber decided to honor Arthur by naming the awards after him. So the Arthur S. Flemming Awards have been an annual feature of life in Washington ever since. They are given at a large public luncheon and are highly prized by the recipients. Arthur and I take great pleasure and pride in attending these occasions whenever we are in Washington. At the 1984 awards party, the Jaycees honored me with a lifetime membership.

The year 1972 marked the twenty-fifth year that the Arthur S. Flemming Awards had been made, and for the first time two of them went to women. Arthur and I were there to enjoy the celebration. Elizabeth Hanford, later secretary of Transportation in President Reagan's cabinet and secretary of Labor in President Bush's cabinet, married to Senator Robert Dole of Kansas, was one of the awardees. At the time she was in the White House Consumer Affairs Office.

Arthur's favorite extracurricular activity was, of course, the church. During the war years, his church involvement was chiefly confined to Foundry United Methodist Church, where we were members. The minister was Doctor Frederic Brown Harris, who was for many years the chaplain of the United States Senate. Arthur and Doctor Harris became close friends. Frequent and long were their discussions about Foundry personnel matters and about the various programs of the church.

It sometimes happens that meetings of church groups form the setting for bitter personality clashes and battles over policy.

Several such situations occurred during these years, and Arthur's part in these different crises was to support fully the proposals of Doctor Harris and to plead for quiet, reasonable approaches to problems.

As the children came along, and as each one reached the age of two, Arthur started taking them to the Foundry Sunday school. In those days we didn't have a car, so going to Foundry on Sunday mornings had nightmarish aspects for me. There was breakfast to get, six people to get properly dressed and combed (big Arthur did get himself dressed), a six-block walk to the bus, and when we got off, another six-block walk to the church. Sunday dinner was supposed to appear miraculously on the table within minutes after we got home.

Truly, Sunday was a day to live through, and by the time dinner was over, all I wanted to do was fall in bed.

The fact of the matter is that I was not as religious as Arthur. I was quite content to let him do the organizational work. He loves meetings; I hate them. My role might be described as a sort of habeas corpus one, that is, I "deliver the body." Over the years I'm sure I've delivered him to thousands of church meetings and have taken him to many a church dinner where he was the speaker. But my one experience as president of a church women's organization was a really unpleasant one, and I've remained aloof from them ever since. Occasionally I've taught Sunday school classes, but not on a regular basis. I left that sort of thing to Arthur, and I insisted to him and to others that since I had to take care of his children and the house single-handedly, that he'd have to do my church and civic work, and I'd hope to go to heaven on his coattail! My Presbyterian friends tell me this won't work.

After the war wound down, Arthur was making many speeches at churches all over the Washington area. Churches of all denominations invited him to speak at their services. It was a handy way for the ministers to have a holiday now and then since Arthur always said "Yes" when asked to speak.

It was natural, therefore, that he should become involved in the capital city's cooperative church organization, the Washington Federation of Churches. His first job in this group was to head up the annual financial campaign in February of 1946 and, as night follows day, the next year he was elected president of the federation, the second layman to head it.

One of my clear memories of this event is what Doctor Frederick Reissig, the executive secretary of the federation, said to me. "It won't take much time," he explained in his effort to get my approval. "You know, we believe in family life, too."

But it did take too much time, with endless meetings to attend in connection with the work of the federation. Besides, whenever Arthur was president of anything, the momentum picked up, and he had all sorts of ideas and projects to propose as part of the federation's program.

His special project during his two years as president of the federation was to get it to agree to support a chaplain at St. Elizabeth's Hospital, the government's hospital for the mentally ill. He had many consultations with the hospital's administrators and the federation executives over this proposal and later over the selection of the chaplain.

And of course being president of the federation brought him additional invitations to speak to church groups. Sometimes I went along.

I still have a particularly vivid memory of one such occasion, and it involves an evening service when Arthur spoke at one of the large downtown Black Baptist churches. This was in 1947, when Washington was still a completely segregated city.

When we arrived at the church, Arthur was escorted up to the front, and I was shown to a seat right in the middle of the church and entirely surrounded by Black people. I was the only White person in the church besides Arthur.

The ritual of the service began, and I became aware that a communion service was in progress. When we got to the point in the ritual where the elements representing the body and blood of Christ were passed, a real dilemma presented itself. The bread was passed first. That posed no problem. But the wine! It was served in a common chalice instead of in individual cups as was the custom in our own church. Suddenly I was aware that if I was to participate, I would have to take my sip from the chalice following the sips taken by all the Black communicants, and without even the token wipes that Episcopal clergymen provide between sips.

What should I do? Rapidly, three possible courses of action passed before my mind as I sat there: I could leave, thus showing clearly to members of the congregation that I didn't want to drink from the same cup they did; or, I could just sit there and let the cup pass me, revealing the same attitude; or I could take a sip and pass the chalice on to the next person.

There was Arthur sitting calmly up on the podium, unaware of the truly critical problem facing me down among the Black congregation. Only a Southerner brought up as I had been, with a set of attitudes like mine, can appreciate the enormity of the dilemma I was wrestling with.

Meanwhile, the chalice began to move across the front pew, passing from hand to hand, and through the second row, and then the third, slowly but surely making its way from person to person to the pew where I sat. I honestly didn't know what I would do until the moment actually arrived when I was passed the chalice to take my sip, and I did just that! I look back on that particular incident as the moment in time when I began to conquer my built-in prejudicial attitudes, and from that time on I was able to face many a situation that forced me to grow as far as my racial tendencies were concerned.

Arthur's activities and interest in the field of religion were reaching out into the national arena during this period. One recognition he received was an annual award for National Churchmanship given by *Zion's Herald,* the only independent journal of religious news and thought in American Methodism.

His involvement with organizational work on the national level began in September, 1947, when he accepted the chairmanship of the department of church and economic life of the old Federal Council of Churches of Christ in America. The department was concerned with helping local churches to hold conferences on the relationship between American churches and community economic problems. A basic technique of the department's program was to bring together outstanding leaders in various segments of economic life to discuss the responsibility and program of the church.

Clearly Arthur was joining the liberal churchmen of the day in promoting the active involvement of the church in the great social, economic, and political issues that confronted the country. He was not content with viewing the church as an isolated institution unconcerned with issues that affected all of the people. He gave many a sermon on "Love thy neighbor as thyself." In fact, it became a sort of theme song with him as he constantly related the work of the church to public service and good citizenship.

In late May of 1948, stories began to appear in the Washington papers suggesting that Arthur's resignation as a member of the Civil Service Commission was imminent. And on May 29, *The Evening Star* carried the story of his resignation to accept the presidency of Ohio Wesleyan University.

Arthur's friend Doctor Frederick M. Davenport invited him to go to England with him in July. We were to leave for Delaware, Ohio, the end of August. Doctor Davenport was eighty-four years old, and it was his annual custom to go abroad by ship and to take along as a companion a younger man. I feel sure this arrangement was also a sort of safety precaution which made Doctor Davenport's family more comfortable about his taking such a long trip.

On the night of July 15, 1948, Arthur telephoned me from New York. He was scheduled to board the *Queen Elizabeth* at ten o'clock for a midnight sailing. He simply wanted to check to see if everything at home was all right before he mounted the gangplank to the *Queen Elizabeth*. He asked if I thought I had enough money to keep the home front solvent during the three weeks of his trip to England. I assured him I had enough.

But for some unexplained reason I added, "But if we have any unexpected emergency such as a bad accident or operation, I don't have enough to cover such a contingency."

Arthur replied: "In case of any such emergency, just call Dad. He'll help you out until I get home." Thus comforted, I went to sleep.

The following morning I awoke feeling more ill than I'd ever felt in my entire life. I was completely inert with dizziness, nausea, and abdominal pain. I really couldn't lift my head.

Lib, then twelve, took over and called our family doctor. Doctor Dortzbach arrived shortly, and his initial diagnosis was probable appendicitis. But there were some factors present that made him hesitant. So, during an excruciatingly painful morning, two more doctors appeared at my bedside to investigate the cause of my sudden illness. In these days of strict clinical medical practice, I can hardly believe that three doctors bothered to come to the house, but that is exactly what happened. At the time, I was hardly aware of their presence, all of them nodding their heads in puzzlement.

By noon, all were agreed on one thing: I must go to the hospital immediately for surgery. The surgeon, Doctor Caulfield, a Spring Valley neighbor, thought I had a hemorrhagic ovarian cyst.

I was really too uncomfortable to care what they did to me, and also too ill to be more than vaguely aware of what would happen to the children while I was hospitalized. Some wonderful friends and neighbors came to the rescue.

Nobody on either side of the family came to assist or in any way offered to help, though they all knew that Arthur was on his way to Europe, and I was alone with the children. The whole experience was grim indeed, but friends cared for the children, brought food, and gave me abundant loving support in this crisis. And we all survived.

The operation was performed in the late afternoon. One friend took me to the hospital. Another came to wave me off to the operating room and to remain there until I reacted to the anaesthetic. Several friends offered to help me out financially. Our grocery merchant even came to the hospital and offered to supply food for the family as long as necessary. If Arthur had been home, this sort of thing would not have happened. But he was on the *Queen Elizabeth* somewhere out in the Atlantic Ocean, and our friends simply took over. I look back on my hospital stay as a rather pleasant experience.

On the third day after the operation I was wheeled down the corridor to the office where the telephone was. In that day hospital rooms did not have telephones as standard equipment.

There I placed a trans-Atlantic telephone call from the hospital in Bethesda, Maryland, to the *Queen Elizabeth,* which was by then approaching England. Arthur couldn't be reached immediately, but when found, the message he was given was to "call Mrs. Flemming in Bethesda, Maryland." He, too, therefore, had a brief time to wonder what was going on.

When he returned the call, I told him what had happened and assured him everything at home was "under control." He arrived back home on August 8, and by that time I was managing the house and the children as if nothing had happened.

On August 23, Arthur was given a testimonial dinner at the

Mayflower Hotel in Washington. About seven hundred people came, most of them bureaucrats and their wives.

The toastmaster was Congressman Robert Ramspeck, former chairman of the House Civil Service Committee. Speeches were made by Donald Dawson, administrative assistant to the president; Arthur's fellow commissioners Frances Perkins and Harry Mitchell; Attorney General Tom Clark; Secretary of Defense James Forrestal; and representatives of the three government employees' unions: the National Federation of Federal Employees, the American Federation of Government Employees, and the National Association of Letter Carriers.

Messages were read from Ex-President Hoover, Doctor Leonard White, Senator William Langer, and others. It was a great evening for Arthur.

I don't remember much that was said on that occasion, but I do have a clear recollection of Miss Perkins's speech. As she stood at the microphone, she crooked her little finger in Arthur's direction and said: "Arthur, you will be able to run Ohio Wesleyan with your little finger after all the things you've done in Washington. I predict you'll be back before very long." Subsequent events bore out her prediction.

A few days before we left Washington for our new adventure in educational administration, the congregation of Foundry Church gave a testimonial dinner for Arthur and presented him with a pair of sterling silver candelabra. Later, in a letter written by Doctor Harris transferring our membership from Foundry to the William Street Methodist Church in Delaware, he said that "he would rather lose any six other laymen from his church than Arthur."

In December of that year, Arthur returned to Washington to receive the annual layman's award given by the Washington Federation of Churches.

9

OHIO WESLEYAN: PRESIDENT

It was in January, 1948, that the question of our going to Delaware, Ohio, with Arthur as the possible new president of Ohio Wesleyan, became a topic of conversation at our house.

Doctor Herbert Burgstahler, who was selected for the presidency of Ohio Wesleyan ten years earlier when Arthur was a viable candidate for the job, had just retired. And the board of trustees apparently thought that Arthur, now ten years older, was the man to replace him. They were even able to overlook the fact that he was not a minister.

In later years, Arthur always referred to his selection to be president of Ohio Wesleyan as an "experiment," because he was the first non-minister and the first alumnus to be so honored. So far, none of the presidents since Arthur (four, to date) has been a minister, and two have been alumni, so apparently the "experiment" didn't work out too badly.

Arthur was not really anxious to go, as he had been earlier. He was entirely happy at the Civil Service Commission and felt that what he was doing there was serving a lot more people than would be the case if he went to Ohio Wesleyan.

So the question of to-go-or-not-to-go was a really difficult one. He was a trustee of Ohio Wesleyan, and his trips back to Delaware for meetings of the board had kept him in close touch with the college. He was an intensely loyal alumnus, so the emotional pull was strong.

But he had been in Washington for twenty years, the last nine of them in a really key spot in the federal service, and the prospect of returning to a small city in central Ohio did not loom as a very exciting change. He took several months to make up his mind. One part of the procedure I remember is a small black note book. On one page Arthur wrote at the top: "Reasons for remaining at the United States Civil Service Commission." There followed several pages listing the reasons for that possibility. On the following pages he listed, under the heading "Reasons for going to Ohio Wesleyan," all of the justifications he could think of for going to Delaware. He carried this little book around with him for weeks, adding new ideas as he thought of them.

They were leading him toward Delaware, and finally, in May, his mind was made up.

The Washington Post carried a highly complimentary editorial entitled, "Well Done," in which Arthur's accomplishments as a Civil Service commissioner were enumerated. The final sentence was: "The government can ill afford to lose the services of a man of Mr. Flemming's caliber." This carries a hint of future responsibilities later undertaken by Arthur.

The Star, in an editorial entitled, "A Loss to Government," carried a similar hint in closing with this: "In many other ways he has shown unusual capacities for leadership. The Government will be hard put to find a successor as well qualified for his job as Commissioner Flemming."

August 30 was the date set for our departure for Ohio. We were to travel by train, and I well remember that trip.

As the train wound its way through the Alleghenies in Western Maryland, we leaned back in our comfortable streamlined seats and enjoyed the beautiful scenery all around us. The leaves were just beginning their transformation into deep red, yellow, orange, and brown.

I became aware after luncheon, however, of symptoms of train sickness, which was probably the result of fatigue from many nights of inadequate rest, in addition to the emotional strain of farewells to family members and friends. I made several trips back to the lounge room, becoming weaker and more miserable with each trip.

Suddenly my own symptoms became contagious. I had just returned to my seat after about four spasms of up-chucking, and I noticed that Harry was displaying a peculiar expression that could mean only one thing: my malady had struck him, too!

Harry, unfortunately, did not make it to the men's room before the critical moment arrived, and the results on my brand new maroon suit were distinctly unattractive. The stewardess was there in seconds, with papers and wet towels to clean me up as best she could, assisted by the kind-hearted porter. And the train kept right on rolling along the tracks. Eventually we arrived in Columbus. The fresh air restored Harry and me to normalcy, and we were both all right from then on.

I certainly wouldn't have blamed Arthur if he had drifted away into the next car to avoid being associated with his family in that unpleasant display, but he didn't. He took it in his stride, dismissing the incident as just one of those things.

The house we moved into after our harrowing train ride was a so-called gingerbread mansion, with vast high ceilings and sixty-one enormous windows, most of them single-paned windows. There were fourteen rooms and seven bathrooms. We were the sixth family of Ohio Wesleyan presidents to occupy it.

One day, when we had been in Delaware a couple of weeks, a carpenter appeared from the college maintenance staff to rehang a couple of doors that were sticking. He told me some stories about the previous tenants in that house, and by the time he finished his work I had been greatly enlightened about what the various occupants had done to change it, such as making a bathroom out of a sewing room, a breakfast room out of a pantry, and so on.

Pushing his plane up and down the bottom of the bedroom door, he paused long enough to say, "Yes, I've seen them come and go." After that conversation I had a distinct feeling that the tenure of college presidents in general was dubious indeed.

Shifting gears from Washington life to a little place like Delaware, Ohio, meant an entirely different routine for Arthur. He held on to several of his Washington commitments, including membership on the Hoover Commission, and chairmanship of the Personnel Advisory Board of the Atomic Energy Commission. He thus had occasion to return to Washington frequently.

He jumped into his new duties as a college president on the Ohio Wesleyan campus with enthusiasm, and he enjoyed his new role as a college president from the first day in office. His secretary at the Civil Service Commission spent the first month in the house with us and worked every day at the office to help Arthur get organized. Arthur wished to have her remain in Delaware as his secretary, but she felt that the retirement benefits in the federal service were just too attractive to leave.

From the moment of his arrival Arthur got countless invitations to speak to civic, educational, and church groups throughout Ohio, and he accepted as many of them as he possibly could. In fact, it seemed to me that most of the Methodist ministers in Ohio were bent on having Arthur speak in their churches at Sunday morning services. Since Ohio Wesleyan is a Methodist college and derives financial support from the two Methodist Conferences, I suppose they felt they had a right to a share of his time.

Sunday mornings he was rarely with his family—always off in some Methodist minister's pulpit. I'd get the children off for Sunday school and then get myself dressed and meet them for church. I learned that better behavior was obtained by sitting near the front. And I always sat between the twins (who were five when we moved to Delaware) so they wouldn't get in a fight during the service. I often felt as if I were sitting on top of a volcano, and it might erupt at any moment.

132

It bothered me a great deal that Arthur was away from home on Sundays speaking in Methodist churches all over the state. I really resented this. At least in Washington, I could usually count on his being home on Sundays.

It seemed to me that in Ohio the ministers were actually conspiring to keep Arthur away from his family. Each one felt he simply had to have the new president of Ohio Wesleyan in his pulpit, with no regard whatever for the effect these fatherless Sundays had on the children and me. I still feel this way.

Occasionally I was asked to make a speech, too, and if I consulted Arthur, his advice was always to do it.

One such invitation came to me even before we left Washington. The president of the Ohio Wesleyan University Women's Club invited me to talk at the traditional opening dessert meeting of this group when the new faculty wives are honored. She suggested that I direct my remarks to my reactions to living in Delaware after the years in Washington. Arthur insisted that I accept this opportunity.

The president of the club that year was Mrs. George Gauthier, wife of the director of athletics. In her introduction she referred to the fact that Mrs. Burgstahler, my predecessor, had often said "that to live in the house at 23 Oak Hill [the president's home] was to be the loneliest woman in town. And now, girls," Mrs. Gauthier went on, "let's not let Mrs. Flemming ever have occasion to make a remark like that." I was to recall that statement in later years.

There were some things about life in Delaware that were a bit unnerving for me. I said goodbye to my precious big city anonymity the very first week when, on a walk to orient myself to our new surroundings, I was accosted by a woman who said, "You're Mrs. Flemming, aren't you?"

I admitted I was, and then asked, "Why?"

"Just curious," she replied. At that moment I decided I had to

133

be really careful how I looked, what I said, how I acted. Curiosity is found in abundance in places like Delaware.

I was also made aware of the fact that alumni of Ohio Wesleyan are uniformly excessively proud of that fact and tend to regard others as sort of second-class citizens. At my very first alumni reception held in Columbus for the new president, Arthur and I were standing in the receiving line when one eager lady coming down the line asked me, "And did you go to Ohio Wesleyan too?"

"No," I replied, somewhat apologetically.

She looked me over up and down, apparently quite unprepared for this confession on my part. Then she said, "Well, I suppose there are nice girls at other places, too."

"Maybe so," I said, and off she went.

Soon after this I encountered this same feeling of alumni pride in another connection when two Ohio Wesleyan graduates from Arthur's class called on us one Saturday afternoon. It turned out that they had a daughter attending a state institution in Pennsylvania, and they wanted to talk about the possibility of her transferring to Ohio Wesleyan to complete her courses. It came out in the conversation that the daughter herself was quite happy where she was, and that it was the parents who were anxious that she shift to Ohio Wesleyan.

As an old college admissions officer, I ventured to suggest that perhaps the daughter might be better served if she remained at the state institution until she graduated.

The mother's reaction made it clear to me why they wanted her to transfer. "But you don't understand," she said. "It's the kind of people she associates with that we want to change. We want her to associate with the sort of students who go to Ohio Wesleyan. You know—the kind of people her father and I went to college with."

As a graduate of another state institution, my reaction was

immediate. "Don't worry about that," I advised. "Maybe she'll marry a graduate of Ohio Wesleyan, like I did, and she can make up for it that way."

I found this sort of thing amusing, and after a few years savored the truest acceptance when the alumni association of Ohio Wesleyan made me the recipient of an Alumni Award (the first non-alumnus to receive one) for making the greatest contribution (along with three other awardees) to the university that year.

I was not lonely, however. The children's various activities and interests plunged me into many situations in Delaware—the boy and girl scout organizations, three different parent/teacher associations (one year I held offices in all three simultaneously), band parents, church youth groups, and so on. In addition, I was from the first a regular volunteer nurses' aide at the Red Cross Bloodmobile, and later on the board of the Community Chest. There was no time to be lonely.

The round of faculty and student meetings, alumni groups, and attendance at university and city affairs was a very different sort of life from the bureaucratic routine, but Arthur enjoyed it all.

We also had many guests that first year. One of the most enjoyable was the visit of Sir Percival and Lady Waterfield, in whose home Arthur had been a guest the previous summer in England. Sir Percival had been a civil service commissioner of Great Britain since 1939, and Arthur was proud to confer on him an honorary doctor of laws degree.

We took the Waterfields to the train in Columbus when they left. By this time we felt we had known them always, so easy and comfortable had been their visit with us. As Lady Waterfield mounted the steps to enter the train, she looked back over her shoulder and waved to us. "Don't ride yourself too hard, Arthur," she called. I like to remember that. We did not see them again, but kept up a Christmas card exchange for many years.

The marks of the crusader were apparent in one of Arthur's first actions in Delaware. At that time there were very few Black students enrolled in so-called White colleges and universities, but even then Arthur took an interest in this facet of his new job. When word came to him that none of the local barber shops would give haircuts to Black students, he joined with other faculty members to canvass the barbers and make arrangements for the Ohio Wesleyan Black students to get haircuts in Delaware rather than to have to go twenty-five miles to Columbus for this service.

Making as many alumni contacts as possible was an early priority with Arthur. He went to numerous meetings—in Ohio, New York, Washington, Chicago, and elsewhere—and explained to these groups such problems as faculty salaries, admission policies, fraternity and sorority situations, and invited their questions about any and all Ohio Wesleyan affairs.

He undertook the promotion of an alumni fund as a means of helping solve some of the financial problems at the college. He set a goal for this fund, increasing it each year, and always reached it. The income from this fund was increased so dramatically during his tenure that it became a major source of support. He insisted that the money obtained from alumni giving be used for improving faculty salaries.

He decided also to urge the trustees to support the establishment of a Reserve Officers' Training Corps on the campus. This was at the time when the draft hung over the heads of college students, and he felt that the ROTC offered a very positive opportunity to carry on a college course as well as prep-aration for military service.

A long-range plan for a definite salary schedule, with minimum and maximum rates for each faculty rank and a clearly defined progression system became a matter for much attention. Arthur felt that reasonably definite assurance should be given the faculty as to the future.

The ceremonial occasion known as the inauguration of the new president of Ohio Wesleyan did not take place until June of 1949. The reason for this was that Arthur wanted ex-President Hoover to be the speaker, and it could not be fitted into Mr. Hoover's schedule until then. Saturday, June 11, was set as the inauguration date.

The preparations for the visit of our illustrious guest occupied us for many weeks. Arthur was very proud that Mr. Hoover had agreed to come to Delaware for the occasion, and he was also deeply sensitive to the responsibility of being host to the country's only living ex-president.

His mother and father came for the inauguration, and so did our friends the Frederic Brown Harrises from Washington. To her dismay, his sister Betty came down with the mumps and couldn't come.

The night before the induction ceremony Arthur and I and our nine-year-old Susan took a walk down to the Oak Hill cemetery. Arthur pointed out to Susan the grave of one of Ohio Wesleyan's presidents. "Just think," I said to Susan, "Daddy will be the ninth president of Ohio Wesleyan." "Yes," Susan answered without a pause, "and there'll be a tenth." This became one of Arthur's favorite stories over the years.

Arthur left the house at seven o'clock on Saturday morning for Columbus to meet Mr. Hoover. Lowell Thomas was in the official party, and so was Congressman John Vorys, of Columbus.

There was considerable scurrying around at home to get everybody dressed, fed, and the house in order to receive our visitors. On my final look around, I noticed something a bit unusual sticking out of the ground at the top of the steps along the sidewalk. Closer inspection revealed it to be a curtain rod, and flying from the top of it was a white banner proclaiming HERBERT HOOVER IS STAYING HERE. This turned out to be Harry's idea of alerting any passers-by to Mr. Hoover's visit, just in case anybody could possibly have missed all of the huge pictures in downtown store windows, newspaper stories, and so on, that had flooded our town since the announcement was made that he would speak at Arthur's inauguration.

I expected Arthur and our guests to be back at the house by 9 AM, but long before that our front yard was the setting for considerable activity. Newspapermen, photographers, state highway patrolmen, and curious townspeople were all over it. Flowers and telegrams began arriving, and, in general, excitement ran high by the time Arthur returned, bringing with him the cause of all of the unusual activity.

Mr. Hoover began his day with us by graciously posing for the photographers with the Flemming children on the front porch. All of the children but Lib, that is. She, at thirteen, did not wish to be associated with the family in all the fanfare, even foregoing the opportunity to be photographed with the ex-president of the United States. The other four children were absolutely delighted with this occasion to bask in the limelight with Mr. Hoover.

When the picture-taking was over, the party came into the house. Mr. Hoover had no sooner taken a seat in the living room than he pleased us all by calling Tom, then five, over to him. "Tom," Mr. Hoover said, "if you will empty the contents of your pockets on this table," pointing to the coffee table in front of him, "I'll give you a dime."

This seemed like a pretty good proposition to Tom, and he accommodatingly emptied his pockets. In a moment there was a collection on the table consisting of a pair of handcuffs, a pencil, stones, and a small notebook. He looked expectantly at Mr. Hoover, and true to his promise, the ex-president gave Tom his dime.

This was too much for the other boys, who by this time had gathered around the table too. Mr. Hoover made the same bargain with them. Harry emptied his pockets and also received his dime.

But young Art had a worried look on his face. "Mr. Hoover," he said, "I don't have anything in my pockets."

At this point Mr. Hoover showed that he had had a lot of experience with small boys. He noticed that Art was carrying a small receipt book in his hand. "Well," said Mr. Hoover, "if you'll just write me one of those receipts, I'll give you a dime too." So Art made a few scribbles on the receipt, and then walked away happily with his dime.

Mr. Hoover also provided additional pleasure by signing autographs for the children. A couple of pieces of paper he placed on the corner of the leather-topped table as he signed them, and there, several days later, we noticed the distinct impression in the leather of "The Good Wishes of Herbert Hoover."

Mr. Hoover showed no disposition to retire to the guest room for rest or for quiet reflection on his afternoon speech, but instead remained a relaxed member of the household all morning, though many people came in and out. The photographers waited patiently for further opportunities to take pictures, and before we left for the alumni luncheon in the gymnasium, he willingly posed for them with Arthur in the living room and in the yard.

It was a gloomy day, and on every side the conversation piece at the time was, "Is it going to rain?" The inauguration ceremony had been planned for Selby Field. The field is surrounded by trees and bushes and provided an attractive setting for the solemn occasion. Though it was dark and threatening, no raindrops had fallen by the time we entered the gym for the luncheon. People were advising Arthur very freely to give the word to transfer the ceremony from Selby Field to Gray Chapel, even though this meant that about four thousand people would be disappointed by not being able to be seated. The chapel seated two thousand; the stadium, six thousand.

At two-fifteen Arthur left the luncheon table and went outside to take an appraisal of the weather, and then he gave his decision. "We'll proceed with the plans to have the program at Selby Field," he announced.

The weather report had predicted rain. This decision of Arthur's, in defiance of the prediction, gave rise to one of our favorite family sayings. Harry's comment was, "But God doesn't always do what the weatherman says." He didn't that time!

The academic procession began to form. And the rain began to fall, not hard, but gently and persistently for a few moments. The die was cast, however, and the college orchestra began the strains of the march for the academic procession across the field to the stands. A few moments later, the rain ceased, and the sun came out for the first time that day. It remained shining brightly for the rest of the afternoon.

Mr. Hoover made some generous remarks about Arthur. "I have worked with him intimately for two years," he said. "He was better fitted for the work of the Commission on the Organization of the Executive Branch of the Government than any of the rest of us. He brought high statesmanship and great understanding of its human problems."

After the inauguration ceremony was over, Arthur drove around the downtown area of Delaware with Mr. Hoover to give further opportunity to the townspeople to see our very special guest.

The next issue of *Life* magazine carried a full page of pictures and a story about Arthur's inauguration as president of Ohio Wesleyan. The story pointed out the fact that both Mr. Hoover and Lowell Thomas, who was a member of the platform party too, appeared to be dozing, but it was facing the bright sunlight that made them close their eyes. Later that evening, Mr. Thomas told of the inauguration on his evening newscast.

We settled down quickly to normalcy after Mr. Hoover left.

Arthur began that year the custom he continued during all of his years as a college president at three different institutions. He taught a regularly scheduled course in the political science department. He maintained that this was a good way to get to know how the college actually served the students. Besides, he enjoyed teaching, and he particularly enjoyed this sort of student contact.

He also began another custom, which he continued during his twenty years of presiding at college commencements. At some point in the commencement program he always invited the parents and families of the graduates to stand, asked the graduates themselves to stand and face their parents, and then Arthur would direct a few sentences of appreciation to the parents for their making that day possible for their sons and daughters.

Then, each year on this same occasion, he would take note of all the people with cameras trying to get pictures of the graduate they were interested in. Naturally, most of them wanted a shot of the actual moment the diploma was handed to the graduate. Sometimes a really good shot of this fleeting moment was impossible to get. So Arthur always invited the camera bugs to remain after the academic recessional. He told them he would return to the podium and re-enact the moment of degree conferral for as many of them as wished him to do so. This offer was always taken up by many of the visiting parents.

By the end of that first year Arthur and I, as well as all of the children, had settled down quite happily into the Delaware lifestyle. The children all had new friends and were participating in all of the normal activities for their various age groups. One particularly welcome activity was Delaware's well-organized and highly successful swimming program, which gave all of the children a useful and nearly full-time summer activity.

A special project of Arthur's was getting the Institute of Practical Politics at Ohio Wesleyan moving. Under this program, the students learned about public service by working in public offices or within the

ranks of political parties—some paid, but mostly volunteers. The
institute had three aims: to stimulate persons to make a career of
government service; to train a large group to become active in party
politics; and to give all of the students an appreciation of organized
political action in a democracy.

Each year there was a Democratic Day and a Republican Day,
with office holders in each party coming to the campus to speak
to the students.

Ground for the Memorial Union Building was broken in the
fall of 1949. The large L-shaped building, three stories high, was
constructed across from the main campus on Sandusky Street and
became the focal point of student faculty activity.

That fall, too, Governor Lausche asked Arthur to head a study
of the operation of Ohio's government, with the aim of streamlining its business operation. This was called the "Little Hoover
Commission." It was Governor Lausche's plan to have this commission formed on the same basis as the earlier national commission.

The Hoover Commission on the Organization of the Executive Branch of the Government made its report to the president
and to Congress in February of 1949. It recommended far-
reaching reforms in the methods used by the government to hire,
fire, pay, promote, and treat its employees. Arthur at once
became a vocal protagonist for the changes urged in the report,
and as subsequent parts of the commission's report became
public, he undertook a crusade for the implementation of the
recommendations of the commission at various groups all over
Ohio and elsewhere. He felt that citizen education about the
report was imperative, and that the only real hope for change
depended on the awareness of citizens and their willingness to
lobby for the changes recommended by the study commission.

Arthur's administration of Ohio Wesleyan was definitely
affected by his Hoover Commission experience. He identified

three areas that he felt applied to the administration of a college, as well as to the government. They were:

1. Fix responsibility for various activities.
2. Having fixed responsibility, delegate sufficient authority to act to those to whom responsibility has been assigned to carry forward their work in an effective and efficient manner.
3. Establish controls to make sure those who act do so within the framework of established standards.

He felt that these sound principles of management could be applied to the field of education. Accordingly, he named three vice-presidents of the university: one to be in charge of academic affairs; one with authority over business affairs; and a third who acted for the university in the public relations field.

This meant promotion for the three men chosen, and the result was an improved working climate.

A highlight of our second year at Ohio Wesleyan was a trip to Kingston where "Flemming Day" was held on February 1, 1950. The Kingston Chamber of Commerce sponsored a dinner with Arthur's former teachers, classmates, and friends, and other townspeople given a chance to hear a person *The Ulster County News* and *The Kingston Leader* called Kingston's favorite son. After a reception, Kingstonians filled two dining rooms for the testimonial dinner. Arthur's theme in his speech on this occasion was the Hoover Commission's report. It was a truly heart-warming evening—and a proud one for Arthur's parents.

On the lighter side, that spring Arthur took a whole day off and devoted it to the children. He was, in fact, a great sports fan and loved all forms of athletic competition.

Perhaps this is as good a time as any to insist Arthur deserves the description of sports nut. In fact, if physical infirmity should ever deny him the ability to participate actively in outside affairs, he would be content to remain at home indefinitely as long as television provided him with sports events to watch.

He absolutely loves all sports. Baseball is the number-one favorite, followed closely by football and then basketball. Even golf tournaments, bowling—whatever—he watches them all. Every Saturday afternoon while we were at Ohio Wesleyan and later at the University of Oregon, he was at the football stadium, whether at home or away games.

He can spend an entire day watching baseball games or football games. He knows who coaches the pro teams and the top college teams, as well as the most important players. He can recite team standings in the national baseball leagues.

Though never a sports participant, he is the most avid spectator I've ever known.

When we moved to Delaware, the children began to develop an interest in sports, too, and he enjoyed taking them to the Saturday afternoon football games at the college. He, and all of them, began to follow the big league baseball schedules, and often dinner table conversation centered around the record of the Yankees, the Dodgers, the Indians, and so on. The children became loyal Indian fans, and Arthur's loyalty usually followed whatever team Branch Rickey was managing. Branch was a friend of his, a graduate of Ohio Wesleyan, and a trustee during the years we were there.

The older children had extracted a promise from Arthur to take them to see a big league game sometime, but the nearest city having a team in either professional league was Cleveland, 120 miles away. So one Friday night he asked the children if they would like to go to a baseball game in Cleveland the following day. At this time the twins were about six years old, and their sports sense not so keenly developed as it later became, so they agreed to stay home with me. The three older children excitedly entered into the plans for the trip. "We'll go up on the 8:30 train in the morning, have lunch in Cleveland, and then go to the game," Arthur said.

"Can we take Carol along?" asked Lib. She was at an age when nothing was worth doing that wasn't shared with at least one of her pals.

"Of course she can go," promised Arthur.

So, the next morning the twins and I drove Arthur and his four excited charges to the railroad station and waved them off on their trip to Cleveland.

It was a happy group of baseball fans that Arthur returned with that night. The game was a wonderful treat in itself, but for Arthur to throw in a three-hour train ride each way, with dinner in the diner, made the day a very special one for them all to remember.

Lib and Carol got off the train first, with dark, curly heads covered with pert little red and white hats bearing Cleveland Indians on the front. Sue was next, waving a Cleveland Indians banner. Lib proudly showed a candid camera shot of her and Carol taken with their new hats on.

"How did you get along?" I asked Arthur.

"Fine," he said. "Everything went along fine." He seldom exaggerated; understatement was his trademark.

And the children were positively aglow with memories of their day's experiences, and smiles of deep satisfaction were spread over all four faces. The girls were fairly bursting to tell about one humorous incident. Sue started to tell about it before we reached the car.

"You should have seen Harry, Mom," she said. "Dad sent him to get some root beer, and he had to go up a long flight of steps to reach the concession stand. The girl at the stand put the five glasses on a cardboard tray, and Harry started down the steps with it. Someone passed him and bumped his arm. This caused one of the glasses to fall off the tray. A couple of steps later a second glass spilled, this one over a baldheaded man sitting on the aisle, and was he mad! Then, he kept on coming down the steps, dropping another glass every few steps, until when he got back to our row he had dropped all five of the root beers. You should have seen him, Mom. It was the funniest sight I ever saw." And she and Lib and Carol fairly whooped with laughter at Harry's plight.

I could imagine Arthur's embarrassment, but he indicated no distress at all. The incident, as far as he was concerned, fell into the category of things past, and hence not worth worrying about.

For the children, this particular incident at the Cleveland ball park furnished theme material for all of them.

Though I attended many of the college sports events, both in Delaware and at games away, I was never a real sports enthusiast. The college athletic program did, however, furnish an opportunity for development along this line for the boys and for Lib too. For the most part, Sue, like me, was a take-it-or-leave-it sports fan.

My education along another line continued to get a few pushes from Arthur. One such occasion occurred when Doctor Benjamin Mays, then president of Morehouse College in Atlanta, came to Ohio Wesleyan as part of the lecture series. His lecture was scheduled for a cold Sunday evening in February in Gray Chapel.

After church that particular Sunday we were standing outside talking with Doctor William Quillian, chairman of the college lectures committee. The topic of conversation was Doctor Mays's expected appearance that evening.

"Oh, by the way," Arthur said to Doctor Quillian, "where is Doctor Mays going to stay while he is in Delaware?"

"At the Delaware Hotel," was the answer.

"That's no place for him to stay. We'll have him stay at our house, won't we, Bernice?" said Arthur, looking sideways at me to gauge what my reaction was.

"All right," was all I contributed to the conversation.

But when I got home, after giving the family luncheon, I scurried around to get ready for our guest—made the guest room bed, put fresh towels in the adjoining bathroom, and set the table

146

for supper. For this I used a beautiful new crocheted doilie set I had recently received from a dear Mississippi friend. My very best dishes and silver further enhanced the setting.

While doing these chores, I was trying to imagine what my Southern relatives would think of all this.

When Doctor Mays arrived at the house around four o'clock, I felt at first as if I were walking on eggs, but the feeling of unease disappeared I listened to Arthur and Doctor Mays talk of their mutual interests—the church and education.

Back home after the lecture, Arthur showed Doctor Mays to the hall closet to hang his overcoat. As he put the coat on the hanger, Doctor Mays said, "Tomorrow morning maybe Mrs. Flemming will lend me a needle and thread. I have a loose button on my coat."

"Bernice will sew it on for you," was Arthur's reply.

Arthur was always *very* generous with *my* time, but this really went beyond the call of duty!

As a matter of fact, Doctor Mays did not even come downstairs the next morning until Arthur had gone to his office and the children were off to school. Meanwhile, I had sewed the button on.

So Doctor Mays and I had breakfast alone—again a really strange situation for me to find myself in. Ten o'clock came, and it was time for him to leave for the railroad station. As he reached into the closet for his coat, he remarked, "I forgot the button." Then he put his coat on and found that the button he had mentioned the night before was quite tight. I shall never forget how he looked at that moment, disbelief written all over his face as he said, "You did it. Thank you very much."

In the years since then, until Doctor Mays's death a few years ago, our paths crossed his a number of times. Each time we met he would recall his visit to Delaware and my sewing the button on his coat. It was a landmark occasion for me, and for him, too.

By 1951 Arthur's name was familiar to most Ohioans, both in and out of the educational world. He began to be mentioned as a possible candidate for public office. In a story entitled "Keep an Eye on This Man," which appeared in *Here in Ohio* in January of that year, Arthur was described as a man "who has the natural vigor, the intellectual honesty, the adherence to principle, and the knowledge of government which the voters showed they wanted in government and places of party responsibility."

Many persons spoke to him about the possibility of running for the United States Senate or for governor of Ohio.

At this time, Charles Taft, of Cincinnati, was also prominently mentioned as a candidate for governor. He was a brother of Senator Robert Taft and had long been active in Republican party affairs in Cincinnati.

One Sunday afternoon ex-Governor Myers Cooper came to our house to see Arthur. As he was leaving he said to me, "How would you like to be the wife of the governor of Ohio?"

Surprised, shocked, and almost speechless, I managed to reply, "I'll have to think about that. I like being Arthur's wife, no matter what job he has."

Governor Cooper laughed and went on down the steps.

There was no doubt that Arthur was really attracted by the possibility of entering Ohio politics as a candidate for governor. A factor in his thinking, however, was his friendship and deep respect for Charles Taft, with whom he had first become ac-quainted in the work of the old Federal Council of Churches. He was extremely hesitant to get into a primary fight for the nomi-nation with Charles.

At that time there was some in-party fighting in Ohio over control of the Republican party. One faction supported the possible candidacy of Charles Taft; the other faction did not want him to be the candidate.

And, of course Charles heard of the efforts under way to get

Arthur to run for the nomination. He wrote Arthur a letter telling him he intended to run for the nomination. "I am going to run unless I get hit by a truck, or some other eventuality turns up, which is equally unexpected now," he said.

So Arthur decided not to get into the state political maneuvering. Besides, another opportunity for service in Washington was even then brewing.

I have mentioned Arthur's total (almost total, anyway) physical stamina. I can remember only three times in our entire married life when he actually gave up and went to bed. One of those times was in late January of 1951. He was running a fever of 101°, was achy all over, and feeling absolutely miserable. But he wouldn't let me call the doctor.

A long-distance call from Washington made him forget all about his symptoms. I heard him agreeing to do something that required his leaving Delaware the following day.

When he hung up the receiver, he announced that he was going to fly to Lackland Air Force Base in Texas to conduct an investigation with Assistant Air Secretary Eugene Zuckert and Hearst newspaper vice-president Merrill Meigs into charges of over-crowding and bad health conditions at the base. Rumors had circulated that men were dying from pneumonia contracted from lack of decent clothing and housing. Poor quality of food was also cited.

The message came at a time when the entire central part of Ohio was covered with ice, and most activity was at a standstill. No planes were flying, no busses running. Besides, he was sick.

But, remember, there is no such word as "can't" in his vocabulary. He responded to this appeal like a race horse at a race track. He began making telephone calls to see what sort of travel arrangements he could make to meet Secretary Zuckert at Wright Field in Dayton the next day.

I remonstrated loudly, but it did no good. The following

morning he was off for Wright Field to carry out his assignment at Lackland.

A couple of weeks later, at a dinner party, he, for the first time in my presence, described the flight and the difficulty they had landing at Lackland. It happened that a wide area in Texas where the Lackland Air Force Base is located was also covered with a blanket of ice. As the plane in which Arthur was flying approached the Lackland Field, and as the pilot asked for landing instructions, Arthur heard this message come to the pilot: "No one has landed here today. You will have to land at your own discretion."

The pilot decided to land at the base, and when the plane came down, there were already parked near the landing strip two ambulances, and some fire engines—grim notice that the base personnel feared real trouble in landing. I guess it is just as well I don't always know what goes on!

The investigating committee found the conditions at Lackland were not as bad as pictured, but they did make some recommendations for improvement.

The trip home to Delaware was made in adverse weather conditions, too. The last lap had to be made by bus. It is that bus trip that is also fixed in my memory.

Arthur had telephoned to let me know about his transportation difficulties resulting from the icy weather. He was detained many hours in Chillicothe, Ohio, and really didn't know just when he would reach home.

That was in a day when telephone operators put through long-distance calls. The do-it-yourself long-distance dialing system was far in the future.

And, on occasion, long-distance operators can be very persistent. Early in the morning I began getting calls for Arthur from Washington. I told the operator she couldn't reach him, and that I didn't know when he would be home. But all day she kept trying

150

to reach him, so I was aware that something important was afoot. When I queried her as to who was trying so persistently to talk to Arthur (thinking I could relay a message to him in case he called me again), the operator said that General Lucius Clay had placed the call. General Clay was then the executive assistant to Defense Mobilizer Charles Wilson.

General Clay finally did track Arthur down at the Chillicothe bus station. He told Arthur that Mr. Wilson wanted him to become his assistant in charge of manpower problems at the Office of Defense Mobilization.

So Arthur, with the approval of the executive committee of the Ohio Wesleyan board of trustees, delegated much of the day-to-day operation of the college to his three vice-presidents, and off he went to Washington and ODM. He did not take a leave of absence. Instead, he began a two-year commuting program in which he left Delaware every Sunday evening for Washington to help Charles Wilson run ODM, and he returned to Delaware Thursday or Friday around dinner time. He spent Friday evening, Saturday, and much of Sunday in meetings and conferences connected with the operation of Ohio Wesleyan.

This schedule had nightmarish aspects for me and the children. Some of them were into the teen-age period, which is not generally regarded as the happiest time of the growing years. There was no time—absolutely none—left over for the family. The boys were getting into their share of mischief, too. It was a very difficult time for us left at home.

But we all survived.

One of Arthur's most enjoyable extracurricular activities during this time was as moderator of an hour-long radio-telecast called "Columbus Town Meeting." Public issues were aired on this program each Sunday, with experts on opposing sides expressing their viewpoints. Then, the listeners had an opportunity to telephone in questions they desired to have answered. It was an interesting format, and it had a wide audience throughout central Ohio.

Prior to the 1952 election, Senator Bricker of Ohio, a Republican, appeared on the "Town Meeting" program with Michael DiSalle, a Democratic hopeful for senator from Ohio. Mr. DiSalle used the occasion to "needle" Senator Bricker about his law firm's representing a railroad, and in the ensuing exchange Senator Bricker became quite noticeably angry. Later, he took the view that Arthur, as moderator, should not have allowed Mr. DiSalle to prod him the way he did—in other words, he held Arthur responsible for the poor showing he made that day. This attitude on the part of Senator Bricker was subsequently reflected in his failure to give Arthur his blessing for appointment as secretary of Labor. Later, however, he did not stand in the way of his appointment as director of Defense Mobilization, and in 1958, when he was appointed secretary of HEW.

I want to mention another incident that occurred about this time. One day Doctor Arneson came into Arthur's office and told him that the Ohio Wesleyan chapter of Phi Beta Kappa wanted to initiate him as a member. Arthur's scholastic performance as an undergraduate student had not been of Phi Beta Kappa caliber, but Doctor Arneson explained to him that his election was based on his record of more than twenty years of high-quality accomplishment since his college graduation.

Arthur listened to him, really impressed and deeply moved by this recognition, and also very sensitive to its implications in an academic community where Phi Beta Kappa membership is especially revered.

Slowly he shook his head. "No, Doctor Arneson," he said, "I cannot accept this honor. Membership in Phi Beta Kappa normally signifies exceptionally high-quality scholarship. I did not achieve that standard in college, and I do not feel that I am entitled to it now. I appreciate it very much, but I shall have to decline."

Doctor Arneson could hardly believe what his ears were hearing. Declining honorary membership in Phi Beta Kappa was something he had not counted on from Arthur. But he understood Arthur's reasoning, and he respected his decision, although very disappointed by it.

Another little flurry in our lives occurred in the spring of 1952 when Arthur was asked about his interest in the presidency of American University. But this opportunity was turned down without any real stress. Life was too interesting and full at Ohio Wesleyan and ODM to contemplate a change at that point.

As we got into the period of change of power following the 1952 presidential election when Dwight Eisenhower defeated Adlai Stevenson, the quadrennial speculation over the top bureaucratic appointments in the new administration occupied a lot of newspaper space. The situation became a matter of particular interest to us one day in late November when Senator Robert Taft telephoned Arthur and told him that he had submitted his name to the president-elect as his choice for appointment as secretary of Labor. This idea remained a viable one only until Senator Bricker, acting under his senatorial courtesy privilege, decided not to go along with it. There is no doubt that Arthur was interested in the possibility that Senator Taft had suggested to him.

Then, at about the same time, Arthur was summoned to President-elect Eisenhower's headquarters in New York. He was informed that the president-elect was naming a special commission to study proposals for streamlining the executive branch of the government. In addition to Arthur, the commission included Nelson Rockefeller and Milton Eisenhower, the president-elect's brother.

Though all three of the members of this newly appointed commission were present, and were told that they were to confer with General Eisenhower about his ideas for the commission's work, it turned out that they were to be a kind of "cover" to hide the fact that the president-elect had already left the country on a secret mission to Korea. His schedule had been set up to look as if he were in New York simply as a protection to him as he began his famous effort to end the Korean conflict in response to a promise made during the election campaign. Arthur enjoyed this episode in which he was a part of a conspiracy.

After the inauguration, one of President Eisenhower's first actions as chief executive was to create and give official status to the commission to streamline the executive branch of the federal government.

Another of President Eisenhower's early decisions was to name Arthur acting director of the Office of Defense Mobilization, and when the college year was over in 1953, Arthur was sworn in as the permanent director of ODM.

This was the year of Lib's graduation from high school—an occasion for which Arthur very nearly missed being present. The fact is that our lives are strewn with incidents when Arthur, with his strong tendency to hairbreadth scheduling, almost missed some important family celebration, and a few when he actually did miss one. Lib's graduation was one of the "near misses."

Arthur had been invited by the superintendent of schools in Delaware to be the speaker at the graduation exercises, scheduled for the evening of June 3, a Thursday, at eight o'clock. Of course he was happy to have this opportunity to participate in this big night in Lib's life, and he cheerfully accepted the invitation.

He was to be in Washington on June 3, and he made a reservation to fly from the capital city to Columbus in the late afternoon. Allowing time for the thirty-mile drive from the Columbus airport to Delaware, he would possibly get to Delaware a half-hour before eight o'clock—if the plane was on time.

I kept after him, as did Lib and his secretary, to change these arrangements and take an earlier plane so as to be sure to be present, instead of running the risk of being delayed until after the hour set for the graduation on account of bad weather or other adverse conditions. Just a month before plans had to be changed several times because of delayed plane arrivals, and a half-hour leeway didn't seem like much to spare when such an important engagement was at stake.

But Arthur is a man of great faith, and he kept quieting us all down with his insistent reply, "I'll be there on time. Just stop worrying about it. I'll be there."

He did promise that if there was any question at all of possible delay for any reason, he would take an earlier plane.

At twelve o'clock on June 3, the big day, Arthur telephoned me from Washington and soothed me by telling me that he had checked with the Trans-World Airlines office and with the weather bureau and had been assured that the late afternoon plane for Columbus would take off on time and would arrive in Columbus on time, thus guaranteeing that he would be in Delaware a half-hour before the time set for the graduation exercises.

So we calmed down a bit and tried to bring our own faith up to the level of Arthur's. But I didn't succeed, and the feeling of unease persisted.

About mid-afternoon Arthur's sister Betty and her husband Donald arrived from Pittsburgh for the graduation.

And at five o'clock the blow fell. Arthur's Washington secretary telephoned with the information that the flight Arthur was scheduled to fly to Columbus on would be at least an hour late taking off from Washington, and maybe even later, because of mechanical difficulties. So, she said, Arthur had decided to charter a plane for the trip to Columbus in order to be in time for the eight o'clock date. "He said to tell you not to worry," she added. "He'll be there on time."

Whew! Not to worry! This was the kind of thing that was guaranteed to send me climbing the walls. With only a couple of

155

hours until the most important event in Lib's life thus far, and with her father—the speaker—still four hundred miles away! He was well aware of my aversion to charter flights and my state of near panic whenever he resorted to this means of meeting an engagement—which was of course why he had his secretary telephone me instead of calling himself.

Well, we went ahead with dinner as placidly as possible under the circumstances, and at seven-fifteen we were all dressed and ready to leave for Gray Chapel on the Ohio Wesleyan campus where the exercises were to be held. Lib looked very serious and mature in her spotless white academic robe and mortar board, and she showed no trace of apprehension that her father might not get there on time. In fact, none of us risked mention of our fears on this score. We set out confidently for Gray Chapel, as Lib had to be there at seven-thirty for the formation of the academic procession.

Hundreds of people were milling about when we got there— the graduates, their parents, relatives, friends, teachers, and other interested persons. I hardly dared to look at anybody lest my face betray my concern over the fact Arthur was somewhere between Washington and Delaware—there was no telling just where.

Everybody looked happy and expectant. I felt simply dragged down with the weight of worry over this predicament.

Ten minutes of eight. Still he hadn't put in an appearance. What should I do? I felt it was time for me to tell somebody what the true situation was about the graduation speaker.

I decided to seek out the superintendent of schools. I would tell him what had happened. As I started toward the area where the academic procession was waiting to begin its march into the chapel, my imagined opener was, "Look here—I'm worried to death. Arthur hasn't arrived from Washington yet. His scheduled flight was delayed, and he had to charter a plane, etc."

At precisely eight minutes of eight o'clock I spied his tall figure making his way through the crowd of people in the corridor. I felt like shouting.

Nobody looking at him would have guessed that he hadn't been in Delaware all day and that he hadn't just left our house a few blocks away. He looked as serene and untroubled as a small child.

"You weren't worried, were you?" he asked in passing. "I'm here in plenty of time." And with that he went out to join the procession and was shortly on the platform ready and waiting to give his graduation address.

Certainly. In plenty of time. Oh, ye, of little faith!

This split-second timing in which Arthur scheduled his various commitments was a fact of life I had to live with always. Since he didn't drive, I usually took him to the airport to catch planes (except in those wonderfully lush days when he had a driver at Ohio Wesleyan and later when he was secretary of Health, Education, and Welfare).

He would tell me what time the plane was scheduled to leave and when to pick him up, bringing his suitcase along. Unfailingly, I was waiting in the car in front of his office at the time he told me to be there. I waited . . . and waited . . . and waited, and more often than not he would not appear until the very last second when he thought he could make it. My habit was always to have a book in the car so I could at least be partially diverted from watching the clock as the minutes passed away.

He was fond of saying that he never put pressure on anybody to get him any place. If he didn't allow enough time, he'd say, he could make some other arrangement or adjustment. He would never admit that it was the very act of waiting until the last possible moment that was a form of intense pressure in itself. Then he would rush out, get in the car, look at his watch, put on his glasses so he could watch the passing street signs, toss out a few "Watch its," "Be carefuls," "Get in the left lane," "Get in the right lane," and expect me to get him there on time. Oh, no, he never put any pressure on anybody!

Just once in all the years I staged a rebellion and absolutely refused to take him to the airport when he delayed leaving too late for me to feel I could safely deliver him for a departure. This was one Saturday afternoon in Delaware, when he sat in his office reminiscing with his old Bible professor while the minutes ticked away when he should have been on his way to the Columbus airport. I managed to convince him that we were not going to start on that thirty-mile trip when there were only thirty minutes until plane takeoff time.

The years at Ohio Wesleyan were the children's growing years, and even though Arthur was often an absentee father, he nevertheless was a father, and a good one. I remember one day toward the end of our stay in Delaware, Supreme Court Justice Harold Burton and his wife Selma came to town, and we took them to lunch at Bun's. The Burtons were Ohioans, and he was a former mayor of Cleveland. Her life during her children's growing years was not unlike mine.

One thing she said to me has remained with me ever since. "Remember, Bernice," said Selma Burton, "the quality of a father's relationship and influence in his children's lives is not determined by the amount of time he spends with them, but by its character."

As far as their physical care was concerned, they were mine. Arthur was the specialist in administration. He delegated all baby and child care to me. He never "baby sat." He remained as free to pursue all of his own interests as when he was a bachelor. He made more and more speeches, chaired more and more meetings, and took many trips away from home for his various activities and interests.

It would have been easy indeed for me to have developed a feeling of being "put upon." And often I truly did feel hemmed in by the constant round-the-clock demands of five young children.

I developed a few tricks to help me. One was that I insisted to myself that what I was doing was important, so I decided to upgrade myself from simply a "housewife" to a "coordinator of domestic affairs." Over the years I've used this designation for my occupation when filling out various forms and have enjoyed the reactions of people reading this. Also, I kept myself supplied with good books, and in my lonely evenings when Arthur was away, I'd read, read, read.

I also developed various handwork skills. While I sat in the yard watching small children during their early years I sewed, made quilts, luncheon sets, pictures, and the like. I did cross-stitch, crewel embroidery, and needlepoint. I made all of my own clothes and the girl's clothes. I sometimes referred to Arthur as the head-man and I the hand-maiden.

One thing must be made clear, however. Though Arthur devoted little time to the children, he somehow managed to make that time count. He seemed to have a special talent for doing things that produced the maximum of pleasure for the children; or, if it was gift he was buying, he always turned up with the perfect selection and one that was sure to delight the person who received it. And, if he had an idea for giving them a special treat, no obstacle was too great to overcome to accomplish it.

He, unlike many men, actually liked the children even during the early years of babyhood, and when they began to walk, he'd take them all over the neighborhood.

Arthur had only two rules he adhered to in dealing with his children, and later his grandchildren:
1. Let them do anything they want.
2. Let them have anything they want.
Indulgence became his most consistent trait in dealing with them.

Early on he assumed responsibility for the children's Christmas gift shopping. I did the shopping, wrapping, and mailing for our families and friends, but kept strictly out of the children's gift selecting, though Arthur always asked for suggestions as to suitable gifts for them.

The year that Harry joined the family we began another tradition that has continued to this day. We decided to have Santa Claus visit us in person and give out the gifts on Christmas morning. Accordingly, I purchased a Santa Claus suit, and we persuaded one of our friends to impersonate Santa. Later Arthur began to assume this role, though a couple of times in recent years one of the grandsons has played Santa.

When Lib was about ten, Arthur began taking her along on his Christmas Eve shopping expedition. He never shopped before Christmas Eve.

By the time we moved to Delaware, Sue joined the Christmas Eve trip to the stores with her father. There was never a Christmas when this schedule varied. December 24 was absolutely sacred for his shopping except when it fell on Sunday.

The second year we were in Delaware, there was considerable argument as to who would go shopping. The girls both wanted to go, and Harry insisted it was his turn. Tom and Art, six at the time, took the view that they ought to be included, too. I talked it over with Arthur, and he settled it without any hesitation whatever. He'd take them all! Then Lib, true to form, asked if she could take her friend Shirley along, and to this Arthur also agreed. So all six children accompanied him on his Christmas shopping expedition. Only Arthur would have tackled that!

Thus began Arthur's most cherished Christmas tradition, and it continued for over thirty years. As each child has married, their spouses often joined the expedition. And as the grandchildren outgrow the fantasy period, they are also invited to join. On this day, Arthur truly resembles the Pied Piper, sometimes trailed by as many as a dozen shoppers.

They leave the house right after breakfast and go to the largest shopping area available wherever we are celebrating our Christmas reunion that particular year. There is much whispered conversation as to appropriate gifts for everybody. The group breaks up into smaller groups or pairs in the morning hours, and then all meet at an agreed-on time and place for lunch. Afterward, more hours of shopping.

All come home for supper, laden to the ceiling with the gifts they have selected. And, oftentimes, Arthur will persuade one or two of them to go out again with him after supper to get some forgotten items. Many family stories center around incidents that have taken place on these shopping trips. I have never been included on these shopping orgies. I've never been invited to go, and I doubt my ability to make any sort of contribution. On the contrary, I'm sure that I would do so much worrying about the cost of it all that nobody would have any fun. So it is best that I stay home.

Christmas Eve is for me a day spent in doing the advance preparations for the Christmas dinner. When the shopping expedition was over and all the purchases delivered at home, then I got into the act. Arthur would insist that I drop whatever I was doing and immediately listen to him tell me who-was-to-get-what before he forgot himself who the recipients should be. As a result, I was wrapping and writing identifying cards well after midnight. Frankly, by the time it was all done, I was so worn out I really didn't care who-got-what. Sometimes I felt that once a year was entirely too often for Christmas anyway.

Often, along about eleven-thirty, Arthur tried to persuade one or more of the older ones to go to the midnight Christmas eve service at the nearest Episcopal church. He usually succeeded in getting the company he sought.

Christmas morning tradition dictates that a breakfast of sweet rolls and fruit juice is served upstairs while Arthur is on the

161

lowest level transforming himself from Dad (and Grandad) into Santa Claus, assisted by me. I am absolutely indispensable when it comes to pinning that pillow on to give him the necessary girth. When the transformation is complete, we ring the make-believe sleigh bells, shout "Merry Christmas," and the gift distributing ceremony begins.

The big old house we occupied on Oak Hill in Delaware had twelve-foot high ceilings. Each Christmas season brought out other facets of Arthur's character. For example, he always insisted on our having a balsam fir tree.

A recital of the beauties of long-needle pines fell on deaf ears as far as he was concerned. And spruce was no satisfactory substitute either. A Christmas tree was a balsam. Nothing else would do. Moreover, it must reach the ceiling. On a couple of occasions when I selected a tree in his absence from home, these specifications were not satisfactorily met, and he insisted that we exchange my selection for a tree that suited his twelve-foot high specifications.

Setting up these huge trees was a major project, especially since Arthur was seldom present at the time to erect it. Making fast a twelve-foot tree was a tiresome and difficult task, but as Harry and Art and Tom grew older, they became quite expert at it.

Years later, when we were living in St. Paul, one of our Speese grandsons began to exhibit signs of respiratory distress each Christmas, and after some testing procedures, the doctor determined that Johnny Speese was allergic to trees, particularly cut trees. When Lib told us about this, she said, "I know it will be really hard for Dad, but could you have an artificial tree this year?" It was indeed a traumatic experience for Arthur to agree to have an artificial tree, instead of his beloved balsam, but he went along with me to select the substitute.

Later that evening he sat reading the paper in the library while I sat on the floor with the pieces of the artificial tree laid out all around me, and with the instruction sheet in my hand, trying to figure out how to put it all together and make it resemble the one we had seen in the store. When I was about half way through, Arthur looked up from his paper and said to me, "I'm glad one person in this family is mechanical." I am not mechanical, and I absolutely hate reading instructions, but when it was all assembled, trimmed, and the new lights added, it was hard to tell the difference between it and a real live tree.

Much of Christmas day throughout the years was spent by Arthur on the floor helping the children work out the games he had bought the preceding day. And always his selections proved to be the most popular of all that came to the house at Christmas.

The forty-eight-hour period that included Christmas eve and Christmas day belonged to Arthur. He created it; he carried it out; he paid for it; and, best of all, he always loved every minute of it!

Arthur was always generous with the children. He'd pay their library fines (without the accompanying lectures I felt compelled to give them), get them triple-decker ice cream cones and banana splits, and handed out money for any reasonable whim (and many I thought unreasonable).

One night after a week when Arthur had been away, Lib came into our bedroom and seated herself on the corner of her father's bed. She was about sixteen at the time. She had a number of specific requests requiring financial backing to lay before him, and earlier in the week, when she had taken up her needs, real or fancied, with me, I had been very dubious about her getting the items she wanted.

As she leaned on the foot of the bed swinging her feet in mid-air, she began. "I need a new pair of saddle shoes, Dad."

"All right. Get them," he replied agreeably.

"Then I need a new green skirt," she continued.

"Well, get it."

"I also want a new bathing suit before I go to Lakeside," Lib went on.

"It's all right with me," Arthur said.

Lib smiled, a trifle triumphantly, at me and pulled herself up off the bed. She started out of the room.

"Thanks a lot, Dad," she said over her shoulder. "I'd rather deal with you than Mom."

Even the frequent accidents that seem to be a part of family living where there are growing children, and which oftentimes required a considerable outlay of money, always failed to arouse in Arthur any emotional impact whatsoever. Whenever something was broken, he refused to waste any energy groaning about it. Instead, his immediate reaction was invariably, "Get it fixed."

There was the time when Susan left her precious flute carelessly lying across the seat of a chair, and Harry just as thoughtlessly sat on it. A peculiar V-shaped instrument was the result. This bit of youthful heedlessness failed to excite Arthur, but the resulting repair bill sent my blood pressure skyrocketing. Replacing broken eyeglasses were part of every months' expenses. The "get it fixed" response was Arthur's only reaction. My reaction usually included a lecture on exercising more care.

It might even be said with complete accuracy that anything to do with finances actually bored him. For example, he would always put off coming to grips with his annual report to Uncle Sam until March 15, and later when the law was changed to April 15, found him struggling to get his income tax return in shape to mail. Many's the time it was minutes before midnight when the job was done, and a hurried trip to the post office in the nick of time saved him from paying a penalty. There were even times when he got the tax return in late. My suggestion that he get an accountant to do this chore for him failed. He always insisted on doing it himself.

Sometimes he would hold large checks for weeks, or even months, before depositing them. And he seldom accepted an honorarium for the countless speeches he made. If an hono-rarium was offered, his practice was to suggest that it be given to some worthy cause. He was also dilatory about collecting for his travel expenses, often paying them himself with no thought of reimbursement.

To Arthur, money was something to use for the necessities of life and for pleasure—not to hoard. He had no acquisitive instinct whatever.

Way back in 1946 when he was offered the presidency of Dickinson College, I wanted him to take the job. To me, it offered a means of insuring the children's education, as sons and daugh-ters of administrative officials and faculty members at Dickinson had free tuition privileges. "Let's go to Dickinson," I argued, "it will provide us security."

"Security?" he repeated. "Security is a will o' the wisp. People chase it all their lives, and never find it."

The Dickinson opportunity had to be justified on some other ground. In the end, his decision was not to go.

Quite frankly I worried about money. Arthur had always been able to have anything he wanted, and so to him money was something that was always there. On the other hand, I had a healthy respect for money, as it was habitually scarce in my family. I was a much more careful spender than Arthur, and I did not have quite the same compulsion to let everybody have everything they wanted.

Indulgence of his children, and later his grandchildren, was Arthur's hallmark. If they wanted something, they should have it, and they all knew it.

Well, as I said, I worry about money!

When President Eisenhower appointed Arthur the permanent director of the Office of Defense Mobilization, the trustees of Ohio Wesleyan granted Arthur a leave of absence, and the family moved back to Washington. Dean Ficken, the academic dean, was appointed acting president.

This leave was extended a second year, and then a third year. Arthur, though technically on leave during the entire first term of President Eisenhower, was constantly on call in case of emergencies needing his advice at the college. And he made many trips back to Delaware to attend board meetings and other campus meetings.

Dean Ficken asked to be relieved of the responsibilities of his acting presidency after two years, and Doctor Frank Prout, an Ohio Wesleyan alumnus and president emeritus of Bowling Green University in Ohio, was named acting president for the year 1955–56.

In 1955, Arthur was elected to serve as chairman of the board of trustees for one year to succeed Harvey Yoder. Mr. Yoder had been chairman since 1947. In this capacity, Arthur retained an active decision making role at the college while serving his last year on leave from Ohio Wesleyan.

The college certainly did not stand still during the period Arthur was on leave. Several new dormitories were built, and also the Kathryn Sisson Phillips Hall to house the departments of education, philosophy and religion, and psychology.

Early in February, 1957, Arthur submitted his resignation as director of the Office of Defense Mobilization to President Eisenhower and returned to Ohio Wesleyan. It was no small adjustment for him to leave the excitement of sitting around the president's cabinet table and exchange the tremendous responsibility of the nation's defense preparedness effort for the somewhat limited area afforded by Ohio Wesleyan. The pull toward public service apparent from his college days made it very difficult for him to turn his back on Washington.

He was warmly received by faculty and townspeople, however, and after a few months had firmly established himself again as an Ohioan. He did all of the customary college presidential chores, including pep rallies, welcoming fathers to the campus at half-time ceremonies on Homecoming-Dads' Day, making frequent speeches, attending endless meetings, and so on.

He was also continuing as a member of President Eisenhower's Commission on Government Organization with Nelson Rockefeller and Milton Eisenhower.

Also that year the American Council on Education asked him to chair its Commission on the Survey of Dentistry in the United States. All U.S. dental education, research, and services were to be under scrutiny by the commission.

And all the while he was working for Ohio Wesleyan's increased salary plan, a new science center for the college, and an up-to-date little theater, radio, and television communications center on the campus. He had worked hard with one of Ohio Wesleyan's affluent alumni in California to get financing for the little theater and had just about achieved this goal when the winds of change started blowing again—and, as before, toward Washington.

1928: Arthur stands with the members of the American University debating team outside the White House. President Calvin Coolidge is in the center of the photograph, with AU's Dean Woods to the right, followed by Arthur. Earlier that year, Arthur had chosen to come to AU to coach debating instead of going to Harvard Law School. It was a decision he never regretted.

July, 1939: Arthur takes the oath of office as a U.S. Civil Service commissioner. Appointed by FDR, Arthur was thirty-four at the time, the youngest Civil Service commissioner since Theodore Roosevelt, who was thirty when he was appointed. Lucille Foster McMillan and Harry Mitchell, the other two members of the commission, are seen standing behind him.

In the summer of 1947, Congress authorized the Commission on the Organization of the Executive Branch of the Government, thereafter referred to as COEBG. President Truman's appointees included Secretary of the Navy James Forrestal; former Undersecretary of State Dean Atchison; an industrial executive from Dayton, Ohio, George H. Mead; and Arthur. Ex-President Hoover was one of the appointees of the Speaker of the House, and he became, at seventy-eight years of age, the chairman of COEBG. Arthur enjoyed getting to know Mr. Hoover, whom he admired greatly.

June, 1949: Arthur and ex-President Herbert Hoover sit on the front porch of our house in Delaware, Ohio, awaiting the start of ceremonies inaugurating Arthur as president of Ohio Wesleyan University. Arthur's acquaintance with ex-President Hoover, the invited speaker of the day, was through their work together on the Commission on the Organization of the Executive Branch of the Government, the so-called Hoover Commission. Later, much to their delight, Mr. Hoover gave a dime to each of the Flemming children.

June, 1949: Arthur is inaugurated as president of Ohio Wesleyan University. Although he had been in the post since August, 1948, his official inauguration did not take place until June of 1949. The reason for this was that Arthur wanted ex-President Hoover to be the speaker, and it could not be fitted into Mr. Hoover's schedule until then. Pictured in the photo below are, from left to right, Herbert Burgstahler (retired president of Ohio Wesleyan), Bishop Herbert Welch, Ex-President Herbert Hoover, Arthur, Lowell Thomas, Dean Ficken, and Frederic Brown Harris.

July, 1953: Arthur is sworn in as director of the Office of Defense Mobilization under President Eisenhower, who looks on as Supreme Court Justice Burton administers the oath of office.

1958: Arthur had been back at Ohio Wesleyan less than a year after a four-year leave of absence to be director of the Office of Defense Mobilization when a telephone call informed him that President Eisenhower wanted Arthur to take over as secretary of Health, Education, and Welfare. He accepted, but it was the most difficult decision he ever made. Arthur attended his first cabinet meeting as secretary just before he was sworn in. Vice-President Nixon was present and also representatives of each of the divisions of HEW.

August, 1958: Arthur is sworn in as secretary of Health, Education, and Welfare in President Eisenhower's cabinet. Supreme Court Justice Whitaker, looking on, administered the oath of office on that occasion. A former Ohio Wesleyan colleague had this to say: "I suddenly forgot how upset we were upon learning that Arthur Flemming was going back to Washington. When I met President Eisenhower and realized what a tremendous honor had been conferred upon Ohio Wesleyan, my feeling (i. e., of annoyance) changed to one of pride. Not since Charles Fairbanks was vice-president, and without cabinet status, has our university made such a contribution to the national government."

November, 1959: As secretary of HEW, Arthur was often required to take stands that were distinctly unpopular. Up to that time he had enjoyed good press, but he was to taste public wrath several times during his cabinet years. The famous "cranberry incident" memorialized in this AP wirephoto followed one of Arthur's unpopular rulings. Immediately before Thanksgiving, Arthur had banned the sale of a large portion of that year's cranberry crop until it had been tested and certified by federal regulators as free of taint from a weedkiller.

1959: Arthur, as secretary of HEW, represented the U.S. as host to King Bhumipol and Queen Sirikit of Thailand. During their state visit, one item on the Thailand royal visitors' agenda was the dedication of the Division of Biologic Standards Building of the National Institutes of Health, as King Bhumipol had expressed a particular interest in seeing this part of our government's activity.

1960: Arthur's most important responsibility during the last days of the second Eisenhower term was to chair the first White House Conference on Aging. Twenty-five hundred delegates attended the conference to discuss the problems older people face, and hundreds of recommendations came out of it. Here, Arthur visits with actress Mary Pickford, a delegate to the conference.

1960: Arthur stands with (left to right) Bertha Adkins, Frances Perkins, Marion Folsom, and William Mitchell during a celebration of the twenty-fifth anniversary of the Social Security Act.

1962: As president of the University of Oregon, Arthur hosts his friend and colleague Nelson Rockefeller at a University of Oregon football game. Both men are avid sports fans.

November, 1963: The National Commission on Health Care for the Aged, convoked at the behest of Senator Clinton Anderson of New Mexico and Senator Jacob Javits of New York, was asked to take a "new look" at health insurance for the aged. As chair of the so-called Javits Commission, Arthur went to Washington to present the report to President Kennedy. The president was enthusiastic about it, and it later played a significant role in the passage of Medicare in 1965. President Kennedy was assassinated a week later.

1967: Arthur came to the attention of President Johnson in his role as president of the National Council of Churches. LBJ, for whom Arthur had voted in the elections of 1964, had asked Arthur to accompany the official party to oversee the elections in Vietnam in August of 1967. I was really afraid my vacation plan to take Arthur to Alaska would sink under this presidential request, but it didn't. I think Arthur wanted to go as much as I did.

May, 1969: Arthur hands the gavel to Wilbur J. Cohen during the highly confrontational ninety-sixth annual forum of the National Conference on Social Welfare in New York City. The two former secretaries of HEW shared the podium as Arthur's term as president of NCSW was ending, and Wilbur's beginning.

1973: Arthur shares a light moment with President Nixon. In April, 1973, the president nominated Arthur to be U.S. commissioner on aging. Arthur's experience as chairman of the 1971 White House Conference on Aging, his appointment in 1972 as White House consultant on aging, and his deep and longstanding interest in issues affecting aging Americans made this appointment a perfect fit.

June, 1973: Arthur is sworn in as U.S. commissioner on aging in Health, Education, and Welfare Secretary Casper Weinberger's reception room. Weinberger is standing on Arthur's right.

August, 1974: Arthur, as U.S. commissioner on aging, greets President Ford in the Oval Office. Appointed to this post by President Nixon in 1973, Arthur reached the mandatory retirement age of seventy during President Ford's administration. Both President Ford, and later President Carter, issued waivers to permit him to continue his public responsibility beyond that age.

July, 1977: Arthur, as chair of the United States Commission on Civil Rights, meets with President Carter and the other members of the commission. President Nixon asked him to assume the chairmanship of the commission in 1974. The Commission on Civil Rights gave Arthur's crusading instincts full play. It is my belief that he enjoyed being in this post as much as any he had ever undertaken, and probably more. He had tremendous respect for his fellow commissioners, and I don't believe he ever missed a meeting or a commission hearing during the eight years he served as chairman.

November, 1981: Arthur stands with four of his fellow former HEW secretaries (left to right): Elliot Richardson, Patricia Harris, Wilbur Cohen, and David Mathews. The former secretaries were asked to return to HEW to give advice on some pending issues.

February, 1982: Benjamin Hooks of the National Association for the Advancement of Colored People and Dorothy Height of the National Council of Negro Women honor Arthur with the Hubert H. Humphrey Civil Rights Award of the Leadership Conference on Civil Rights. In the spring following his firing from the Civil Rights Commission, he received awards and honors from civil rights organizations throughout the country. All were accompanied by generous appraisals of his contribution to civil rights.

1989: Arthur shares the podium with the late Congressman Claude Pepper and Congressman Edward Roybal of California to announce a new bill to provide public support for long-term care. Arthur chairs the National Health Care Campaign, a coalition of over one hundred national organizations that has just one objective: the enactment of legislation that will provide for universal right of access to adequate health care, including long-term care.

September, 1989: Arthur is honored at a dinner celebrating the memory of Congressman Claude Pepper, who died in May of that year. Bob Hope was the entertainer that night, and Geraldine Ferraro, as master of ceremonies, presented the award. Arthur received the first Pepper Distinguished Service Award by the Mildred and Claude Pepper Foundation.

10

THE OFFICE OF DEFENSE MOBILIZATION

The Office of Defense Mobilization was the brain-child of President Truman. It was set up in December of 1950 to meet the Korean crisis, and was part of the Executive Office of the president.

The president felt the need for such an office because of problems arising in World War II. It was hoped through this office to guarantee economic and industrial blueprints for defense could be developed, and that the implementation of these blueprints could be coordinated more effectively.

He had persuaded Charles Wilson to resign his job as president of General Electric Company and head up the new Office of Defense Mobilization. Mobilization Director Wilson, through General Lucius Clay, asked Arthur to return to Washington. His assignment was to assume responsibility for mobilization manpower problems. Editorial comment on his appointment was uniformly favorable—in *The New York Times*, *The Washington Post*, *The Cleveland Plain-Dealer*, *The Columbus Dispatch*, and others. So he began a commuting schedule between Washington and Delaware, spending Monday through Thursday or Friday in Washington, and returning to Delaware each Friday evening for a continuous weekend round of meetings and appointments to keep Ohio Wesleyan functioning as smoothly as possible.

In his new capacity, he was to preside at meetings of the Office of Defense Mobilization's Manpower Policy Committee. One of his major jobs was to help establish policy on the problem of deferring essential workers from military duty.

Labor leaders were very displeased over this development, and so was Secretary of Labor Maurice Tobin. For weeks these men had been trying to get President Truman and Defense Mobilization Director Wilson to place a big labor man in with the big business men in the mobilization high command. They felt that Arthur's appointment took too much power from the secretary.

Mr. Wilson did appoint Secretary Tobin to be on the Manpower Policy Committee, but the chief role went to Arthur as chairman. Others on the committee were representatives of the Department of Agriculture, the director of Selective Service, the chairman of the Civil Service Commission, the deputy administrator of the Defense Production Administration, and the chairman of the Wage Stabilization Board of the Economic Stabilization Agency. Mr. Meany, the president of AFL-CIO, at Arthur's request, designated one of his top officials to work with Arthur.

One of Arthur's first decisions was to support a new policy prepared by General Hershey, the director of the Selective Service, permitting postponement of military service for college men, the postponement to be based on scholastic achievement. He made it clear that this was not a plan to permit students to avoid service, but simply to defer it. He explained that "the armed services would thus have the benefit of men trained to serve more effectively. Also, when these men have served in the armed forces for the required period, the nation will have a store of highly trained young men who have had the benefit of a formal education and practical experience in the armed services."

In a speech before the closing session of the American Council on Education in May, 1951, Arthur (who is not given to crying "Wolf, Wolf") declared that the forces of communism were so strong that "there is a distinct possibility of their being able to wipe out our liberties." He appealed to the educators to cooperate in defense mobilization by helping in these fields:
1. Awakening the country to the danger of communism;
2. Turning into constructive channels the interest in economy

and good management in government;

3. Teaching that sacrifices are worthwhile if liberties are to be preserved; and

4. Giving the constituencies detailed information on the best use of manpower. He said those seeking jobs should find out where they can make the maximum contribution to the defense mobilization program.

This theme that "never before in our history have we been faced with such a serious threat to our basic freedom" was reiterated again and again in speeches of this period.

Balancing the country's needs for the armed forces and needs for arms production and nondefense production was a big problem, and Arthur's job was to work on this without weakening the nation.

It was in this mood of fear of losing our liberties that Dwight Eisenhower was sworn into the office of president of the United States on January 20, 1953.

One of President Eisenhower's first official acts was to request Arthur to become the acting director of the Office of Defense Mobilization. A short while later, under a White House reorganization plan sent to the Congress for approval, the Office of Defense Mobilization was converted from a temporary agency into a permanent one. This office absorbed the National Security Resources Board, created by previous legislation, as well as part of the stockpile purchasing functions then handled by the Department of Defense through the Munitions Board and the Department of Interior.

The order establishing the new ODM made the director a member of the National Security Council in recognition of the vital strategic importance of defense mobilization.

The president asked Arthur to become the director of this reorganized and greatly enlarged ODM. The proposed new ODM thus became a statutory body in which all mobilization of nondefense resources for the nation was to be centralized under one director. By invitation of the president, the director of Defense Mobilization became a cabinet member, and from then on attended all cabinet meetings.

The swearing-in to his new job took place on June 25, 1953, at the White House. Arthur's parents, his sister and brother-in-law, and all of our children were present. Supreme Court Justice Harold Burton, an old friend, administered the oath of office.

Justice Burton caused considerable consternation and comment by using on this occasion the so-called "long oath." Before he was through, Arthur had given not only the customary pledge to support the constitution, but had also disavowed communist and fascist leanings, promised not to strike against the government, and affirmed that he had not paid anything for his job. This particular form of oath taking surprised even the president, who remarked, "That's a new one. I've never heard that before."

Arthur's responsibility was to reorganize the Office of Defense Mobilization so that it would operate as the lead agency in coordinating the development and implementation of plans for the mobilization of the nation's nondefense resources if we should become involved in hostilities. In this connection it had responsibility under the Defense Production Act for the stockpiling of strategic and critical materials. It also had responsibilities in the area of human resources.

It was an awesome task. One of Arthur's first jobs was to develop plans for decentralizing the price and wage programs that were in operation throughout the Korean conflict and to develop standby price and wage control plans to be implemented in the event of another conflict.

The first picture of the Eisenhower cabinet shows Arthur sitting between Budget Director Joseph Dodge and Secretary of Labor Martin Durkin.

We hadn't been back in Washington but a short while when

the mail brought us one of the coveted square white envelopes with "The White House" embossed in gold in the upper left-hand corner. It contained an invitation to a dinner honoring the vice-president.

We both went to great pains to get ourselves properly outfitted for the occasion. In Delaware, Ohio, we had no need whatsoever for the kind of apparel customarily worn to White House social events. Arthur had to get "full dress" white tie equipment, as all White House affairs in the Eisenhower days were true formal occasions.

For me, it required a new floor-length gown, long white kid gloves, and a new evening wrap.

When the evening of the dinner arrived, the children were all lined up at the front door to watch us leave. Art called after us, "Well, I hope you two get your money's worth!" We did.

That first year back in Washington also saw another adjustment in our family. Lib was married to George Speese and returned to Ohio to live. It was a real wrench for all of us.

Arthur's schedule was busier than ever. In addition to the three-man Committee on Government Organization, which consisted of Arthur, Milton Eisenhower, and Nelson Rockefeller, another study group similar to the one set up in the Truman administration came into being. Its composition and scope were, like the first reorganizing board, to recommend changes in the executive branch. There were four members appointed by President Eisenhower, four by Vice-President Nixon, and four by Speaker of the House of Representatives Joseph Martin. Ex-President Herbert Hoover was asked to be the chairman. Arthur was one of the president's choices. The others were the former Postmaster General James Farley and Attorney General Herbert Brownell.

The death of Senator Robert Taft in the summer of 1953 gave rise to speculation that Governor Lausche might appoint Arthur to replace Taft as the United States senator from Ohio. *The Evening Star* and

Time magazine both printed stories about the possibility.

Also, when Secretary of Labor Durkin resigned in a controversy over proposed Taft-Hartley Labor Law amendments, both *The Post* and *The Star* headlined stories with Arthur's name as a possible choice for his successor. But neither possibility came to pass.

He was kept busy indeed with his responsibilities at ODM. Fear of Russia's build-up of thermonuclear bombs was grim motivation. In October, 1953, the president himself issued this warning: "The Soviets now possess a stockpile of atomic weapons of conventional types, and we must furthermore conclude that the powerful explosion of August 12 last was produced by a weapon, or a forerunner of a weapon, of power far in excess of conventional types.

"We therefore conclude that the Soviets have now the capability of atomic attack on us, and such capability will increase with the passage of time."

This statement marked our entry into a new phase. The United States faced the kind of threat of major devastation that for centuries had hung over Poland and France.

Arthur was directing all of his energies into planning for such an eventuality. *The Reporter*, dated January 27, 1955, called Arthur's area of responsibility the "Department of Just-In-Case." "Without straining facts," it said, "it can be called second only to that of the Secretary of Defense in the power that it carries. This is because he [i.e., Arthur] writes basic policy for a broad sector of the national economy, partly because he sits in both Cabinet and National Security Council meetings, and partly because he acts for the President on a wide range of problems, making policy that binds all of the other departments and agencies."

We even had a special telephone installed by Arthur's bed (called a "white" phone) connecting us directly with the White House, and I was instructed in the special emergency "lingo" used in operating it. Fortunately, I never had to put my ability to the test.

A massive build-up of weapons on hand and capacity in reserve was the first phase of mobilization. The second phase was that of perfecting and protecting the industrial base. Arthur had to make many difficult decisions regarding the use of coal, oil, and other products.

How to insure that the government would keep operating in case of war was another project of Arthur's. By the spring of 1954, an elaborate plan to operate the government by remote control was complete. The president himself led the drill for an atomic raid.

In this setting, he flashed orders to some two thousand top administration officials who had fled the capital to secret emergency headquarters in an atomic preparedness exercise. The band of ranking government officials had fled to some thirty secret standby headquarters in four nearby states (Maryland, Virginia, West Virginia, and North Carolina) to see how they would carry on essential wartime operations in the event of advance warning of a real attack on Washington.

The emergency government plans focused on two points: one was the "underground" Pentagon, which was running the military side of the government; the other was primarily a test of a communications network connecting each hideout with the White House. The president himself, who had directed the invasion of Europe by remote control from England, was greatly interested in the exercise, particularly the communications aspects.

In June of 1955, another "Operation Alert" was ready for trial. That time, at the sound of a warning siren, President Eisenhower was evacuated by helicopter to a secret command headquarters. Arthur and fifteen thousand other government workers also fled to refuges outside the city.

A third "Operation Alert" took place in July of 1956.

In all of these exercises President Eisenhower was well

satisfied with the way the plans had been worked out by the Office of Defense Mobilization.

These occasions were for me a time of strain, even though I knew that the emergencies were "make believe." But as I had learned to do through the years, my own salvation lay in planning and carrying out some elaborate household project, such as the recovering of a sofa, making new draperies, making a folding screen, or whatever—something to keep my hands and my mind busy. My own description of Arthur and me is: "He's the head man; I'm the hand-maiden."

The president's heart attack in 1956 cast considerable gloom over the entire county, and there was a great deal of uncertainty and speculation as to whether he would run for a second term. His recovery was excellent, however, and he decided to run. By the time the first Eisenhower term was over, Arthur had been in Washington with the Office of Defense Mobilization six years, four of them on leave from the presidency of Ohio Wesleyan.

It was time to go back to Delaware. Actually, the children and I had returned to Delaware in the fall of 1956 so they could begin the school year. Arthur stayed in Washington until the end of the first term in January, 1957. I had thoroughly enjoyed the years in Washington with the ODM and was really loath to return to middle America. But return we did, and I soon settled down into the academic routine.

When Arthur returned, he was wearing in his lapel the insignia of the Medal of Freedom. The president had gone to the Defense Department the day before to confer this on Arthur, citing him for contributing "immeasurably in coordinating the efforts of the government in forging a position of strength in the everlasting fight for peace."

A few years later, when we were clear across the country in Eugene, Oregon, Arthur's years at the Office of Defense Mobilization again played a major role in his life. He became the focus of a Senate Special Committee investigation in the spring of 1962. It had strong political overtones.

There is nothing—absolutely nothing—that delights the heart of a political party more than to point the finger of shame at the opposite political party. To be able to catch the opposing party in any action that smells of corruption in public office is great sport.

It doesn't really matter much whether the charges are proven or not; it often serves the same purpose politically if enough suspicion is created in the public mind to swing voters from the political party under scrutiny.

President Kennedy, in the spring of 1962, announced that he was "astonished" to find, in his first year in the White House, that the government had $7.7 billion in stockpiled strategic materials. "Stockpiles" is the term given to inventories owned by the government of some ninety-five commodities deemed to be strategic and critical. They are deemed critical because experience in World War I, World War II, and the Korean War had shown that without resources of strategic and critical materials in readily usable form, the country's defense efforts can be hampered, delayed, or even fail.

The president said that the United States needed only about $4.5 billion in stockpiled materials, and that, therefore, the previous Republican administration had unnecessarily increased the stockpiles. He said he was "astonished" at the amount of stockpiling completed during the Eisenhower administration.

Senator John Williams (R-DE) looked into the record and found that President Kennedy, as a senator from Massachusetts, had voted eight times on roll call votes between 1956 and 1960 for subsidies for stockpiling. Only once had he cast a negative vote for such a subsidy.

Nevertheless the administration requested Senator Stuart Symington (D-MO), chairman of the Senate Armed Services Subcommittee, to conduct an investigation into the stockpiling program of the previous Republican administration.

Senator Symington, a former secretary of the Air Force and therefore presumably an expert on defense preparedness, had himself also voted affirmatively on the various decisions in the Senate regarding the elevation of stockpiles of strategic materials. He too turned pious and willingly agreed to proceed with the investigation the president proposed.

During the period Senator Symington was charged with investigating, Arthur was director of the Office of Defense Mobilization. He charged that Arthur had made a decision on stockpiling in 1954 that had resulted in "windfall" profits for copper mining firms. The General Services Administration had testified earlier that private mining companies picked up a three million dollar "windfall" when the government, pursuant to a decision of Arthur's, allowed them to postpone or cancel deliveries of copper to the stockpile, and then to sell the metal to private industry at a higher price.

The loss of potential copper profits occurred in 1956 and 1957 and was therefore said to be traceable to a decision by Arthur as director of the Office of Defense Mobilization. Some half-dozen mining companies allegedly made huge profits as a result of this decision.

So the Democratic members of Senator Symington's subcommittee set out to have a field day as they went after the Republicans in an attempt to prove (1) that the stockpiles had been unnecessarily increased and (2) that the Republicans had permitted huge profits to be made by certain companies.

The Republican members of the subcommittee openly accused their Democratic colleagues of defaming former Eisenhower officials in an attempt to reap political advantage. Senator Prescott Bush (R-CT) charged that Arthur was being unjustly accused and made the "object of defamatory criticism and that the Symington hearings had been conducted in a vendetta style to find scapegoats and to cast blame upon the former administration." More-over, the counsel for the subcommittee made a statement that the Eisenhower administration's stockpiling program had been ex-tended for political purposes. But Senator Symington continued to hold hearings and declared that Arthur had been at fault in using the stockpiling law as he did.

It was in this climate of bickering that Arthur's turn to testify arrived. In his opening statement to the subcommittee he outlined in detail the guidelines he kept in mind as he discharged his responsibilities in the materials area, in each case carefully explaining that the various actions taken were in pursuance of acts passed by the Congress of the United States. He further explained that his decisions were discussed with President Eisenhower and that the president was in agreement that acquir-ing the strategic and critical material would guarantee that the nation would be strong if a crisis were to develop.

He flatly rejected the previous testimony of the General Services Administration officials who said that the government should have collected the three million dollar "windfall" by accepting the scheduled deliveries and then reselling the copper on the open market. Arthur declared this would have been "dangerous governmental activity of the trading of strategic and critical materials."

Senator Symington kept pressing Arthur to reconstruct very minute details about stockpile transactions which had taken place eight years earlier, and finally Arthur angrily accused him of questioning him unfairly. Arthur said it was the first time he had ever been accused of being less than candid before a congres-sional committee. He insisted that the frailties of human memory prevented him from recalling specific conversations with gov-ernment officials regarding stockpile policies, rather than any deliberate intention to hide facts from the subcommittee investi-gating the situation, as Senator Symington inferred.

Arthur said that the so-called "windfall" profit resulting from his directive was secondary to his concern to strengthen our defense mobilization base without consideration of profits or losses in administering the nation's defense stockpile. He said that the government occasionally could have profited from the stockpile operations by "playing the market" itself, but that he had rejected such transactions because he believed it would constitute a dangerous practice. He insisted that cancellations and deferrals were intended to relieve a tight supply situation in industry at the time.

Being pushed by Senator Symington, without advance warning, for minute details of a transaction that occurred such a long time ago really bothered Arthur. He offered to obtain a leave of absence from the University of Oregon in order to spend a couple of months, if necessary, in Washington to recheck files in order to answer the committee's questions with complete accuracy.

Senator Symington pretended surprise at Arthur's annoyance at being asked for such wide-ranging details about meetings and conferences that had long since vanished from his memory, without any advance indication of the scope of the questions to be asked. "I have never been placed in this position before," Arthur said. "I have never withheld any information from Congress."

But Senator Symington preferred to let the inference remain that Arthur was deliberately being vague about his answers to the questions. Arthur's offer to take a leave to check the files to refresh his memory, and then to testify later, was never accepted.

Other Eisenhower cabinet officers were declared by the investigating committee to be active in the then-secret policies and contracts that built up the stockpiles, with most of the blame falling on former Treasury Secretary George Humphrey, Secretary of Commerce Sinclair Weeks, and Secretary of the Interior Douglas McKay.

Ex-President Eisenhower sent a letter to the subcommittee strongly defending his stockpile policies and decisions. He said he firmly rejected the policy of "too little-too late" stockpiling, and that "when he left office in 1961 the nation was strongly situated in this regard to deal with the forces of international communism." He further declared in his letter that when he became president, he was determined that we benefit from the mistakes of prior years (i.e., that previous stockpiling had been confined to mere talk instead of implementation). His long-term stockpiling policy evolved, and Congress supported his efforts by considering the programs the administration presented and by appropriating yearly funds for the purchase of stockpile materials.

As a result, by the end of the Eisenhower term, the country had, for the first time in our history, stockpiles of strategic and critical materials—enough, President Eisenhower said, "to deal with any emergency situation."

The investigation droned on for months, with Senator Symington draining every ounce of political advantage from his insistent questioning about details and his insinuations about Arthur's motivations in his stockpiling decisions.

Finally, in September of 1963, Senator Symington made available a draft of a blistering one hundred-page report attacking the management of the multimillion dollar national stockpile under the Eisenhower administration.

The Republican members of the committee charged that the report was slanted to embarrass prominent Eisenhower administration figures and was completely lacking in objectivity.

The draft released by Senator Symington was so intemperate, in fact, that he couldn't even get his committee to approve it. In an executive session, the report failed because of a 3-3 tie vote. Even one Democratic member refused to approve it.

One commentator, in a column about the draft, declared that Senator Symington had attempted to indict a handful of Eisenhower cabinet officers as though they were members of a "corrupt and greedy political gang." He added that nothing in the report made this a believable determination and declared that the Republicans were entitled to cry "foul" over its very partisan nature.

Arthur issued his own reaction to the draft. He said the stockpile investigators virtually ignored their colleagues (i.e., the Republican members of the subcommittee) in drafting the highly critical report on Republican stockpile policies. He further said that Senator Symington also had virtually ignored detailed stockpile reports available from the Joint Committee on Defense Production. He concluded by declaring that "I am glad that when the Eisenhower administration left office, our nation finally did have substantial stockpiles of strategic and critical materials. Our strategic resources materials should not be dissipated until determinations have been made by competent authorities as to what our present objectives should be. This the Kennedy administration has not done."

One editorial in the *Portland Oregonian*, in commenting on the Symington draft of the stockpile subcommittee of the Senate Armed Services Committee, said it had "as foul a political odor as any such document in a long time. It may be credited almost wholly to Senator Stuart Symington who has been pushing the stockpile investigation in the hopes, presumably, of making the kind of political strike that projected Harry Truman into the national limelight as the exposer of defense production waste." (It was, of course, a fact that in 1960 Senator Symington had been one of the viable "hopefuls" for the Democratic nomination for president.)

And, further, the editorial said: "The clear purpose of Senator Symington's one-sided presentation is to invite the inference that the Eisenhower administration in secret manipulation of the federal program of acquiring stockpiles of strategic materials, acted to enrich its friends both inside and outside the administration."

After a discussion of the nature and reason for stockpiling standards, the editorial concludes with: "Senator Symington, however, has apparently set some standards of his own—political standards—and they are woefully low."

11

THE PRESIDENT'S CABINET

Arthur has said that the decision to leave Ohio Wesleyan and go to Washington to become secretary of Health, Education, and Welfare in President Eisenhower's cabinet was the most difficult one he ever made.

He had been back at Ohio Wesleyan less than a year after his four-year leave of absence to be director of the Office of Defense Mobilization when a telephone call from Governor Adams, the president's administrative assistant, informed him that then-Secretary of Health, Education, and Welfare Marion Folsom desired to leave the cabinet for health reasons, and the president wanted Arthur to take over that post.

Arthur was deeply sensitive to the fact that it is no small honor to be invited to serve in the president's cabinet. Besides, the department he had been asked to head covered all of the areas of his special interest.

In addition, Arthur felt a particular closeness to the department since he had had a hand in the creation and naming of that newest executive department. As a member of President Eisenhower's Advisory Committee on Government Organization, along with Nelson Rockefeller and Milton Eisenhower, he had helped work out the organizational details to merge the Federal Security Administration, the Public Health Service, and the Office of Education into a cabinet-level department.

Arthur had gone, along with Oveta Culp Hobby, then the Federal Security administrator, to see Senator Robert Taft and present to him the proposed plan for the new department, with the result that Senator Taft agreed to sponsor the departmentalizing of the three independent agencies. Senator Taft also agreed to see to it that the necessary money and congressional backing were provided. The name of the new department was also agreed on at that meeting, with Senator Taft himself suggesting that it be called the Department of Health, Education, and Welfare.

It was Senator Taft's prestige among his fellow Republicans that got the project moving, since many of the conservative Republican senators of the time took a dim view of the idea. Mrs. Hobby became its first secretary, and Mr. Folsom was the second. And now, five years later, the president was offering Arthur the opportunity to head it.

Naturally it was an attractive possibility for Arthur, but the most obvious drawback was that he had been on leave from the presidency of Ohio Wesleyan during the entire first Eisenhower term, and his strong sense of duty and obligation and loyalty dictated that he remain at his post in Delaware.

I shared this feeling, even though the idea of returning to Washington had great appeal too.

Arthur talked the matter over with his number-one confidant and counselor, his father; with the president of the Ohio Wesleyan Board of Trustees, Charles B. Mills; and with other key people whose judgment he trusted. But nothing came of these consultations to shake his conviction that he was morally obligated to remain at Ohio Wesleyan.

He reported his decision to Governor Adams. And Governor Adams said, "Think about it a while longer, Arthur. The president wants you to take this job."

So Arthur struggled with the matter a few weeks longer. But he came out at the same place, and again he reported his decision to Governor Adams. Again, in his turn, Governor Adams made the same reply he had earlier: "Think about it some more. The president wants you—not anybody else."

By this time many people knew that Arthur had been invited

to become a member of the president's cabinet. Many of the Ohio Wesleyan trustees were putting considerable pressure on him to turn down the cabinet opportunity; so did the president of the Alumni Association; and the faculty got up a petition, signed by nearly every member, urging him to remain at Ohio Wesleyan.

From an economic standpoint it didn't make any sense at all for us to leave Delaware. Susan was then a sophomore at Ohio Wesleyan, on free tuition. We had all of the boys to educate, and free tuition was available for them too. In all, this amounted to about $20,000 in free tuition. (Remember, this was 1958.) Besides, the job at Ohio Wesleyan was a permanent one, assuming good performance, of course. (Realistically, a college president's job is never assured.) The HEW job was a political appointment, with a probable tenure of two and a-half years. After that, what?

As the pressures mounted to keep Arthur at Ohio Wesleyan, and with virtually everyone knowing exactly what Arthur should do (except Arthur himself), that is, that he should remain in Delaware, I began to have second thoughts about my original feeling that he should stay at Ohio Wesleyan. Should a president of the United States, I asked myself, have to beg men to come into his cabinet? Rather, shouldn't this kind of opportunity take precedence over all others, and shouldn't citizens asked to serve in this way respond willingly, even though it meant making sacrifices, financial and otherwise?

The weeks passed, and Arthur's intense struggle went on. He simply couldn't make up his mind to leave Ohio Wesleyan. But neither could he, finally and irrevocably, turn his back on the HEW opportunity.

Four months had passed since Arthur was first approached by Governor Adams. Something had to give!

Arthur made an appointment the first week in May, a Wednesday, to go to Washington and give his final decision. The night before he left I asked him what he was going to do.

"I don't know," he replied. "I still have a few more hours to think about it."

"Well, I know what I think you should do, so I might as well say it. I think you should go to HEW." It was the first time I had allowed myself the luxury of making a positive statement about going, and my attitude represented a complete about-face from my earlier conviction.

"Why?" Arthur asked.

"Because I think if the president wants you badly enough at HEW to come back and ask you three times, he deserves to get the man he wants. His needs should have precedence over all other considerations in this case."

But Arthur only shook his head.

After he had left for Washington, his father telephoned from Kingston, and I told him what I had said to Arthur about his taking the HEW job. And he, too, for the first time, said he had come to the same conclusion. That made me feel really good, as I always felt on firm ground when Dad Flemming agreed with me.

The next day, Thursday, Arthur telephoned me in the early afternoon to say that he had told the president he would take the job as secretary of Health, Education, and Welfare. There was no exhilaration in his voice, no relief even. He simply sounded tired. I asked him what had led him, finally, to tell the president he would take it. "I don't know," he replied somewhat wearily, though he, too, had concluded that one should not say "No" to the president of the United States when he made such a request.

"Well, I'm glad. It was the right thing to do."

That evening the news stories all carried items about Arthur's appointment. And immediately we began getting telegrams, telephone calls, and special delivery letters from our friends all over the country, all expressing happiness and congratulations over this new opportunity for public service for Arthur.

But in Delaware a strange thing happened. Nobody, absolutely nobody, mentioned it to us.

The story broke on Thursday, May 8. It was the day before the annual three-day Mothers' Day weekend celebration, called the Monnett Week-End—the biggest and most festive commemoration of the college year. It was a period filled with open houses, the May Queen crowning, plays and dance recitals, style shows, athletic contests, and so on—all planned and executed by the students to provide their mothers with a good time. Each dormitory and fraternity house had a mother-daughter or mother-son banquet on Friday evening to set the tone for the weekend gaiety. Each year I went to one of these banquets and also to nearly all of the other events on the crowded schedule.

Thursday evening, at home, though I received several long-distance congratulatory calls, I received no calls from faculty friends or Delaware townspeople. Friday the same was true.

Friday evening I dressed and went to the dormitory our daughter Susan lived in to attend the banquet with her. Several administrative wives and faculty people were also guests at the banquet. Not a single one of them said a word to me about Arthur's appointment. Several students extended congratulations, and several of the out-of-town mothers did also, but the strange silence persisted as far the faculty and administrative people at the university was concerned. It was as if a vow of silence had been taken by all of the Ohio Wesleyan people.

On Saturday, too, I went as usual to all of the scheduled events in connection with the Monnett Week-End. And though I met many, many "friends" as I went about the campus that day, absolutely no one spoke of our leaving Ohio Wesleyan for the cabinet appointment in Washington. Meanwhile, from outside of Delaware, the telegrams and phone calls kept coming.

On Sunday, after the annual Mothers Day convocation, it was our custom to receive the visiting mothers and faculty people in Arthur's reception room following the service. Then, for the very first time, the wall of silence had a slight crack in it when one faculty wife said as she went down the line, "We're going to miss you." It wasn't much, but it did help a little.

For Arthur, too, that weekend was a strange experience indeed. He called a faculty meeting for Friday night following the announcement of his appointment to explain his decision to them, hoping that he would be able to get them to understand his motivation. There were nearly 150 people present, nearly all of whom a short while before had signed the petition asking him to remain at Ohio Wesleyan. When the meeting was over, all but two of the faculty members present left without even speaking to him. Two members did go up to him afterward and generously expressed their understanding of his decision and wished him well.

It is still hard for me to understand their behavior. The faculty's farewell gesture was to organize a dinner where they presented us with a water-color painting of a portion of the campus.

We did not leave Delaware for Washington until the end of July, nearly three months after the announcement of Arthur's appointment. In that entire time not a single faculty person came to see us, or called to say goodbye. It was as if we were total strangers. A group of younger faculty wives who had lived in the temporary housing behind the president's home did give me a coffee party and handkerchief shower, and that cheered me a lot.

I suffered acutely during those weeks. Often I found myself remembering what Mrs. Burgstahler had said about being the wife of Ohio Wesleyan's president: "To live in the house at 23 Oak Hill was to be the loneliest woman in town."

We had lived in Delaware seven years out of the previous ten. Active involvement in numerous college and community activities had accompanied all of those years. At one annual alumni luncheon after we had been at Ohio Wesleyan about four years,

I was presented with an Alumni Award for outstanding service to the university, the first non-alumnus to be so honored. So I was completely unprepared to find myself virtually friendless at the time of leaving Delaware.

A couple of wonderful neighbors did help a lot. One of them, a trustee's wife, attempted to cheer me by saying that "no president's wife ever left Ohio Wesleyan with any friends." She explained that the reason was that Delaware and Ohio Wesleyan have traditionally regarded the president of Ohio Wesleyan and his wife as "different from them, not really one of them, and sort of untouchable."

The death of Arthur's father occupied our minds much of the time. He had a stroke two days after commencement and died the following Saturday. It was a severe shock to Arthur, who throughout his life had kept in close touch with his father and depended on him for helpful counsel many times. Dad Flemming was eighty-four when he died. He was still doing a full day's work in his law office in the morning, and spending each afternoon at the Rondout Savings Bank where he was president. Just a few weeks before his stroke he had tried an important case and won. Arthur was very proud of him.

Arthur, Tom, and I went to Kingston and were there when Dad Flemming died, though he never regained consciousness after he suffered the stroke.

After the funeral we lingered in Kingston a few days to help Arthur's mother. Then we stopped in Washington to locate a house. We found a lovely new split-level in Chevy Chase, Maryland, which ideally suited our needs.

I remember with particular vividness our move back to Washington. The van had an accident on the mountains on old Route 40, and was forty-eight hours late in arriving at our new home. This made it necessary to unload on Sunday.

Arthur and I had previously been invited to have dinner after church on that Sunday with Doctor and Mrs. Frederic Brown Harris and Madame Chiang Kai Chek. We had accepted because we had expected that the van unloading process to be well past by that time. When I visualized that huge van unloading in front of our house on that particular Sunday, I knew I had to be there. Attempts to persuade the man in charge of the van to delay unloading until Monday had failed.

When I told Arthur I would have to be excused from the dinner engagement with the Harrises and Madame Chiang, he brushed aside my objections as of no consequence at all. He insisted that I go with him, and said that a little thing like a van unloading could be handled by somebody else.

So we went to dinner as scheduled and left Susan and the boys to deal with giving the unloading instructions to the movers. The resulting placement of furniture around in our new ten-room house was interesting to say the least!

On Wednesday, July 7, 1958, according to *The Congressional Record,* the legislative clerk of the Senate read the nomination of Arthur S. Flemming to be secretary of Health, Education, and Welfare. Without objection, the nomination was confirmed.

August 1 was the date set for the swearing-in ceremony. The oath was administered by Supreme Court Justice Whitaker in President Eisenhower's office. Arthur had attended his first cabinet meeting as secretary just before he was sworn in. Vice-President Nixon was present and also representatives of each of the divisions of HEW. Arthur's mother was there and all of our children. Charles and Rachel Mills, from Marysville, Ohio, came for the swearing-in.

Later, "Chid" Mills sent a letter to all of his fellow Ohio Wesleyan trustees which included this paragraph: "I suddenly forgot how upset we were upon learning that Arthur Flemming was going back to Washington. When I met President Eisenhower and realized what a tremendous honor had been conferred upon

Ohio Wesleyan, my feeling (i. e., of annoyance) changed to one of pride. Not since Charles Fairbanks was vice-president and without cabinet status has our university made such a contribution to the national government." In the light of the expressed attitudes of nearly everybody at Ohio Wesleyan, including faculty and trustees and alumni, it is hardly accurate to say that Ohio Wesleyan "made a contribution."

One matter I feel I should clarify is the shift I made to the Republican party at this time. I have mentioned earlier my lifelong leaning toward, and my membership in the Democratic party. Arthur had never once suggested that I change. But when we arrived in Washington to join President Eisenhower's cabinet, things began to happen that I had not counted on. One was the notification that I had been named an honorary vice-president of the Ohio Republican Women. Another was an invitation to be the guest of honor at a luncheon at the Capitol Hill Club, the Republican party's social club. How could I, a "card-carrying" Democrat, respond honestly to such honors as were coming my way as a result of Arthur's cabinet appointment?

Without consulting Arthur on the matter, I decided I owed him my final loyalty—that is, changing my registration in Ohio from Democrat to Republican. So on a trip back to Delaware in the fall of 1958, I made a visit to the elections office. I explained my intention to the official there, whereupon he said that I couldn't change my registration until the next regular election (two years hence) since Delaware is what is called a non-registering county, meaning you can register only at election time.

I insisted to the election official that I wanted to change my registration right then, not two years hence. He could offer me no help or any suggestion to carry out my plan, so I ended up leaving a note, which he attached to the page in the registration book where my name was, signifying my wish to change my registration from Democrat to Republican. I can't say that I felt any differently, or even that my attitudes toward public questions changed.

Arthur took charge of the Department of Health, Education, and Welfare at a time when many educators were deeply concerned about the field of education at all levels. This followed the general alarm felt over Russia's Sputnik, the discovery that launched the space age.

Congress had reacted to the news about Sputnik by placing great emphasis on scientific training as the overriding objective of education. Before Mr. Folsom left office, the administration had worked out a program to spend about $800 million of federal funds in the next four years to strengthen the teaching of mathematics, science, and foreign languages, and for the expansion of graduate studies. Arthur took over in time to carry the ball for the Sputnik-inspired education assistance law.

In his position as secretary of Health, Education, and Welfare, Arthur found himself often in situations that required him to take stands that were distinctly unpopular with many of his fellow citizens. Up to that time he had, for the most part, enjoyed what is called a "good press." Newspaper writers had dealt very kindly with him, but he was to taste public wrath several times during his cabinet years.

In a feature story which appeared in the *St. Louis Dispatch* at the time of his appointment, Edward Woods, the Washington correspondent for the paper, referred to this aspect of Arthur's public service, and said, "Flemming, who has held many government positions since President Roosevelt appointed him to the Civil Service Commission, seems to have led a charmed life politically. No one here in or out of Congress seems to be mad at him about anything."

Asked to comment on his extraordinary immunity to political sniping, Arthur said, "I am not going to brag about never having my head knocked off. High government position is a hazardous occupation. But I've always tried to work out problems. I recognize fully the rights of Congress under our system of checks and balances, and I think it is a good thing because it keeps one on his toes, and that's all to the good."

A wise statement indeed. Political sniping really caught up with him when he was at HEW.

Here is a case in point. School closings, because of the refusal of some Southern states to comply with desegregation directives, were a big problem when Arthur took over. Almost immediately he had to become the interpreter of the federal position on the school integration struggle. He deplored the threat of school closings in Virginia, Arkansas, and other southern states, and he outlined the circumstances under which states and communities could or could not continue to receive federal financial assistance.

Arthur regarded the school closings as absolutely indefensible. He incurred the wrath of Governor J. Lindsay Almond, of Virginia, who branded Arthur's statement blasting the school closings as "Federal NAACP [National Association for the Advancement of Colored People] propaganda to divide and conquer." Governor Almond further said, "Mr. Flemming deplores the effects, when the administration of which he is a servant established the cause," an interesting face-saving turnabout. Governor Almond then reaffirmed his stand on massive resistance (to desegregation of the schools) declaring that "I have not weakened, I do not intend to weaken" in his view that "desegregation would destroy public education in the years ahead."

Nevertheless Arthur continued his efforts toward compliance with the Supreme Court's school integration decision. He appealed to the citizens of the communities where the schools were closed to insist on decisions being made that would result in schools being re-opened under policies that would be in harmony with decisions of the courts.

Another controversial question involving education on which Arthur spoke out forcibly was on aid to federally impacted school systems. Arthur felt that the aid program should be reduced. He felt that the federal government was contributing too much to the educational cost for his own children in Montgomery County (Art and Tom were then in Bethesda-Chevy Chase High School) on the aid program for impacted children. He felt that these grants should be allocated to families who live and work on federal property and not for persons whose homes were on local tax rolls. The people who benefited from this program didn't like this stand.

Improving education throughout the country was a constant concern of Arthur's. He took a firm stand on such questionable activities as "diploma mills"—that is, institutions that provided college diplomas for a fee. These "mills" became the focus of a drive by the government to eliminate this dishonest practice. Arthur published a list of these "degree mills" and vowed to see that this fraudulent practice was discontinued.

Another problem that was current at the time was flouridation of water. Even before Arthur was sworn in, he was bombarded with demands by conservative groups to fight flouridation. Acting on advice from the Public Health Service, whose opinion was based on many years of scientific testing, Arthur actively promoted flouridation of water from his first day in office and throughout his tenure.

Pollution as a national issue was also coming to the fore. Arthur felt even then that federal government resources should be used to help states and communities to build treatment facilities.

He also used the influence of his department to crack down on misrepresented vitamins, minerals, and food supplements. He announced that he would cooperate personally with the Food and Drug Administration in publicizing and prosecuting "those who deliberately seek to deceive the people with false medical claims." At the time, the Food and Drug Administration was involved in some twenty-three court claims against firms and individuals who were charged with false labeling or inferior contents of their products.

A real furor in the field of public health arose in November of 1959 when the Food and Drug Administration presented Arthur with evidence that a weed killer used by cranberry growers caused cancer in rats.

On Thanksgiving Day, 1959, an Associated Press picture carried this caption under it: "Mrs. Arthur Flemming passes a dish of cranberry salad as they posed November 26 with table set for their Thanksgiving Day dinner. Several weeks ago Flemming in his official capacity announced that some of the cranberry supply had been tainted with weed killer. Since then, cranberries on sale have been stamped as government approved."

The AP wire story quoted above sums up one of the really bizarre episodes in our lives, remembered as the Great Cranberry Crisis of 1959. This particular story was printed in newspapers all over the world, complete with a picture of Arthur and me and the cranberries, as indicated in the quotation above. Washington, New York, Amsterdam, and Paris papers carried stories. We have copies of the pictures clipped from newspapers from all of these cities and more. The cranberry crisis grew out of the fact that tests on cranberries carried on by the Food and Drug Administration in HEW indicated that large quantities of them showed traces of aminotriazole, a weed killer known to have caused cancer in rats.

The examination of the first series of samples from the newly harvested 1959 northwestern cranberry crop (from Oregon) was completed early in November. Some interstate shipments were found to be definitely contaminated.

George Larrick, the Food and Drug Administration administrator, presented the evidence to Arthur. Arthur's responsibility in the matter stemmed from a so-called Delaney Amendment to the Food, Drug, and Cosmetic Act of 1938. This amendment barred the use of any carcinogenic agent in food processing. And, if such an agent were found, it was mandatory for the secretary of Health, Education, and Welfare to take appropriate action.

True, all of the cranberries harvested were not contaminated; only a portion of them were.

So, pursuant to instructions in the Delaney amendment, Arthur at his regular press conference issued a warning to the public not to buy cranberries until some sort of plan could be developed that would indicate which berries, and which cranberry products— packaged, canned, or otherwise—were not contaminated by the weed killer.

Arthur said, "It is a serious action to take. But I have no alternative on the basis of the evidence we have. Even though only a small portion of the cranberries may be contaminated, it is my duty to the public to present the evidence. I don't have any right to sit on evidence of this kind."

This directive set off an explosion that hit the front pages of the newspapers all over the country. The cranberry growers, through their organizational representatives, and also the members of Congress from cranberry-growing states, and even the secretary of Agriculture (whose department had cleared the weed killer) all started screaming their defenses and their innocence of any misuse of chemicals.

With one voice they denounced Arthur as an alarmist and declared him to be misinformed. Some of the more vocal protesters demanded that President Eisenhower replace Arthur as secretary.

The story broke just two weeks before Thanksgiving, the season the cranberry growers depend on for their major sales for the entire year. On the day the cranberry fracas broke into the public press, Arthur's sister Betty was visiting us, and I had invited some friends for tea at our house. During the brief tea hour the telephone rang eighteen times, and each time it was a newspaper reporter posing certain questions to me:

"What do you think of your husband's order banning the sale of cranberries?"

"Will the matter be cleared up by Thanksgiving?"

"Do you plan to serve cranberries at Thanksgiving?"

"Do you have a favorite cranberry recipe?"

And so on.

The calls came from reporters from as far west as San Francisco, all looking for a new angle to build a story around. Of course, I could have stopped answering the telephone, or I could have had somebody else answer it, but it was my first exposure to this sort of thing, and I was intrigued by it. Naturally, I was very careful how I answered the questions and really didn't answer any of them directly. It was the first time the press had ever attempted to involve me in any of Arthur's official decisions.

That same evening, on the National Broadcasting Company's Huntley-Brinkley nightly newscast, David Brinkley's last little quip before his "Goodnight, Chet" was, "And Mrs. Flemming says she is going to serve cranberries on Thanksgiving." I didn't hear this myself, but several friends told me about it.

Now, Mrs. Flemming had said no such thing. In fact, David Brinkley had not even checked with me. And the fact that he used that sentence makes me wonder if he is always as careful as he should be.

The cranberry producers were up in arms and bitterly accused Arthur of unjustly throwing a cloud over the entire cranberry industry and jeopardizing a fifty-million-dollar-a-year-business.

Ambrose E. Stevens, the executive vice-president of Ocean Spray Cranberries, a cooperative of some 75 percent of the producers, charged the government (i.e., Arthur, as the representative of the government) with "killing a thoroughbred to destroy a single flea."

Ocean Spray members had agreed previously to hold off the shipping of some millions of tons of cranberries from areas where the Food and Drug Administration had suspicions of misuse of aminotriazole. What contributed to the trouble, apparently, was the breaking of the voluntary embargo on suspected lots of cranberries by some growers on the West Coast and in Wisconsin, New Jersey, and Massachusetts. Cranberry industry spokesmen were vehement in protesting that they had been unfairly treated.

A conference of representatives of the industry and government officials was called by Arthur to develop a plan for testing the berries. These tests were designed to guarantee "pure, wholesome, and nutritious fruit for the buying public." The growers, represented by Mr. Stevens, promised to (1) bar the use of aminotriazole; (2) segregate suspected berries; (3) test the 1959 crop then in possession of the handlers; and (4) destroy all berries found, by scientific research, to be contaminated.

Immediately, an elaborate testing program was put into operation so that consumers could determine whether the cranberries they were buying had been tested and cleared by the Food and Drug Administration. Thanksgiving was then only a week away.

The clamor continued, both in and out of the government, with Arthur the focal point of severe criticism and laudatory cheering. I have an impressive collection of editorials from *The New York Times*, *The Washington Post*, *The Philadelphia Inquirer*, *The New York Post*, and others. Without exception they supported Arthur's action in warning the public of the possible health hazard from eating contaminated cranberries. Columns of "Letters to the Editor" almost uniformly expressed appreciation that a high-level bureaucrat was so conscientiously looking after the interests of the citizens.

The procedures for testing were sped up so that cranberries

labeled "tested and approved" were on the grocery store shelves in a matter of days.

A couple of days before Thanksgiving I received a telephone call from a *New York Herald Tribune* reporter asking for permission to take pictures of the Flemmings eating cranberries. My initial reaction was to scream a loud "No." By this time I was heartily sick of cranberries. I didn't want ever to see one again, or hear the word—much less eat them. However, Arthur persuaded me to permit the reporter to come to our house, as he felt it might stimulate the sale of the tested cranberries and help counteract the public fear from the earlier warning. So I agreed, and the result was that picture that made news all over the world.

Cranberries became a by-word for weeks—nay, months, even years—on all sorts of occasions. I've listened to many a chairman at various meetings where Arthur was to speak, and to toastmasters at banquets, too, build the cranberry incident into their introduction of Arthur. It was always sure to get a laugh.

It affected me in various ways, too. At a luncheon given at the Capitol Hill Club to honor Mrs. Eisenhower's birthday, the cabinet wives were seated at the head table. During the luncheon Frances Lewine, of the Associated Press, passed a note up to me which read: "Mrs. Flemming, are you planning to serve cranberries for Thanksgiving?" And, the next day, the newspaper account of the birthday luncheon included a list of the cabinet wives present and said that "Mrs. Flemming was wearing a cranberry red hat."

Another side effect of this famous crisis was that I was called by a representative of *This Week* magazine and asked if I would write a story for that publication built around the decision making process that Arthur used—how he struggled over whether to make the information public that the weed killer used on cranberries had been found to cause cancer in rats. My caller obviously visualized Arthur pacing the floor, wringing his hands, tearing his hair, sweating out what his decision would be.

I told my caller that I wasn't even aware of any struggle going on and that I didn't even know anything about the cranberry decision until it was made. There was no struggle at all that was obvious to me. Arthur simply was convinced that, under the Delaney amendment, he had a responsibility to act; and, to him, there was only one course to follow. The *This Week* man could hardly believe this! Anyway, he told me to write it up, and they would then decide whether to use it in the magazine.

I got to work right away and reconstructed the background and the actual decision to release the Food and Drug Administration findings, and then the furor that followed. The representative of *This Week* came out to the house to see me. When he read my account, his reaction was that there was certainly no drama in the account of Arthur's decision about the cranberries; hence, nobody would be the least bit interested in reading about it.

The influence of cranberries in our lives didn't stop when they reappeared on the grocery shelves with their "tested and approved" labels on them. Everywhere we went those cranberries followed us.

One incident occurs to me. For the first time in his life, about mid-December of that year, Arthur, who had developed some noticeable physical symptoms, agreed to do what the doctor told him, and we went to Atlantic City for a few days' rest. While there we did some boardwalk shopping. We bought a teakwood carved screen. The salesman who did the paperwork about shipping the screen raised his head when Arthur gave the name "Arthur Flemming." "Arthur Flemming," the salesman repeated. "Where have I heard that name?"

He scratched his head as he searched his memory. He got no help from us. Finally, he nodded in satisfaction. "Oh, I know," he said, "didn't you have something to do with cranberries?"

There it was again! And this sort of thing happened almost

daily for a long time thereafter.

When we left the cabinet after the election of John Kennedy as president, and Arthur was invited to the University of Oregon as president, the Oregon cranberry growers who had been hit by the 1959 cranberry decision were quite vocal in their opposition to Arthur's becoming president of the university. But they didn't keep the Oregon Board of Higher Education from appointing Arthur to that position.

The dishes were hardly out of the dishwasher after the Thanksgiving dinner when another crisis arose—this one over chickens. It involved a drug named disthylstilbestrol (stilbestrol, for short) which was being used to caponize young chickens. The drug artificially caponized the fowl and caused them to gain weight faster than surgically castrated ones.

A prolonged study indicated that in rare instances use of stilbestrol causes cancer. So again a great hue and cry arose when Arthur approved banning the sale of chickens that had been given the drug.

Charles E. Shuman, president of the American Farm Bureau, took out after Arthur at the annual meeting of the Farm Bureau Federation then in progress. He accused Arthur of using cranberries and poultry to further his political ambitions, including possibly the vice presidency. He said Arthur "had put up a lightning rod to attract attention." The Farm Bureau, he said, would seek a change in The Food and Drug Act in the next session of Congress to "clip Arthur's wings. We're going to try to get some changes that will put him [i. e., Arthur] out of the business of scaring people out of eating things." The changes involved making the secretary more "responsible in a judicial sense. The secretary should be compelled to prove in court that seized foodstuffs contain harmful substances."

Mr. Shuman, in accusing Arthur of creating a furor to get public attention and thus promote his "political ambitions," obviously didn't know what makes Arthur tick.

Color additives in lipstick also came under review. Testing had proved some of these additives to be unsafe. Arthur therefore asked Congress to extend the ban on cancer-inducing chemicals to include color additives.

Arthur's stance through all of these critical decisions was that since "no one can tell how much or how little of a carcinogen is required to produce cancer in human beings, the American public should not be put in the position where they include in their diet any substance that has produced cancer in rats." And he insisted on following this point of view as long as he was secretary of HEW.

It was in the fall of 1959 that Arthur's long hours at the office and his round-the-calendar schedule began to catch up with him. He developed symptoms that he simply had to pay attention to. He had severe pains in the chest and shoulder, which motivated him to see the doctor for the first time in many years. In the ensuing testing procedures two rather severe ailments were diagnosed: angina and diabetes.

Our family physician, Doctor Dortzbach, summoned us both to his office to hear the report on the findings. He seated us on the sofa along the wall in his office. Then he very seriously emphasized what Arthur had to do. He pointed out that the long years of constant rush-rush-rush living by Arthur, with no periods of rest from his grinding routine, had taken their toll and that Arthur simply had to change his habits. He insisted that failure to do this would inevitably result in even more serious physical deterioration.

Then he proceeded to outline what he considered to be an absolutely necessary change of pace. In addition to the internal medication he intended to prescribe, he told Arthur that he must take a rest period every morning and every afternoon on a couch in his office and that he must curb considerably his customary schedule of out-of-town speaking engagements and meetings. He urged that I see to it that Arthur follow this new routine.

We were both in a very sober frame of mind when we left Doctor Dortzbach's office that November day. He had certainly succeeded in making us realize the serious nature of Arthur's physical condition.

The next day Arthur did follow the suggested routine of morning and afternoon rest periods. I questioned him about that when he returned from his office that evening.

The second day, however, previously scheduled meetings made the rest periods impossible to follow. And the day after, and the day after that, no rest periods were taken. By this time he had completely gotten over his initial fear of the dire consequences Doctor Dortzbach had predicted and forgot all about the pre-scribed rest periods.

He did, however, get the prescriptions filled and took his medication faithfully. He also began to make a real point of taking long walks.

In the ensuing thirteen or fourteen years he did not return to the doctor for any regular physical checkups, but continued to take the same medication in the same dosages prescribed in 1959.

Each time we moved—to Eugene, to St. Paul, and back to Washington—I picked up the prescriptions from the druggist and took them along with me to the new location. I get the prescrip-tions filled regularly, and Arthur takes them faithfully.

As for the regular vacation periods the doctor also insisted on, that never has been and still is not a part of Arthur's plan of living. I am certainly not recommending this apparent physical neglect for anybody else, but it seems to work for Arthur. He is never sick—at least, if he is, he never says so. He is careful what he eats, watches his weight and maintains the same weight year after year, and is careful to get a good night's rest most of the time. Observing him has convinced me that, for the most part, good health results from "positive thinking."

I'm sure nobody at HEW noticed any change or any reduction

in the long hours Arthur put in because, of course, the problems falling in that department continued unabated.

Medical care for the aged was a subject of prime concern to Arthur during these years. He worked diligently at trying to draft a plan that would be acceptable to the Budget Bureau. He was particularly concerned with providing help in cases of catastrophic illness. A Democrat-sponsored health plan had already been introduced in Congress by Representative Forand, of Rhode Island.

President Eisenhower wanted the federal government to do something about this problem. At one point he had Arthur work on a social insurance plan, but when reminded by the American Medical Association that he had said he wouldn't take this approach in a campaign speech in 1952, he asked Arthur to work up a federal-state plan that would be financed through general revenues.

In May of 1960, the Eisenhower administration sent to Congress a comprehensive voluntary health plan for approximately twelve million aged persons. The plan proposed $1.2 billion to set up a federal-state insurance program that would pay most of the cost of long-term illness for most persons over sixty-five years of age.

Arthur unveiled the long-awaited administration program at a meeting of the House Ways and Means Committee, and this offered an alternative to the compulsory features of the Forand bill. But the Republican congressional leaders took a dim view of the proposal, called "the Flemming plan," to insure the aged for medical care, though Arthur urged its acceptance. He was still plugging for medical care for the elderly in his final days as secretary of HEW. But Congress took no final action on either proposal.

Arthur also got into the problem of trying to do something about automobile smog. As early as February, 1960, long before Ralph Nader's emergence as the consumers' advocate, he used his office to urge automobile manufacturers to make an inexpensive smog-fighting device standard equipment on all new cars.

Even at that time the Public Health Service had identified automobile-caused air pollution as harmful to human health and vegetation. They said that experiments with animals showed that smog-borne irritants can heighten susceptibility to lung cancer and other respiratory ailments.

He also got behind the early promotion of seat belts in automobiles as a safety device in case of collision. He ordered seat belts in all cars belonging to his department. And he insisted that, since he was promoting seat belts as an official policy of HEW, we had to have them installed in our family car. Moreover, we were to use them. He was so successful that our family members are regular users of seat belts, and to this day I am actually incapable of turning on the ignition until after my seat belt is fastened, even if I am going only as far as the corner.

The first year Arthur was secretary of HEW, Congress passed legislation authorizing Washington's new cultural center. According to the terms of the bill, the secretary was to be a trustee. The president asked him to serve as chairman.

It was an exciting extracurricular activity and provided many stimulating contacts. Under Arthur's chairmanship, Edward Durell Stone was selected to draw the plans for the center, and a handsome design was unveiled in May of 1960. Cost limitations made severe revisions necessary, however, and the final cultural center, later named for John Fitzgerald Kennedy, bears little resemblance to the original grandiose design.

An occasional personnel problem with unpleasant implications had to be dealt with too. A particularly distasteful problem of this kind involved the chief of the department's Antibiotics Division of the Food and Drug Administration, Doctor Henry Welch. Doctor Welch's income from outside sources dwarfed his government pay of $17,000. Most of his outside income came from his connection with certain publications, which relied heavily on advertising by pharmaceutical companies.

Doctor Welch's activities outside the FDA were widely publicized during hearings before the Senate Anti-trust and Monopoly Subcommittee. As a result of these disclosures Arthur demanded the resignation of Doctor Welch on the ground that the FDA official had deliberately misled his superiors in receiving compensation "far beyond what is the commonly accepted concept of an honorarium."

Twelve-to-fourteen-hour days, six days a week—holidays included—were the rule during the years at HEW. But they did not keep us from enjoying many of the fringe benefit social advantages of being a member of the president's cabinet. We participated in many truly exciting occasions.

The White House functions we were privy to were, of course, at the top of the list. The annual dinners honoring the vice-president, the cabinet, and so on were occasions we looked forward to with eager anticipation. We never became sophisticated enough to outgrow the wonderful feeling of awe and pride that was part of each time we entered the White House.

The state dinners when the president and Mrs. Eisenhower were hosts to visiting heads of state from other countries were special privileges. Normally about three or four of the cabinet members and their wives were invited to these functions, so we all had a turn now and then. Among the official state dinners we were invited to were those honoring General Charles deGaulle, Emperor Haile Selasie of Ethiopia, Queen Frederica of Greece, the King and Queen of Thailand, and the President of the United Mexican States and Mrs. Lopez Mateos.

We were invited to the dinner honoring Premier Kruschchev also, but Arthur was out of town that evening. We made up for that disappointment the next night by going to Premier Kruschchev's dinner at the Russian Embassy, a rare privilege indeed. I also went to a luncheon Mrs. Nixon gave for Mrs. Kruschchev.

When the Princess Beatrix of The Netherlands visited Washington in September of 1959, Mrs. Eisenhower invited the cabinet children in her age group to a luncheon at the White House in the princess's honor. Harry and Susan were both in college at the time, but they came home for this special occasion and were among the guests on that day.

After a year that included a number of White House invitations, as well as invitations to parties given by other cabinet members and their wives, I decided it was time for me to give an official party. I wanted to do it a bit differently from the usual routine of ladies' luncheons, which was to adhere pretty rigidly to just the cabinet wives on the guest list. My idea was to honor Mrs. Eisenhower by also including the cabinet daughters who, as far as I knew from my own experience, had no opportunity to meet Mrs. Eisenhower or Mrs. Nixon. I talked it over with Arthur, and as usual he said, "Go ahead."

Accordingly, I telephoned Mrs. McCaffrey, Mrs. Eisenhower's social secretary, and explained to her what I had in mind. She thought Mrs. Eisenhower would be delighted to meet these young women, about ten in all. So a date was agreed on, and then Mrs. McCaffrey asked where I planned to have the luncheon. I replied that I could either give it at a hotel, or I would be happy to have it at our house. To my delight, Mrs. McCaffrey said, "Mrs. Eisenhower would like to come to your house. She gets a great many invitations to do public things, but not so many to go to private homes. So, why don't you give it at your home?"

This pleased me very much. I have a conviction that home entertaining, no matter how modest, is the very best kind of entertaining and truest expression of one's self. So it was agreed on. The invitations were issued and nearly everyone invited was able to accept.

Then I set to work to make it a truly beautiful party. Since our dining room was not large enough to seat so many people, I cleared the recreation room and set up tables in a "T" shape. A caterer provided the table and gold chairs. My florist friend, Paul Bauer (who often supplied flowers for White House functions) provided the most perfect yellow roses, gladioli, and spider mums. The table bouquets were really gorgeous creations in yellow, as were all the flower arrangements throughout the house. Paul helped me with them.

A few days before the party, the White House secret service men came out to "case" the house and the environs, a standard precautionary procedure whenever Mrs. Eisenhower went out for an engagement.

The great day arrived, a perfect June day. By twelve-thirty our block in Chevy Chase was lined with all of those impressive chauffer-driven limousines assigned to cabinet members. Though I had told absolutely no one what was going on at our house, it was not hard to tell that something special was happening at 7108 Lenhart Drive.

It was an unmitigated success in every way. Mrs. Eisenhower is a very gracious lady indeed, and she obviously enjoyed the occasion. So did I, and my own enjoyment of any party I give is the yardstick I use in measuring its success.

One of my favorite memories of that afternoon is of the large number of children who came out and took their places in the neighborhood yards in order to get a glimpse of Mrs. Eisenhower when she left. No doubt their mothers were watching from behind the draperies in their homes!

Another of our never-to-be-forgotten experiences was the occasion on which we acted as host and hostess to King Bhumibol and Queen Sirikit of Thailand.

On all state visits, the Department of State plans the schedule for visiting heads of state. One item on the Thailand royal visitors' agenda was the dedication of the Division of Biologic Standards Building of the National Institutes of Health, as King

Bhumipol had expressed a particular interest in seeing this part of our government's activity. He was therefore scheduled to make the dedicatory address.

A luncheon preceded the dedication and was held at the Stone House on what is called "the reservation" by NIH people. Arthur and I met Their Majesties at the curb as they alighted from their car, and escorted them to the terrace at the south end of the Stone House. There the luncheon guests were presented to the visiting king and queen.

I was seated next to King Bhumipol at the luncheon table, and Arthur beside Queen Sirikit, certainly one of the world's most beautiful women. They were both young, attractive, interesting people, with four young children, so conversation was not a problem. Besides, the State Department leaves nothing to chance and had provided us in advance with several mimeographed pages of material to help us.

After luncheon we proceeded to the new building where the dedicatory program was to take place. And following this, the farewells were said. A proud day indeed, and one we'll not forget.

Another visiting dignitary left an interesting momento in his wake. This was Premier Nikita Kruschchev, and his visit to Washington set a lot of social activity in motion. We participated in that.

Premier Kruschchev presented Arthur and each member of the cabinet with a handsome shotgun, carefully packed in a beautiful hand-tooled leather case. Custom dictates that all such gifts remain at the State Department until that particular administration is out of power, so Arthur did not actually receive the gun until we were at the University of Oregon.

One night after a dinner party at our home in Eugene, Arthur was telling about the Kruschchev visit and the gift of the Russian shotgun. Of course everybody wanted to see it. Until that evening the gun had never been removed from the case. It was found to be unassembled, so the men present, including Governor Hatfield, tried their hands at putting it together. They all failed.

"Antoinette can put it together," Governor Hatfield said. "She's good at this sort of thing." So the gun was brought into the living room. Mrs. Hatfield got down on the floor, laid out the pieces, and examined them carefully. While we all watched her, she did indeed assemble the gun.

It is typical of Arthur's complete lack of interest in such things as hunting guns that it had been in his upstairs den for several years in its case, and he had never even taken it out, much less tried to put it together. A couple of the men present on that evening were hunting enthusiasts, and they had a hard time understanding this.

One fringe benefit of the cabinet years that I particularly enjoyed was the privilege of attending the joint sessions of the Congress when the president delivered his annual State of the Union message. The cabinet wives sat in the executive gallery of the House of Representatives chamber just behind Mrs. Eisenhower and Mrs. Nixon.

It was exciting to watch from the gallery as the members of both houses of Congress wandered into the House chamber and took their places. The members of the Supreme Court and the Diplomatic Corps came too.

And then the doorkeeper of the House, William "Fishbait" Miller, intoned, "The President of the United States." The members of the cabinet had already been announced and were in their places when the president was announced. On these occasions I was fairly bursting with pride as I watched Arthur walk in with the cabinet and take a seat in the front of the chamber.

On three occasions I watched this historic ceremony, each time marveling at the priceless experience I was privileged to share.

There were other privileges, too, that we enjoyed during those years, such as going to Andrews Field in Maryland when the president left on an official mission, or returned from one. Watching with the other cabinet people in anticipation of the arrival of the president was a tremendous thrill. When that giant silver bird which was *Air Force One* came swooping down out of the sky, with its unspoken message, "The president is home safe," we who were waiting felt a great swell of gratitude and pride.

Then the door would open, and there appeared the president. A moment later he would greet each one of us personally before entering his limousine to drive to the White House. How we treasure those wonderful memories!

I had a few extracurricular activities of my own that provided considerable satisfaction, too. Cabinet wives are invited to virtually all of the charity fundraising events in Washington, such as the Salvation Army Benefit luncheon, the Heart Association luncheon, and countless others. At most of these we were guests and had no responsibility.

The cabinet wives were also asked to chair many of these financial drives, though it was left to the individual whether she regarded the acceptance of such an invitation as a real working assignment, or a purely honorary one.

Over my years with Arthur, the example he set was always to answer "Yes" whenever he was asked to take responsibility in special areas of the church, government, civic projects, or whatever. The words "No" and "Can't" simply aren't in his vocabulary. My own instincts were not always so positive, but some of his driving sense of responsibility did rub off on me.

And so, when I was asked early in 1959 to chair the District of Columbia's American Cancer Society drive for funds, I accepted. A committee was set up to help, and it was decided to sponsor a champagne dinner dance at the Shoreham Hotel in May. Tickets, I believe, were twenty-five dollars apiece, and an elaborate entertainment was planned.

The sale of the tickets lagged. There were so many such affairs in Washington, most of them for good causes, but one simply has to choose! A lot of telephoning did result in increased ticket sales, however, and as we neared the date, it looked as if the benefit would be a success.

The illness of Secretary of State John Foster Dulles was very much on our minds at the time, as his illness was related to our cause. He died on the Sunday preceding the Tuesday when our benefit was to take place.

The committee decided to cancel the benefit dinner on account of Secretary Dulles's death, and we offered to return to each subscriber the amount paid for the tickets. It is a most heart-warming memory to recall that every single subscriber agreed that the money should be kept for the Cancer Society. So we ended up making more than if the benefit had been held.

The following year I was again invited to chair the fund drive for the local division of the American Cancer Society. Again I agreed.

We decided that year, 1960, to sponsor the Washington premiere performance of the musical *My Fair Lady* at the National Theater on June 20, asking fifty dollars for each ticket.

It was a special bit of fun for me to go to the Military Air Transport Service landing field a few days before the performance to greet the stars of the cast as they returned from performances in Russia on the Cultural Exchange Program. Lola Fisher and Michael Evans were the Eliza Doolittle and Professor Higgins of the company, and I enjoyed very much the opportunity of welcoming them on their return to the United States. That benefit, too, was a complete financial success.

Another responsibility I agreed to take on was the chairmanship of the District of Columbia March of Dimes drive for the National Foundation in 1960. I gave the opening coffee party at our house to launch the drive and had the year's poster girl in attendance.

These activities greatly enriched my life. I thoroughly enjoyed them and met many interesting people in the process of carrying out these responsibilities.

In mid-year of 1960 Susan's marriage to John Parker was the highlight of the family experience. After that Arthur's attention began to be directed toward the forthcoming presidential campaign. He appeared before the platform committee to plead for the inclusion of some liberal ideas for dealing with problems in the field of health, education, and welfare. It it interesting to note, in retrospect, that he was singled out, along with Attorney General William Rogers, by Senator Barry Goldwater as being "too liberal" to represent the Republican party's over-all attitude on social questions. Senator Goldwater declared that he was "disturbed" that members of the Eisenhower cabinet were pleading the "liberal approach" and insisted they didn't represent the rank-and-file Republican party membership. He even threatened to ask Charles Percy (the platform committee chairman) for equal time for presentation of the conservative approach.

The convention in late July found Arthur present as a member of the Ohio delegation, Harry as a page to the Nixon hideaway quarters (a highly motivating experience, by the way), and I as a fascinated spectator viewing the proceedings from the special vantage point of a box reserved for cabinet wives.

I have indicated before that Arthur was not a truly dedicated political partisan. His first public appointment came through President Roosevelt, and later he continued to serve under President Truman. He had never run for public office, and was as much at home serving in public capacities under Democratic presidents as under President Eisenhower. Nevertheless, in the rash of newspaper speculation as to possible vice-presidential nominees, his name appeared frequently in lists of possibilities for the nomination. *The Wall Street Journal, The New York*

Times, The New York Herald Tribune, The Washington Post, The Washington Evening Star, and *The Detroit Free Press*—to name some whose clippings we've saved—all included Arthur's name in their lists.

Arthur didn't take any of this speculation seriously. The nomination of Henry Cabot Lodge for vice-president ended the matter.

When the convention was over Arthur devoted considerable time and energy in the effort to elect Richard Nixon president of the United States. He made a number of political speeches in various parts of the country, and during the final five weeks of the campaign accompanied the Republican candidate on the special campaign plane helping to delineate the issues, particularly in health, education, and welfare.

I also did a bit of politicking. I made several speeches to various groups promoting the candidacy of Richard Nixon, and I made a trip to Philadelphia with Adele Rogers (Mrs. William) where we spent the day handing out buttons and making brief talks over loudspeakers placed along the sidewalk.

The most exciting political experience of this period for me was going along on a charter plane with Mrs. Nixon, the other cabinet wives, and Mrs. John Sherman Cooper to Lexington, Kentucky. Senator Cooper was up for reelection that year.

We spent the day shaking hands and talking to people about our candidates. It was a real thrill for me to participate with Mrs. Nixon in this sort of activity, and I developed a great admiration for her skill in handling people of all ages. She is a "pro" in making young and older people, and all kinds, feel at ease. Of course, the key is that she really was interested in them.

The people made their choice in early November, and John Kennedy squeaked through as president-elect with about a 100,000-vote majority. At that point we knew for sure that Arthur would be job-hunting. In fact, he humorously told his secretary and me, too, to be especially nice to everybody who called on the telephone.

It is a part of the record of the cabinet years that even the heavy responsibilities associated with being secretary of Health, Education, and Welfare were no reason for Arthur to diminish his church involvements. It was during this time that Foundry Church decided to build a new educational building. And, of course, Arthur was chairman of the building committee. There is a room in that building that bears his name.

His most important responsibility of the last days of the second Eisenhower term was to chair the first White House Conference on Aging. Twenty-five hundred delegates attended the conference to discuss the problems older people face, and hundreds of recommendations came out of it.

John Kennedy's first announced cabinet choice was Governor Abraham Ribicoff, of Connecticut, to be the new secretary of Health, Education, and Welfare. Arthur immediately invited Governor Ribicoff to his office for several briefing sessions to assist the secretary-designate to become oriented to his new duties as head of what Arthur always called "the most exciting department in the executive branch of the government." (When Secretary Ribicoff resigned after two years in the department, he referred to it as "The department of dirty water, dirty air, and dirty looks.")

The curtain fell on the cabinet experience promptly at twelve noon on January 20, 1961. As members of the Eisenhower cabinet, we were given seats on the Capitol steps, but this time behind the newly appointed Kennedy "team."

We had our last ride with our driver friend, John Wood, of whom we had become very fond, that day. We went in the beautiful Cadillac limousine provided for the secretary to the 1925 F Street Club, where Admiral and Mrs. Lewis Strauss gave a farewell luncheon for the ex-President and Mrs. Eisenhower. The defeated Republican candidate and Mrs. Nixon, and the retiring cabinet members were all there. It was a real Auld Lang Syne occasion.

Afterward we were driven home by Wood. (Nearly twenty-four years later, when our children gave us a fiftieth anniversary celebration dinner, they arranged to have us called for and driven to the party by John Wood, whom Tom had managed to track down. That was a glorious reunion!)

Realization hit us with a dull thud that it was all over. After two and-a-half years of being busy with official duties, being feted, having the phone ring constantly, being sought after by many groups and many individuals, it was over! Nobody wanted us for anything, and Arthur had no place to go. It was a truly sobering experience to learn at first hand what the term "change of power" means.

How does one come down from the rarified atmosphere of the mountain top to the common ordinary business of living?

For Arthur, of course, it was a difficult adjustment indeed. He had to make a decision as to where he would direct his energies in the future, so he began right away to explore various possibilities, including the University of Oregon where we eventually went. He rented office space in downtown Washington and spent his daytime hours there. He had a number of speaking commitments, and these gave variety and stimulation to those weeks of reduced activity.

We had many old friends and relatives around to provide special contacts. All of the "official" invitations we had been receiving suddenly stopped.

But I like to recall one particular incident that was important in helping me to "adjust" to my return to private status.

Mrs. Douglas Dillon, whose husband had been the under-secretary of State during the Eisenhower years, became a "hold-over" wife when her husband agreed to become John Kennedy's secretary of the Treasury. She decided to give a luncheon the

218

week after the inauguration of President Kennedy to provide the "old" cabinet wives an opportunity to meet the "new" cabinet wives.

The day before the luncheon Washington had one of its rare blizzards, just like the one that occurred the day before the inauguration. I was not anxious to drive to this party myself, as my imagination pictured my getting stuck in the snow and ice in view of all the drivers of the official limousines who would be there to transport the "new" cabinet wives.

Art and Tom were out of school that day on account of the deep snow, so Tom agreed to drive me to the luncheon in the twins' Volkswagen, and Art agreed to pick me up when it was over.

The party was beautiful, and we all had a really good time under Mrs. Dillon's expert management.

Afterward I left the Dillon home at the time agreed on with Art to call for me to go home, but when I reached the sidewalk in front of the house, Art was nowhere in sight. Instead, I ran head-on into Wood standing beside the HEW limousine and waiting, not for me, but for Mrs. Ribicoff. We greeted each other, asked about each other's health and families, and I think we managed to minimize the strain of the new situation. By this time the "new" cabinet wives were all coming out, taking their seats in those beautiful chauffer-driven cars, and driving off, while I remained on the sidewalk waiting for Art.

And then, making its way along in the midst of all of those Cadillacs, I spied the Volkswagen. I climbed in beside "my" driver, and we chugged along home. After that my adjustment, I felt, was complete.

12

O R E G O N

G oing to the University of Oregon was our BIG adventure.
The idea of going to the West Coast institution was
proposed to Arthur in late December of 1960 when one afternoon
there appeared in his office Doctor John Richards, Chancellor of
the Board of Higher Education for Oregon. Arthur did not know
him. Doctor Richards' mission was simply to sound Arthur out
as to whether he would be interested in the presidency of the
University of Oregon. Knowing that he would be out of a job
after January, 1961, John Kennedy's Inauguration Day, Arthur
was in a mood to explore any opportunity that was suggested to
him.

He wasn't entirely certain he wanted to return to the field of
education, but he did tell Doctor Richards he would be glad to
consider the Oregon opportunity.

It was just before Christmas. Lib and George and three little
ones had already arrived to spend the holiday with us.

When Arthur came home for dinner that evening, he was
hardly seated at the table when he told us about his interview with
Doctor Richards.

"How would you like to go to Oregon?" he asked me.

"Oregon," Lib repeated. "Sounds like a foreign country to
me."

"Doing what?" I asked in reply to his question.

Then he explained that Doctor Richards had asked him to
consider becoming president of the University of Oregon.

I was immediately attracted to the idea. As long as we had to
move somewhere, and with the twins finishing high school and

going to college anyway, I thought it a good idea for us to do something really adventurous. The Oregon opportunity appeared to be this sort of possibility for us Easterners. So at once my reaction was, "Let's go!"

We discussed it a bit with the children and decided at least we'd take a look at the Oregon situation. Doctor Richards had suggested that we fly to the West Coast during the Christmas week for an exploratory visit to see the campus, the president's house, and to meet some members of the faculty and the Board of Higher Education.

So when we flew out of Baltimore's Friendship Airport for Portland, Oregon, on December 29 on our initial visit, I was really excited. I was, however, beginning to have qualms about putting all of those miles between us and the children. I was sufficiently uneasy, in fact, to write out before we left a supplementary statement to our wills, duly witnessed by Donald and Betty Sherbondy, indicating that if Arthur and I should die in a common accident, Art's and Tom's educational expenses should be met before any other disposition of our estate took place. It was obvious that I regarded flying across the country quite differently from flying to Columbus, Ohio, for example.

At that time Sue and John were living in Bethesda, Maryland; Lib and George in Delaware, Ohio; and Harry was in college at Ohio State University. We had always been able to get together at Christmas and in the summer. And, I thought, if we should go to the West Coast, would we ever be together again? To me, at that time, it seemed unlikely that we would. Keeping our family together meant a great deal to both Arthur and me, and on that cold, icy evening when we started across the country, I wasn't quite as enthusiastic as I had been before Christmas. Still, I was intrigued by the idea and was quite willing to investigate it.

Early in the morning after our arrival in Portland we were met by two members of the Board of Higher Education of Oregon and driven the 115 miles to Eugene. I should perhaps explain that all of Oregon's public higher educational institutions were under the supervision of a single board whose members were appointed by the governor for five-year terms.

We had Mount Hood pointed out to us as we were driving south through the lush green of the Willamette Valley, kept green all winter because of the rainy season from October to May. We were told that although it rains a great deal it wasn't very wet rain—more of a mist than actual downpour. We were also coached as to the proper pronunciation of O-R-E-G-O-N and W-I-L-L-A-M-E-T-T-E, and told that we should never, never place the accent on the last syllable of either name. Mount Hood was indeed a majestic sight with its snow-covered, cone-shaped peak standing out against the sky. The giant evergreens along the highway, straight and tall like sentinels, impressed us too.

We were taken to Doctor Richards' home, and after coffee with him and his wife Peg, Arthur went into a conference session, and I was taken on a tour of the university campus and Eugene. Later we were both shown through the president's home. At luncheon later, and at a tea at the home of the chairman of the presidential selection committee, I had an opportunity to meet many of the people who were a part of the university.

That evening we had dinner at a hotel in Salem with other board members. And the next day Arthur had more meetings while I had a tour of the university's Portland schools: the Medical School, the Dental School, and the School of Nursing.

I liked everything I saw and everyone I met. But still I had that nagging fear and hesitation based on the distance from other members of our family. I certainly was not pushing for a decision to take the Oregon job.

Arthur remained completely noncommittal. He was attracted to the university and regarded it as a really excellent institution of higher learning. But he was far from convinced that he wanted to go there, or even that he wanted to be a college president again. He had several other ideas he wanted to explore—in the publications field, with foundations, and so on.

It was actually not until February 22, 1961, that he finally made up his mind to accept the offer of the presidency of the University of Oregon. He decided he would begin his new job on the first of July so we could remain in Washington until Art and Tom graduated from the Bethesda-Chevy Chase High School.

I appealed to him to block out on his calendar a ten-day period in the end of June and plan to drive to Eugene with the boys and me. "This is your last chance to do something of this kind," I urged him. "Art and Tom will be in college after September, and I think it would be great fun for the four of us to drive across the country together." He agreed to do it, and I watched him write it down in the little black engagement book he carries in his pocket.

In mid-April we went to Geneva to attend a meeting of the International Civil Service Commission. Arthur had also been asked to do some work for the National Council of Churches in Paris, Amsterdam, Stuttgart, and London, so a one-day stand was planned for each of these cities.

On June 16 we attended Art's and Tom's high-school commencement; on June 17 the van was loaded; and on June 18 we were ready to go. A last-minute goodbye telephone call to Arthur's mother in Kingston convinced him that she was feeling quite lonely over thoughts of our being three thousand miles away, so he decided to fly up to Kingston and spend Sunday with her. He would then rejoin us in Delaware, Ohio, where we planned to spend Monday night with Lib and her family.

On Tuesday, in Delaware, he got two telephone calls that were to disrupt further our plan for a cross-country trip together. One was from Sargent Shriver, the Peace Corps administrator. He wanted Arthur to meet with him and a group of other college presidents in Washington on June 22 to formulate plans for the newly organized Peace Corps, including methods of recruiting. Arthur (of course!) agreed to do as Mr. Shriver asked, thus usurping another two days of our trip.

The second call was from the governor of Oregon, Mark Hatfield, who wanted Arthur to fly to Honolulu on June 27 to join a panel of educators who were to discuss education before the nation's governors at their upcoming conference there. Again Arthur agreed, though in both cases I remonstrated loudly that he had a prior commitment with me and Art and Tom.

Why, I kept fuming, did the family always have to take second place to requests made by people outside? I never really understood this, but the fact is that this is what usually happened. I still don't understand it. But if the family had come first, I would probably not be writing this account of Arthur's life.

So that's how our family trip turned out. However, he did travel with us the three in-between days, so my family togetherness plan wasn't a complete failure.

The twins and our dachshund Frankie were in their Volkswagen, and I drove the Pontiac. Each morning we would consult our maps and agree on a place to meet for lunch, and then on a place for dinner and to spend the night. Each time but one we all arrived at the agreed-on place within a few minutes of each other.

Our only other visiting stop was to spend a night in Minneapolis with Sue and John, who had moved there a few weeks earlier as John had taken a job as head of the Department of Medical Art and Photography at the University of Minnesota Medical School and Hospital.

In spite of our disappointment over Arthur's not being with us for the entire trip, we enjoyed it mightily. For us all it was a lesson in appreciation of our great and beautiful country. Art and Tom have both driven across the country many times since then, taking various routes, but I have not repeated the driving experience since our maiden trip in 1961. It is one of my favorite memories.

Arthur met us in Portland on June 28. The next day we drove to the famous Timberline Lodge on Mt. Hood, a Works Progress Administration project built during Franklin Roosevelt's administration and which he personally dedicated. As we sat at luncheon there we were amazed to see snow falling all around us. Mt. Hood is never without snow, and to watch it falling on the 29th of June was an unusual experience for people geared to hot, humid Washington, DC, summers.

The van didn't arrive in Eugene for a week after it was promised, so we spent our first week in Oregon at the Eugene Hotel. Arthur went off to his office on July 1, a Saturday, and regularly thereafter, but the boys and I spent our first week getting acquainted with our new environment. It was a long week for them, although several of the faculty members offered diversion.

One special recollection of such diversion is our attendance at the National Collegiate Athletic Association track meet on the university campus. We all went. As soon as we had taken our seats, the administrative dean's wife, Mrs. William Jones, pointed out one of the track officials. "There's Governor Hatfield," she said, "in the maroon jacket."

"Oh," I replied. "Does your governor do this sort of thing regularly?"

"Often," she answered. I watched him from then on doing all of the chores a track official customarily is responsible for. Later I watched him walk off the field, apparently to his car. No one accompanied him. Accustomed as I was to the pomp and circumstance of official Washington, it struck me as very strange that the state's top official had no escort from the field to his car. I expressed this concern to my seatmate. "The governor is leaving, alone. Doesn't anybody escort him?" I asked.

"Oh, no," she replied. "In Oregon, the governor is just one of the people."

Before we left Washington Art had been admitted to the University of California at Berkeley. So his college plans were all set. Tom, however, had not applied anywhere, preferring to wait and look the college situation over after we arrived on the West Coast. He decided to apply to both Willamette University, in Salem, and the University of Oregon, and he was accepted to both institutions. He decided that the course offerings and the faculty at the University of Oregon were superior to Willamette, so that was the basis on which he made his choice.

The first scheduled event of each college year at the University of Oregon is a convocation for new students and their parents. Arthur, as the new president of the university, was to give a welcoming, inspirational talk on this occasion. I went with Tom.

We had seats next to a talkative lad from Roseburg, Oregon. He began at once: "Do you have a son or a daughter entering the university?" he asked as soon as we had taken our seats. Apparently he didn't associate me with Tom.

"A son," I answered.

"Where are you from?" he kept on.

"Eugene."

At that moment the door to the right of the platform opened, and the procession of deans and other administrative officials began to enter the hall. My new friend nudged me. "There's Flemming," he said. "He's the new president of the university." And then, in a burst of feeling, he added, "Our first look at old Flemming."

I tried to look properly impressed with this information.

Later, Arthur and I stood in line at a reception to greet the new students and their parents. I was curious to see the reaction of my friend when he met Arthur and me standing together. Finally he came nonchalantly down the line. Arthur greeted him cordially, asked his name and where he was from, said he was glad to have him at the university, and then, turning to me, said, "And this is

Mrs. Flemming."

The boy smiled, shook hands, and then with a look of complete consternation, looked at me again, shook his head in disbelief, and then passed on. I cherish the memory of the expression on that young student's face as he realized that that evening had not provided my first look at "old Flemming."

That first fall at the University of Oregon we found ourselves privy to some fringe benefits. Since the university was not then a member of a regional athletic conference, the football schedule included games with institutions all over the country. That particular fall the schedule, made up years before our ever thinking of being in Oregon, had games scheduled with Stanford, the University of Minnesota, and Ohio State University, among others. Moreover, Arthur was an avid football fan, and he was told that both he and I were invited to travel with the team on its chartered plane to all of the "away games." Arthur accepted the invitation, and going with the players and officials to these games became a regular part of our fall program.

That year it was a particular godsend, as we had an opportunity to visit Art, then a student at Berkeley, when we went to the Stanford game, Sue and John in Minneapolis when we went to the University of Minnesota game, and the Speeses in Ohio when we went to the Ohio State game. Much bantering centered around the president's scheduling of football games in places where he could visit his children.

We enjoyed these trips very much indeed. Arthur justified them on the ground that each trip gave him an opportunity to enlarge his acquaintance with the University of Oregon constituency as he always spoke to an alumni group in each location we visited.

That fall, too, Arthur continued to have a voice on the national scene by writing a monthly editorial for the *Good Housekeeping* magazine. He wrote on such controversial subjects as: Here's

What the Public Schools Can Do about Religion; The Public Must Be Protected against Worthless Drugs; The Shame of Mental Hospitals; Must Children Pay the High Price of Prejudice; Our Schools Should Be Open All Year; The Truth about Public Welfare Chiselers; Why Can't a Woman Be Paid Like a Man; and Let's Win the Fight for Flouridation. He gave this up after about a year and a-half as meeting the publication deadline became too demanding.

His many invitations to speak before Oregon groups of various kinds gave him further opportunities to speak out on issues of the day. One such occasion was a talk before the Oregon State Dental Association. He used this as a chance to set forth his support of flouridation, then a hot issue in our new state. Arthur, leaning on his experience as secretary of Health, Education, and Welfare, cited thirty years of study by the United States Public Health Service and the conclusion that flouridation did no bodily harm and reduced cavities by two-thirds. He urged the Dental Association to launch a program of education about the matter.

At that time flouridation had been rejected by the Oregon voters in a referendum. Later Arthur, on a television program, said he favored a referendum proposal to bring the issue again to a public vote. The dentists were virtually unanimously behind flouridation, but many of the public at large were critical of Arthur's speaking out as he did.

He was also very vocal in urging support for the federal higher education bill sponsored by Representative Edith Green of Portland. This bill would provide $300 million a year in matching federal money for buildings and other needs. Many conservative Oregonians, fearing federal control of education and ever fearful of dependence on federal funds, opposed the bill.

Another issue he kept hammering on was the Food and Drug Administration's policy on chemicals used in agriculture. He defended the FDA and reiterated his position on the famous

Delaney anti-cancer amendment to prohibit the use of substances in any quantity if they are found by appropriate tests to cause cancer in man or animals. This revived the antagonism the Oregon cranberry growers felt so keenly in the fall of 1959, and they were again critical of Arthur for his part in removing Oregon berries from the market until tested.

Then Arthur, right off, jumped into state Republican politics. Addressing a Multnomah County annual Lincoln Day dinner, he said he was looking forward to preserving his membership in the Republican party in Oregon. "It was one of the strongest declarations of political partisanship by a top Oregon professional educator in a good many years," said the *Oregonian*. Arthur compared Kennedy's approach in office to Eisenhower's in administration, civil rights, economics, and the operation of the Health, Education, and Welfare Department. He said there wouldn't have been a Cuban Bay of Pigs fiasco if President Kennedy had made use of the National Security Council as Eisenhower did.

He also accused President Kennedy of not pressing for civil rights as he said he would and pointed out that he had not issued the civil rights executive order on federal housing he said he would. He said the administration was willing to set aside civil rights for political considerations.

With all of these, and other, pronouncements during his first months in Eugene, he stepped on a lot of toes.

One of the state legislators, Senator Walter Pearson, then a candidate for governor, announced that he thought that the president of the university talked entirely too much about partisan matters. He actually stated that if he was elected governor he would insist that Arthur "either stay at the university and run it or be fired." Senator Pearson's antipathy to Arthur went back before he came to the university when, in a public statement, he said there were plenty of good educational administrators in

Oregon, and he didn't see why the Board of Higher Education had to go all the way to Washington to get a president.

Another member of the legislature, State Representative Tom Monaghan, said he thought the president of the university should be nonpartisan, like a judge.

Defense of Arthur's right to speak out on public issues came from Chancellor Lieuallen, who had been appointed to replace Doctor Richards as the State Board of Higher Education's executive officer. He insisted that educators should be encouraged to participate in politics. "Doctor Flemming is not only eminently qualified to speak out on public issues," he said. "He has both the vigor and the capability to do this without interfering with the performance of his duties as president of the University of Oregon."

While Arthur was being verbally flogged by the likes of Senator Pearson and Representative Monaghan, several editorials in support of his right to speak out on public issues, and even on his right to be an active political partisan, appeared in the newspapers. An editorial in the *Eugene Register Guard* as early as October undertook to assess the performance of the new president of the university and described Arthur as a "human dynamo." It then cited his many speeches and said he "runs a tight ship, teaches, and is available to anyone who wishes to see him, writes a column for a national magazine, serves on numerous boards and commissions, is outspoken on such hot potatoes as flouridation, welfare, and federal aid to education. . . . His performance speaks for the twelve-hour days, seven-day weeks, for dedication to his work, for a talent for organizing, for knowing what to skip and what to do. It's admirable, enviable, hardly believable. Yet, there it is."

In a later editorial, in March of 1962, the *Register Guard* specifically defended Arthur's political activity. It said: "Arthur Flemming, president of the University of Oregon, has stood himself up as an example of a public employee who is not going to abdicate the full responsibilities of citizenship. A number of people, chiefly Democratic politicians, have been trying to shoot him down. Mr. Flemming's example should give courage to those who, for one reason or another, are squeamish about expressing their opinions on public matters."

The *Oregonian* and the *Oregon Educational Journal* also gave full editorial support for Arthur's political activity.

Arthur also insisted on the right of faculty members of institutions of higher learning and teachers in public schools to participate in political activity, or even to run for office if they chose to do so. "Any law which discourages this should be amended," he said. (He referred to an Oregon law on which basis the attorney general had made recent rulings that it is illegal for a faculty member or public school teacher to make contributions of money to a candidate, his committee, or to a political party.)

Another area in which he spoke out was religious education. In a speech before the Oregon Education Association, he urged that students be taught about religion and the Bible. "The Bible is as fundamental to the study of western civilization as Homer and Shakespeare. [Pupils] can study the Bible without violating the basic concept of separation of church and state."

One of Arthur's *Good Housekeeping* articles got him in the bad graces of the Oregon State Medical Society. The article was entitled "Medical Care for the Aged—and This Nonsense about Socialized Medicine." Arthur wrote that it is "irresponsible nonsense" and "is simply not the truth when the American Medical Association labels a proposed administration medical bill as 'socialized medicine' in paid advertisements." He said the proposal includes a specific prohibition against governmental interference in the practice of medicine, and leaves it to the patient to select his own doctor, his own hospital, or his own nursing home. "By persisting in labeling as socialized medicine something that is not socialized medicine the AMA does a disservice to the nation," he said.

This article raised the ire of many members of the Oregon Medical Society, and they became openly antagonistic to Arthur. At the Society's House of Delegates' meeting in Portland in the spring of 1962, Arthur's *Good Housekeeping* article was a common topic of conversation. A resolution censuring him for it was introduced at the meeting, and then tabled. But it did indicate the intensity of feeling on the part of some of the members of the medical profession.

Again the *Register Guard* rushed to Arthur's defense, and devoted an editorial to the matter. It said he was "doing the university and the state a service [i. e., by speaking out on issues]. By his own example, he is demonstrating that a university is the natural home of ideas."

One Eugene doctor, Doctor Carl Phetteplace, decided he would personally set up an organization to rid the state of Oregon of Arthur. With this aim, he sought the help of a newspaper in Albany, Oregon—a paper that had been highly successful in molding public opinion relative to public issues. Doctor Phetteplace's wife, Edythe, was a prolific writer of letters to the editor, and often castigated Arthur in her letters.

Doctor Phetteplace's vendetta against Arthur lasted only until he needed Arthur's help in carrying out one of his own responsibilities. This occurred when he was chairman of the annual cancer drive in Eugene. He needed Arthur's advice on the selection of faculty people for his committee. Arthur was just as courteous to him as could be, not even indicating any surprise that a man who was so bent on getting him out of the state should suddenly be asking a favor.

But that wasn't the extent of Doctor Phetteplace's nerve as far as asking favors was concerned. A few days after this he again telephoned Arthur and asked him if the cancer drive committee could have its kick-off tea at our house. Arthur assured him that we (meaning both he and I) would be happy to lend our house for this purpose.

Well! When Arthur came home that night and told me of Doctor Phetteplace's request, I was absolutely dumbfounded at his nerve. I really sputtered, and told Arthur that I'd do anything under the sun he wanted me to do, but to play the welcoming hostess to Doctor Phetteplace was really going a bit far. What made the situation doubly hard for me was that I really wanted to help the cancer drive, having built up considerable loyalty to that cause when I had twice served as chairman of the District of Columbia's annual drive for funds for the Cancer Society. Arthur succeeded in persuading me that I must view this in terms of the *cause,* and not in terms of the person heading the campaign in Eugene that year.

So I did it. But in all the years I've been doing this sort of thing, often at Arthur's request, at no time has my own enthusiasm been at a lower point. I really had to talk myself into being nice to Doctor Phetteplace.

There was a brief business period during the tea hour, at which Doctor Phetteplace presided. He spoke in lavish terms of Arthur's help to him, and presented a scroll addressed to both of us which expressed the appreciation of the cancer drive committee for our help. Somehow, for me, neither his little speech nor his scroll quite erased the memory of the earlier crusade to oust Arthur from the university. Well, as I've said before, Arthur never held a grudge against anybody.

Harry's wedding in Columbus at Christmas time that first year gave us an opportunity to have the entire family together for the holiday. As Ohio Wesleyan was then without a president, we were offered the use of the president's house—an elegant new mansion built for the president after we left Delaware.

That Christmas was also the occasion for the unveiling of a

portrait of Arthur to be hung in University Hall on the Ohio Wesleyan campus alongside the other ex-presidents. Our seven-year-old grandson, George Speese, pulled the cord that revealed the portrait.

Then, in early February, came the famous Gus Hall incident testing freedom of speech at the university. The first sound I heard on the morning of February 5, 1962, was the rapid four-finger click-click-click of Arthur pounding out something on his typewriter in his upstairs den. Later, at breakfast, he read to Tom and me what he had written.

It was a statement concerning the University of Oregon's policy regarding outside speakers on the campus. The question was pertinent because the executive secretary of the Communist party, Gus Hall, had been tentatively scheduled for a speech at the university as a part of a speaking tour of western colleges. The university sponsoring groups were the Young Democrats and the Student Union Forum Committee.

When word of Gus Hall's proposed appearance in Eugene was announced in the press, controversy broke out all over the state of Oregon as to whether he should be permitted to speak on the university campus. Irate taxpayers were highly indignant over the idea of Hall's being permitted to speak in tax-supported buildings and wasted no time in getting to work to prevent his appearance.

The problem first reared its head when newspaper reports indicated that requests to schedule talks by Gus Hall on five college campuses in the state of Washington had been denied by the administrative officials of all colleges approached.

Gus Hall's Oregon appearances were under the sponsorship of the Focus Club of Reed College. Arthur was out of town when the first stories appeared about the matter. The president of our sister institution, Doctor James Jensen of Oregon State University, joined the group that had refused to permit this well-known

Communist to speak on their campuses. Two other Oregon public institutions, Portland State College and Oregon College of Education, announced that under existing policies Gus Hall would be permitted to speak on their campuses.

It was in this climate of raging controversy that Arthur returned to Eugene. The first thing I said to him was, "You didn't ask my advice, but I strongly feel that you shouldn't let Gus Hall come to the University of Oregon to speak."

"Why not?" Arthur asked.

"Because he's too hot to handle," I replied.

The following morning Arthur was ready with his decision, and he was pounding it out on his typewriter before he got dressed. The statement he read to Tom and me was built around the university's strict adherence to freedom of speech. Here it is:

> If the university deviated from the policy it has followed as to freedom of expression, it would be placed in the category of a second-class university by men and women who understand the true purpose of a university.
>
> The university has traditionally followed a three-point policy on visiting speakers:
>
> It is the group's responsibility to extend the invitation and to provide information on the speaker's background so that his comments may be properly evaluated.
>
> Decisions made by a faculty or student group are not subject to review by any committee or administrative official of the university.

Arthur then indicated his own enthusiastic approval and support of this policy and added that this did not mean that the university put its stamp of approval on all outside speakers. In fact, he said, Gus Hall would be at the top of his own list of undesirables.

He talked the matter over with various student leaders, and they joined him in approval of his stand.

On that same afternoon, Arthur read his statement at the regular faculty meeting. They applauded him vigorously. One member of the faculty told me later that in all of his fourteen years of attending faculty meetings at the University of Oregon he had never before heard the faculty applaud a statement by the president of the university.

The faculty then proceeded to consider the matter and approved a statement similar to the one Arthur had pounded out at home that morning.

This simple statement of the First Amendment protection of freedom of speech set off a full-blown storm of protest throughout Oregon. Governor Hatfield, urged by telephone calls and letters from angry citizens at Arthur's being, in their eyes, "soft on communism," issued his own statement of disapproval of using public buildings as a platform for a communist speaker, though he did refuse to intervene in the controversy.

The chanceller of the Board of Higher Education was also approached by many people who wanted him to step in and countermand Arthur's decision. He, too, reaffirmed the right of the university to be an open forum for all sorts of opinions.

By this time, newspapers in Eugene and Portland—in fact, all over Oregon—were carrying stories and editorials about Gus Hall's expected appearance at the university. Editorial comment on the matter was almost uniformly supportive of the freedom of expression principle. An exception was the Eugene tabloid, *The Emerald Empire*, which carried highly critical and uncomplimentary stories and editorials about Arthur.

Exceptions in the university constituency to Arthur's stand were few indeed. One who disapproved was the director of athletics, Leo Harris. Mrs. Harris came up to the house to see me and explained that her husband couldn't understand why Arthur would lead the university into so much controversy when he could so easily have followed Doctor Jensen's example and denied permission for Gus Hall to speak. She indicated she thought I could use my influence to get Arthur to reverse his decision.

I explained to her as gently as I could that my policy was to stay out of such situations. "It is Arthur whom the Board of Higher Education selected for president of the university—not I," I told her. "If they thought I could do a better job than he, they would have asked me to be president." She got the point.

The John Birchers and the Freedom Center of Oregon (the two most conservative organizations in existence at that time, and both bent on defending us all from "this terrible Communist threat") went into action. A highly organized telephone campaign began—at the office, at home, at the governor's office, the chancellor's office, and at the homes and offices of various members of the legislature.

Our phone at home rang steadily. At first, when I answered it, I innocently carried on a normal conversation, offering to send any caller a copy of Arthur's public statement of principle, and thanking people who called for their interest. However, when we began to realize the real nature of the telephone campaign, I had to force myself to be civil.

I was grateful for the experience the cranberry episode had provided me to become conditioned to explosions of wrath directed at Arthur in the wake of decisions that were so widely misunderstood. However, in the cranberry incident it never really became a personal vendetta, whereas the Gus Hall episode became highly personalized.

Each caller started out precisely the same way: "I am calling to protest Doctor Flemming's allowing Gus Hall to speak on the university campus. . . ." Many made inferences that Arthur was atheistic, unpatriotic, unconcerned about the tender minds of young college students, and so on. I explained to some callers Arthur's long record of service to and interest in his church, but stopped short of telling about his years of service to his country, and the various decorations and awards he had received from the government for his outstanding service in the public arena. I longed to ask my irate callers just what they had done in either the church or the government to help make the world better, but I restrained myself. Many talked interminably about corrupting young people and how Arthur was contributing to this by his Gus Hall decision.

It went on and on. Saturday night—the speech was scheduled for early afternoon on Monday—the phone was still ringing after midnight. By this time we were all pretty sick of being nice to our continuous stream of callers, and Arthur and Tom and I agreed that we would just let it ring. But that, too, was hard to live with, and hard to sleep with, too!

Besides the telephone campaign, the Freedom Center, whose motto was "On Guard for America," was busy in downtown Eugene. They prepared and distributed thousands of flyers with Arthur's picture and the headline "Arthur S. Flemming Leads Oregon's Great University into Communist Trap by Approving Campus Appearance of Enemy Agent." The story covered two sides of a mimeographed sheet and called Arthur consistently left-wing, communist-leaning, and so on, and ended with a plea for everybody to write, telephone, and telegraph Flemming, the university, and the governor, and urged that the governor dismiss Flemming from the university. The extreme conservatives were really having a field day, all wrapped up in their vicious fanaticism and intolerance.

Many vitriolic letters appeared in the *Eugene Register Guard* berating Arthur for his part in the Gus Hall affair.

Sunday it was more of the same, though we did go to church and then down to Cottage Grove, seventeen miles away, for dinner. Arthur had a late-afternoon talk scheduled at the church and a dinner speech at the university in the evening. Tom was home most of the day, however, and answered about every third or fourth call to see if the campaign was still going strong. It was. We stopped answering at all in the evening.

We decided to move into the guest room that night, as it had no telephone and was far enough away from our bedroom to provide quiet. We were all completely worn down and got ready for bed about nine-thirty. Then the door bell rang insistently. I was still half-dressed, so I was elected to go and see who was so anxious to rouse us.

It was Jim Shea, the director of university relations. He told me that the governor had been trying to reach Arthur, but of course he couldn't because we weren't answering the telephone.

So Arthur called Governor Hatfield, and the governor's concern was to talk to Arthur about the safety measures that were being planned to protect Gus Hall on Monday afternoon. Governor Hatfield also offered to send a state police patrolman to protect us at the house. Arthur declined this kind offer, insisting to the governor that we were not afraid. ("Speak for yourself, John.") I confess I was beginning to feel quite apprehensive.

Finally the day of Gus Hall's engagement arrived. We learned that three hundred people in a motorcade were to go to Salem Monday morning to make a last ditch appeal to the governor to stop Gus Hall from speaking.

A committee of the protesters appeared at Arthur's office Monday morning also to plead with him to change his mind. Arthur gave his callers, about a dozen of them, a hearing. He invited them into his conference room, explained again the university's policy on outside speakers to them, and answered their questions. One little old lady walked right out of the conference room after that meeting and told a newspaper reporter that Arthur had refused to see them!

Two bomb threats were also received that morning—one at Arthur's office and one at the police headquarters in Eugene.

Arthur was sufficiently impressed with the possibility of violence that a hurried conference was called of the officials involved, and it was decided to move the speech from Macarthur
Court (the gym) to Hayward Field, as it was felt that security
measures could be more adequately handled outdoors.

As a result of the curiosity resulting from the furor about Gus
Hall's appearance, a crowd of over eight thousand people, most
of them students, turned out to see and hear the nation's top
communist. Some came to listen to what he had to say, but
probably most of them simply wanted to see the man who had
stirred up so much controversy.

Arthur didn't go, as he taught a class on Monday afternoons.

I didn't go either. For the very first time in my life, it was felt
by those close to the situation that the hate-filled protestors might
decide to come up to the house, and that I therefore needed to be
protected. It was, as a consequence, suggested to Arthur that he
"hide" me until after the Gus Hall appearance. Accordingly,
Arthur telephoned me about eleven-thirty in the morning and said
I was to go to the Jones's (he was the dean of administration at the
university and called Arthur "The Hero") for lunch and to remain
there for the afternoon.

Tom went, so we had a first-hand report. He gave us a highly
descriptive account of the occasion. There were a lot of policemen at the field, some carrying night sticks, and many carrying
walkie-talkie radios. Security measures included an elaborate
arrangement to get Hall away from the field after his speech.
Most of the eight thousand listeners seemed decidedly bored.

When it was over, a three-wheeled motor cart was driven to
the back of the speaker's stand, and Hall climbed into it. And off
the field putt-putted the little cart carrying the big man who had
caused so much ill feeling, followed by a half-dozen deputies, a
dog, and a pack of panting photographers.

The audience howled with laughter at the funny sight—glad,

no doubt, that the whole thing was over at last.

It was an impressive demonstration of American democracy, with the main feature being Gus Hall, the top United States Communist.

One of the university faculty members, Roy Paul Nelson, of the School of Journalism, used the cranberry incident and the Gus Hall episode as the basis for an article which appeared later that spring in *The Christian Century*. He staunchly defended Arthur's position in both of these crises, but graphically described the hysteria that followed on the part of many who saw sinister plots as motivations for both decisions.

Three thousand miles across the country, our old friend Doctor Frederic Brown Harris, then chaplain of the United States Senate, read the magazine's account of Arthur's Gus Hall decision and its consequences. He, without consulting Arthur, wrote a long letter to the editor of the *Eugene Register Guard*, which the paper carried in full, and in which he told of his thirty years of close acquaintance with Arthur and called him one of the most patriotic Americans he had ever known.

Others, too, observed what had happened at the University of Oregon where Arthur had acted as defender of the right of free speech. The American Association of University Professors took note of what Arthur had done, and at its annual meeting in Chicago, in April, 1962, this organization presented Arthur with its Alexander Meikeljohn Award for conspicuous support of academic freedom. This award, named in honor of a liberal teacher and educational leader, is given each year in recognition of an outstanding contribution to academic freedom—an area very dear to college professors.

One more result of the Gus Hall visit deserves mention. This was the erection of the "Free Speech Platform" just outside of the Erb Memorial Union Building on the campus. Arthur was invited to speak at its dedication. At that platform anybody could say, read, sing—or whatever—any time he wanted to about anything he wanted to. Students and faculty alike often made use of this special device for the continuing protection of freedom of speech at the university.

The freedom of speech issue kept rearing its head at intervals during our entire incumbency at Oregon. One such occasion was in the spring of 1964 when a group of younger faculty members, most of them in the English department, decided to read some Alan Ginsberg poetry, complete and unexpurgated, from the Free Speech Platform, apparently just to prove how broad-minded they were. The newspapers reported the event, and there was even editorial comment. Some people, of course, blamed this on Arthur, but he paid no attention.

He had to pay attention, however, to another incident that had loud reverberations throughout Oregon that same spring. This was the publication of a poem in *The Northwest Review*, a literary magazine published by the students at the university. The poem was found to include some "dirty words."

Many of the people who were so loud in their criticism of Arthur on the Gus Hall issue saw in this magazine piece another opportunity to "get" him. Walter Huss, the Freedom Center head, reprinted the so-called "smut" and distributed it widely, declaring himself the protector of the morals of the students and everybody else, thus giving the words much wider circulation than they otherwise would have had.

Arthur's first step was to suspend publication of the *Review* pending an investigation, and ultimately publication was resumed with faculty participating as advisers. But, meanwhile, the furor over the "dirty" words continued, and I became increasingly restive as the criticism mounted.

The Oregon Grange, at its state convention in Eugene, passed a resolution asking that Arthur be dismissed from the presidency of the university because of the *Northwest Review* piece. The

Eugene Register Guard had this exciting bit of news spread across the front page, and it plunged me into a state of gloom. I remember being called to the telephone just after I had read the newspaper story, and being asked by my caller if I would agree to talk to an organization she represented. I was so unhappy that I told her "No" right off, without assigning any reason, although ordinarily I should have agreed to her request.

The Oregon Department of the American Legion, holding its annual meeting in Milwaukee, Oregon, in July, had a resolution introduced that called for action "to restore pride in the University of Oregon and to admonish and remove its president, Doctor Arthur S. Flemming." The resolution was unanimously voted down. This particular incident was probably more of a delayed reaction to the Gus Hall affair than a reaction to the *Review* piece, but the motivation was the same.

Editorials again appeared in the Portland, Eugene, Salem, and Medford papers, all of them pointing out the absurdity of holding Arthur to blame for a few bad words in a student publication. And letters to the editor about this were divided between defense of Arthur and criticism of him. All of the people who demanded his scalp obviously held him responsible for the *Review* poetry. In their eyes, he was supposed to read everything written by the students, to exercise prior censorship over it, and of course delete the objectionable words.

Mr. Huss even went about the state trying to organize meetings of citizens in a move to get Arthur fired from the university. One such meeting in Medford attracted about two hundred people, though by no means all of them were enemies of Arthur.

Perhaps the most insistent person in the group bent on removing Arthur from the university was a little old lady in Eugene named Florence Reed Cook. She carried her campaign against Arthur right to a meeting of the Board of Higher Education. For two hours, in a closed executive session, Mrs. Cook castigated

Arthur, and demanded that the board replace Arthur with a president "who would more nearly represent the tenor of the taxpayers who support the University of Oregon"—whatever that means!

In addition to her blaming Arthur for the *Northwest Review* piece, she said the president is also responsible for "other areas of mismanagement" involving student conduct and the use of large sums of money from federal agencies for research grants. She contended "the use of research grants detracts from the university's role"—a queer notion indeed!

When it was all over the board adopted a highly laudatory resolution about Arthur and indicated their full support of him.

I was really annoyed at the board for even giving Florence Reed Cook a hearing, as she was known throughout our area as a number-one troublemaker. She got wide press coverage for her crusade against Arthur, and she obviously enjoyed basking in the light of publicity.

But I thought it unnecessary for the board to dignify her charges by giving her a hearing. In fact, I even sat down one day and wrote a letter to Charles Halloway, the chairman of the Board of Higher Education expressing my feelings. I thought it was a really good letter, but Arthur wouldn't let me send it.

Before I leave the free speech area, there is one other thing that Arthur did I should like to record, as it points up a consistent character trait of his. He made a trip to Portland for the purpose of conferring (at Arthur's request) with the executive officer of the Oregon Grange, Mr. Wheeler. His idea was to try to get Mr. Wheeler, who was presiding at the Grange meeting when the resolution to oust Arthur was passed, to understand some of the problems and issues at the university.

Mr. Wheeler was most friendly to Arthur and said he was truly sorry about the Grange resolution. He further explained that, though he was presiding, he was not fully aware of the implications of the resolution. A strange confession indeed for a presiding officer to make! No public statement to this effect was ever made, however.

Harboring grievances was absolutely foreign to Arthur's nature. You could clobber him, and he would turn around and invite you to dinner.

Oregon found out very early that it really had an activist president at the university, and one that would speak out force-fully in many directions, and one not afraid of provoking contro-versy by the stands he took. One writer, Malcolm Bauer, wrote a news story assessing Arthur's performance that first year and declared that in less than a year he had "emerged as a possible Republican candidate for the governorship, or for one of the state's two Senate seats. At the same time," continued Mr. Bauer, " he has given the University of Oregon one of its most vigorous administrations in its almost one hundred years of history." For, of course, the university was the main job.

Right off, Arthur began his consultative management policy by meeting regularly once a week with key student, staff, and faculty groups. Also, once a week he had his door open to students, who were invited to come in without prior appoint-ments to discuss with him any subject of their choosing.

He also continued the policy he had had at Ohio Wesleyan of teaching a course in political science, a three-term sequence in the evolution of federal policy.

Hazing in fraternities was another problem that arose. Three fraternities on the university campus were found guilty of hazing, and Arthur promised to "crack down" on fraternities involved in this sort of thing.

I recall one irate fraternity alumnus who telephoned our house at two o'clock in the morning one Sunday. I answered the phone, and realized that the caller was obviously emboldened by a bit of alcohol.

"You tell your husband he'd better leave the fraternities alone, or we'll see that he's no longer president of the university," he began. "He's out to 'get' the fraternities, and he'd better 'lay off,' or we'll 'get' him. Besides, he doesn't know anything about fraternities anyway, or he'd know enough to keep his nose out of our business."

Even at 2 AM, or maybe because it was 2 AM, I was annoyed. "Oh, doesn't he?" I said. "Well, let me tell you something. My husband, it happens, does know quite a bit about fraternities. He happens to be a member of one, and so am I."

My caller was not prepared for this news. "Is he?" he said. "Well anyway, you tell him I represent a large group of alumni, and we'll get him out of the university if he doesn't leave the fraternities alone."

"I'll tell him," I promised. And on this happy note, my caller hung up. By then Arthur was awake. "What's going on?" he asked.

"Oh, nothing worth bothering about," I answered. "I'll tell you about it in the morning."

Probably the most controversial development in the area of student life was the idea of a code for student conduct that was the focus of a faculty study in 1963. The establishment of a faculty-student committee to draw up such a code was set up in June. As a result, this joint faculty-student committee finally drew up such a code, which was approved and became effective in the 1963 fall term.

Arthur sent a memorandum to the faculty in which he identified the objectives he felt should guide the faculty-student conduct code committee. Its general aim was to give the students a larger voice and to make them take more responsibility for their own conduct.

Its effect was to remove from the dean of women's office and the dean of students' office their role as sole arbiter in all matters pertaining to student conduct. And, since this meant taking power away from them, these officials fought to retain their control. The dean of women managed to stir up the mothers' organization, by playing on their fears, to fight the proposed new code. But, after months of study, the new student conduct code finally was officially adopted and placed the greater share of responsibility for identifying and for punishing offenders against the mature kind of behavior the code sought to encourage.

Included in the new code was the relaxation of closing-hour restrictions for upper-class women and the establishment of a student court to be made up of five students and two faculty members appointed by the president to deal with student conduct.

Academic matters gave rise to all sorts of problems, too. Arthur's theme song was "the pursuit of excellence," and he made many speeches built around this theme. He saw his job as a mandate to help put the university in a good competitive position so it could get and keep top academic personnel and maintain adequate physical facilities. But sometimes those around him had a different view of excellence from his.

Selecting a new Liberal Arts College dean to replace Doctor Robert Clark, whom Arthur appointed dean of the faculty, brought out some of these different attitudes. A committee was appointed to conduct a search for a new dean. A nationwide hunt was conducted, and several prospective deans were summoned to Eugene for interviews, but no final selection resulted.

Then, all of a sudden, attention focused on one of the Business School professors. The suggestion was seriously proposed to Arthur that he appoint as the Arts dean Charles Johnson, the professor of accounting—an absolutely unheard-of idea!

Arts college faculty people traditionally regard themselves as quite a "cut above" the business faculty. After all, they look on themselves as the real scholars in the university community. And there were a lot of eyebrows raised when Arthur decided to reach into the Business School faculty and appoint Doctor Johnson as the new dean of the College of Liberal Arts.

The wife of the dean of the Graduate School actually telephoned me one day and expressed her view, which she declared was shared by many, that it would certainly never work to have a Business School faculty man in the position of the Arts College dean.

"He has no understanding of the problems of the Arts College people, and they will resent him so much that he won't be able to function satisfactorily," she insisted to me. She wanted me to pass on her advice to Arthur, and I did.

But, in spite of the criticism, Arthur, acting on advice of the search committee, appointed Charles Johnson dean of the College of Liberal Arts. Doctor Johnson's performance in the job was so superior in all ways that when Arthur resigned from the presidency of the university, his Arts dean was the natural choice to be acting president. Sadly, his health broke under the pressures of that office, and he died, in his mid-forties, in 1969.

Another interesting problem was over what to do with the historic pioneer cemetery adjacent to the campus. The cemetery was supervised by the Pioneer Memorial Park Association, which paid no attention at all to it and let debris and trash litter the cemetery.

The idea was proposed that the university take it over, move the graves closer together, and thus provide enough space for several new university buildings. Another suggestion made was that the graves remain as they were and that a building on stilts be erected over them. Both suggestions gave rise to considerable criticism by the older members of the community who accused Arthur of being insensitive to the historical significance of the cemetery. The so-called cemetery controversy raged during the entire time we were at the university. No definite action leading to the university's using that valuable land was ever taken.

Then, the athletic program was a source of friction too. At the time Arthur went to the university all students were required to pay a compulsory fee in support of intercollegiate athletics. Some students opposed this requirement, as did some faculty. It was the subject of heated debate in a faculty meeting with arguments being advanced (with only a portion of the students participating) that the university should not attempt to carry on an intercollegiate athletic program that called for such large expenditures.

Arthur didn't agree with the opponents. He felt that, on balance, the program made a contribution to the university, and that it was appropriate for a portion of its support to come from student fees. In return for the payment of the fees the students, of course, were admitted to all athletic contests.

We had been at the university a couple of years when the director of athletics, backed by an influential group of alumni, began to push for a new stadium. The old athletic field on the campus seated only seventeen thousand persons, and it was not felt that it could be satisfactorily enlarged. So most of Oregon's home games were played in Portland. This meant that on the day of each home game thousands of students and faculty drove the 110 miles to Portland to watch the game.

A proposed new stadium had been in the talk stage for many years, and the university had actually bought a large tract of land across the Willamette River from the campus on what was called the north bank.

From the beginning of the discussion, Arthur had insisted that the home games should be played in Eugene. This alienated a lot of Portland business men who would lose money if this came about. Also, a large number of powerful Portland alumni financial supporters of the athletic program disapproved of any change because playing the games in Eugene would force them to take the 110-mile trip to see the games.

250

And there was opposition to the proposed site in Eugene, too. Many of the Eugene citizens felt that such a valuable and desirable acreage as the north bank property could be more appropriately used for a public park instead of a stadium.

Moreover, where was the money to come from to build a stadium to seat thirty-five or forty thousand people? Arthur had definite ideas on this problem, too. Recognizing that under state law the proposed new facility could not be financed with tax money, he urged all interested parties to work out a financing plan that would involve alumni contributions and contributions from the general public, and would use athletic department reserves, which had accumulated as a result of careful administration by the athletic director.

So, with the athletic department and the alumni supporters pushing for a new facility on one hand; with some faculty and students pushing for deemphasis of athletics on the other; with Eugene citizens fighting the proposed location of the new stadium on the north bank of the Willamette; and with Portland businessmen and alumni supporters there pulling and tugging to keep at least some of the home games in Portland, Arthur engaged an architectural firm to make a study of the alternatives. Finally, the Board of Higher Education accepted Arthur's recommendation to proceed with plans for building the new stadium on the north bank property.

Many people were unhappy with the solution, but once the digging actually got started the interest in the unique design of the new stadium generated considerable excitement throughout the entire community. It was ready for the first game in the fall of 1967. The formal dedication, naming it Autzen Stadium after the largest alumni contributor, took place on a very hot Saturday afternoon with Ohio State University. We lost!

Other buildings were being added to the campus too. One was a so-called humanities building named for a former president of the university, Prince Lucien Campbell. New dormitories were being built; a new education building and a computer science building were in progress.

Lots of things were going on to provide Arthur with respite from university problems and campus debates. One responsibility he undertook was to chair a National Commission on Health Care for the Aged. This twelve-man special panel, convoked at the behest of Senator Clinton Anderson of New Mexico and Senator Jacob Javits of New York, was to take a "new look" at health insurance for the aged.

When the commission finished its work, the recommendation was to care for the older persons' hospital costs through a compulsory social insurance program financed by employee-employer payroll contributions, and to set up a voluntary plan to cover medical costs financed by premiums paid by participants and general revenues. The American Medical Association, through its executive vice-president, issued a statement condemning the report. The Oregon Medical Association joined the American Medical Association in condemning the plan, and again Arthur found himself in a head-on collision with this powerful group of Oregonians.

Arthur went to Washington to present the report to President Kennedy in mid-November. The president was enthusiastic about it, and it later played a significant role in the passage of Medicare in 1965. President Kennedy was assassinated a week later. Homecoming events scheduled at the university were cancelled, and a memorial service held in Macarthur Court at which Arthur spoke.

Another respite from university duties was provided in the summer of 1964 when Arthur was invited to be on the faculty of the Salzburg Seminar. This is a program carried on at the Schloss Leopoldskron in Austria. It consists of four to six seminars each year at which various aspects of American life are explored, such as city government, labor problems, our legal institutions, public and private education in the United States, and so on. These topics are taught in seminars by American experts in each field for the benefit of students who enroll at the seminars. The students are young Europeans from all of the NATO countries, and they have been carefully selected because of their special interest in the particular field to be discussed. Our seminar explored higher education, both public and private, and Arthur was a natural for this because of his expertise and experience in both fields and in the Department of Health, Education, and Welfare.

We lived at the schloss with the other faculty members and the European students, eating all meals with them and really getting to know them well. It was certainly one of our most delightful and educational experiences.

Coming back to Eugene in the leisurely way on the *France* we talked of the possibility of obtaining a vacation cottage on the McKenzie River. Clearly we would never take real vacations. Arthur simply didn't believe in them! Perhaps, we thought, a cottage near Eugene would provide a bit of relaxation.

Accordingly, I set out in search of such a place, and in the late fall we became the proud owners of a lovely four-room cottage, complete with electricity, bath, garbage disposal, and dishwasher. Just our kind of place as we are both definitely room-service kind of people.

It was situated on a point on the river where the water rushes over huge boulders and makes a wonderful singing noise all the time. The previous owners had called the place El Canto Rio, The Singing River. It was completely private, and had a fine view of the Cascade Mountains. I embarked on a redecorating binge, and we had the porch along the river side screened and finished with a translucent roof. It was beautiful.

We made many trips up to the cottage both alone and with

friends for luncheons and dinners on the weekends. But it was certainly naive of me to imagine that we would ever spend more time up there than a few hours at a stretch. In our three years in Eugene after we bought the cottage we spent only three nights there. Arthur's Sunday school class and superintendent responsibilities didn't fit in with weekends at the cottage.

The year 1964 was a presidential election year, and Arthur was a vocal member of a large group of moderate Republicans who found themselves unable to support the Goldwater-Martin ticket. Arthur's old friend Charles Taft, from Cincinnati, Ohio, appealed to him to become a member of the National Committee to Support Moderate Republicans (especially for election to Congress), and Arthur agreed.

He also made the difficult decision to vote in the November election for President Johnson. He was questioned by newsmen as to what he would do, and Arthur said he based his decision to vote for the Democratic nominee on eighteen years of close observation of the presidency and how he believed it should be conducted. He declined to go into Barry Goldwater's merits, or lack of them, saying only, "I based my decision on the positive aspects of Mr. Johnson's qualifications for the presidency."

Throughout our years in Oregon, the university, like its counterparts everywhere, faced the perennial problem of trying to get adequate funding from the legislature. The university was growing fast. The Graduate School was becoming a major institution. Though Chancellor Lieuallen carried most of the responsibility in this area, Arthur did go before various legislative committees to plead for larger appropriations to meet the university's increasing needs for buildings and faculty commensurate with its growth. Rising costs made the situation critical. The Medical School in Portland was a particularly expensive part of the university's operation.

Oregon's legislature tended to be a very conservative one,

loath to provide adequate funding. Often Arthur appealed to alumni groups to help in this area. He also worked constantly at getting support from other sources, and his efforts finally bore fruit.

In March of 1964, the federal government announced a grant of $2.5 million to the University of Oregon to establish a center of educational research devoted to basic and applied research in educational administration and organization at elementary, secondary, and higher education levels. There was great rejoicing at the university over this.

The university, later in 1964, was given a $8.1 million contract to turn the Tongue Point Naval Station into a youth training center, one of three urban job corps centers established as war-on-poverty projects. Arthur jumped into this project enthusiastically as it provided an opportunity to rehabilitate young men who had dropped out of school but who were considered capable of being trained for useful citizenship.

Not everybody agreed that the university was an appropriate place for the job corps idea. For Arthur, it was a perfectly natural aspect of his total commitment to "helping his fellow human beings achieve their highest potential."

But there were many critics of the job corps program and the university's involvement in it. These critics saw no justification at all for the university to administer the government's latest experimental program to upgrade the lives of some of its citizens. Others, including many faculty of the College of Education, saw in it a chance to provide a perfect laboratory for some of their teaching techniques.

Later, in May, 1965, the National Science Foundation made a grant of four million dollars to accelerate the university's science programs, one of four institutions selected for such grants. The money was to be used for seventeen new faculty appointments, research assistants, and for research equipment.

Private gifts were sizable, too, and included a $500,000 bequest from the estate of Maude Kerns, a retired arts department faculty member, and a million dollar gift from Lila Atchison Wallace to finance the start of the university's new School of Community Service and Public Affairs. This was one of the two new schools started by Arthur, the other being the School of Librarianship.

In fact, the university income nearly doubled in Arthur's first five years as president, and he constantly worked to improve both undergraduate and graduate programs in all of the schools.

Plans for future law school expansion were among Arthur's immediate dreams for the university. These included a new law school building and expansion of research activities into a full-fledged legal center to serve the entire state of Oregon. Many meetings were held to promote these dreams. The new building was begun during Arthur's tenure.

By the mid-1960s colleges and universities all over the country were entering the period of intense student protest. In fact, students and faculty alike were beginning to be loudly vocal about such things as our participation in the Vietnam War; the manufacture of war materials such as napalm by the country's large industries; civil rights; army, navy, and air force recruitment on campuses; and so on.

Arthur gave encouragement to this sort of activity in his annual summer session address on June 29, 1965, when he said:

"The spirit of involvement is abroad on the campuses of our colleges and universities. . . . Too many persons are playing it safe by muzzling faculty members, afraid that opinions expressed by faculty will represent opinions by the institution. . . . The university should encourage students to become involved in discussions of major issues, both on and off the campus. . . . The right to civil disobedience is open—if the person is willing to accept the consequences."

In October, 1966, Arthur himself joined a group of interfaith marchers in Portland. This was called a Prayer Procession for Peace. In addition to Arthur, included among the marchers were the president of the University of Portland, Reverend Paul Waldschmidt, and Rabbi Emanuel Rose, of Temple Beth Israel. The purpose was to focus attention on the religious concern for peace, though it did not specifically protest against the Vietnam War.

Arthur also began promoting and teaching a course in understanding the entire Vietnam War situation, using his position as president of the National Council of Churches. He taught a course himself in his adult class at our Methodist church. The idea behind his own course and others sponsored by him was to provide a forum for adults to discuss this very important issue.

There were growing demands for a larger student voice in decision making at the university. The students wanted to play a meaningful and responsible role in every part of the university community. One battle was over teacher evaluation by the students; another was over the question of pass or no-pass grades in certain courses; another was over supplying information about students to selective service boards; and still another was how to deal with campus "hippies" and their activities; and, finally, the perennial problem of Greek discrimination with Arthur always in the thick of things, acting as mediator and trying to keep his pulse on the activities of both students and faculty.

The drug culture became the focus of a *cause célèbre*, too. The managing editor of *The Oregon Daily Emerald*, nineteen-year-old Annette Buchanan, wrote and published a story about the use of marijuana on the campus. Immediately the district attorney, William Frye, was on her trail demanding to know the names of the students who had supplied her with the information for her story so he could prosecute them.

Annette refused to divulge her sources. Arthur backed her up on the grounds that news sources would dry up if reporters were required to disclose their sources of information.

An indictment of Annette for contempt followed, and the subsequent trial resulted in conviction with a fine of $300. William Knowland, publisher of the *Oakland Tribune* and a former United States senator from California, paid her fine.

She appealed her case to the Oregon Supreme Court, and they upheld the conviction.

Annette then appealed her case to the United States Supreme Court, and they refused to hear her case.

We knew Annette well. She came up to our house occasionally, and we both enjoyed her fearless and stimulating approach to the business of living.

The Students for Democratic Society were becoming a strong political force nationally, and this far-left student group provided a bit of excitement at the University of Oregon, too. As a protest against the Central Intelligence Agency's job recruiting on the campus, they set up a Communist party recruiting table on the campus. They brought in a young party member from Portland to test the university's reaction to political recruiting.

As with the Gus Hall incident and the reading of the "dirty poetry" on the Student Union steps, Arthur was never tempted to abandon his free-speech policy. Many people in the Oregon constituency had no understanding at all of the true meaning of the phrase "freedom of speech," and he got considerable criticism from this group. He was actually challenged in the legislature when a member of that body, Representative Lee Thornton, tried to get action to ban speakers he disapproved of at the university, such as George Lincoln Rockwell, Stokely Carmichael, Timothy Leary, and others.

Then, too, there were the growing demands of the Black students for a voice in their affairs at the university. They demanded increased course offerings in Black studies, a voice in the recruitment of Black students, and more recognition in dormitory management.

We had one serious physical encounter when a Black student demanded to see some records in the office of the dean of students. His demand was refused, and he thereupon physically assaulted the assistant dean. He was later tried in court for this offense and found guilty of assault.

A Black activist professor, though contributing to the life of the college, also caused Arthur grief, chiefly because he so blatantly alienated many friends of the university by his belligerent attitude in most of his associations with people in and out of the university.

Crisis piled on crisis during these years. I remember one day when I had driven Arthur over to the coast for a speech. It was on a day when the Dow Chemical Company was on the campus for recruitment purposes. The students objected because of Dow's involvement in napalm manufacture, and actual violence was threatened. On our return drive to Eugene, which normally took about an hour and a half, it took us three hours and a half because Arthur had me stop along the highway just about every time we passed a roadside telephone so he could call his office to check on the campus situation. Fortunately, no violence occurred.

A bit of relief from campus problems was provided when Arthur was asked to chair a commission to study the operation of the Hatch Act. This Act, passed by Congress in 1939, prohibited federal employees from active participation in the political process. They could vote, but that was about all. In 1940, the no-politics act was extended to all state and local government employees supported in whole or in part by the federal government.

The Hatch Act had always been the subject of criticism by those who felt that it made second-class citizens out of public employees. So Congress provided for the study commission, which was also empowered to make recommendations for changes in the Act.

The members of the commission held public hearings all over the country to take testimony on the operation of the Hatch Act. At the conclusion of this process, the members of the commission had a hard time agreeing on how the results should be evaluated in terms of specific recommendations to Congress. They did, however, generally agree that some change was needed.

As is the fate of most government commissions' reports, when completed they are forgotten. The Hatch Act Commission is no exception.

And, of course, Arthur's continued involvement in church activities provided a regular change of pace. He began teaching a Sunday school class soon after we moved to Eugene, and he soon became involved in state-wide religious activities. His contributions to Oregon's religious life led to his selection to be the recipient of the 1967 Oregon Brotherhood Award sponsored by the Oregon Region of the National Conference of Christians and Jews. It was given to him "In recognition of his outstanding personal contribution to the promotion of understanding and good will among persons of different racial, religious, and cultural backgrounds."

There was one difference in Eugene as far as our church involvement was concerned. As I have noted, normally I left church organizational work to Arthur, and I stayed out of it. Our minister there, Doctor Norman Conard, decided he would take a chance on appointing me to a couple of the church commissions. And, when the congregation voted to build a new church, I was appointed a member of the building committee and chairman of the subcommittee to plan the sanctuary. For the very first time, I was in a position to tell Arthur about something going on in our local church. He was on the outside looking in on that building operation, and I was on the inside and privy to all the information, planning, decisions, and so on. I felt really big! As far as church work is concerned, that was my only moment of glory.

Arthur's biggest challenge as a Christian layman came when he was elected to serve a three-year term as president of the National Council of Churches of Christ in America. This took place in December of 1966 at the triennial convention of the council, which was held that year at the Fontainbleu Hotel, in Miami Beach, Florida.

As on college campuses and other institutions over the country, there was ferment in the church, too. As the convention began, there was an air of turmoil in the proceedings. The conservative denominations, with Billy Graham as the most articulate spokesman, were pushing for evangelism as the major theme for the National Council's work. The liberal group, of which Arthur was one leader, were insisting that the council take a position on the big national and international issues that confronted the country. The politics of confrontation had not yet become the technique for urging change that it became during his term of office, but the elements of "hold back-go ahead" were clearly present.

It was in this climate of discord that Arthur assumed responsibility for leadership in the National Council of Churches. In his inaugural address, he identified the issues in which he meant to involve the council.

He called for a nationwide campaign to get public schools to teach courses about religion. He declared that religious illiteracy was rampant in this country and that it was time we launched a frontal attack on it. He declared that the Supreme Court had made clear in its recent ruling against compulsory devotional exercises in public schools that there was no constitutional objection to teaching about religion. This became one of his principal crusades during his term.

He vowed to use his new post to rally public opinion in insisting that our government pass up no opportunity to get the

Vietnam conflict to the conference table. He had sessions with Ambassador Arthur Goldberg of the United Nations and with Secretary of State Dean Rusk in an effort to promote this idea.

He expressed approval of the federal research on birth control and dissemination of information on the subject at home and abroad. He termed it a legitimate activity of the government.

He voiced strong opposition to the Connally Amendment, which restricts United States participation in the World Court by refusing to recognize decisions impinging on United States sovereignty. He said it should be repealed.

He said he would try to improve communication between the council and local churches, so that individuals could be helped to become better acquainted with the great ethical problems of the day and thus be better able to help shape national policy decisions.

An editorial in *The Miami Herald* took note of his election thus:

> The National Council of Churches is an action group which applies Christian principles to the concerns of the day. . . . The National Council has been a force in the civil rights movement and a loud voice for peace. . . . It is fitting that the National Council of Churches has chosen a layman with wide knowledge of public affairs to lead it for the next three years. . . . By experience and temperament Mr. Flemming is well qualified to push the National Council of Churches toward its larger goals.

Time, on December 16, 1966, declared Arthur S. Flemming to be a man who matched the new mood of activism.

Newsweek's story, on December 19, 1966, stressed the same sort of attitude. It also mentioned the problem of bringing Catholics into the National Council of Churches. Arthur called this "the most exciting development of my life time" and vowed to try to bring the Catholic church and the evangelical protestants together. He was also quoted as seeing no real division between "accepting Christ" and "social reform." "The persons who really accept Christ," he argued, "are also interested in social action."

Many of the stories that appeared in newspapers over the country described the sharp cleavage among American Christians over evangelism and evangelistic methods—that is, conservative evangelicals who stress conversion by preaching, and a modern school stressing social activism in the church. Arthur saw his new role as one to bring the worker church and the evangelists together to work hand in hand.

A story appeared in *The New York Times* that gave special amusement to our family. An imaginative reporter telephoned Lib in Delaware, Ohio, and asked for her cooperation in developing a story about her father that would point up facets of his character not found in the dull recital of facts in *Who's Who*. She promptly reacted by giving him a detailed account of the annual Christmas shopping spree her father takes the children on each year. The reporter was delighted with this "inside" story and embellished it in very descriptive language as the lead for his story in *The Times*.

The entire three-year incumbency as president of the National Council of Churches found Arthur involved in conferences and speeches all over the country, pushing for social action by the council and its member denominations.

One footnote to our Oregon years I should like to mention, as this, too, points up special qualities of Arthur's. In the spring of 1965, the newspapers carried stories about a new community college to open in Eugene in the fall. For some time I had been feeling the need to divert my energies to something more rewarding and stimulating than pouring at afternoon teas and going to meetings. I asked Arthur if he would mind if I applied for a job teaching at the new Lane Community College.

"Certainly not," he said. "Go right ahead."

I do not believe that many men in his position would have

encouraged me with such blanket approval as he did. At that time it was not at all customary for university presidents' wives to be wage-earners themselves. In fact, in 1965, I didn't know of any.

So I set up an interview with the president of the new institution, and in September, after a period as a student in the university's summer session to "brush up," I began my second career as a college teacher and kept up this schedule for three years thereafter. I did not teach a full load—only two or three courses per term—and I do not feel that I neglected any of my duties in connection with the university either. I was usually able to attend all of the special occasions scheduled with Arthur, and also to handle the home entertaining required.

Many of the faculty members and their wives expressed approval, but not all. After the first year, one dean's wife said to me, "Are you planning to teach next year, or have you already proved whatever it was you were trying to prove?" Is there a satisfactory answer to a question like that?

Arthur's painful decision to leave the presidency of the University of Oregon to go to Macalester College, in St. Paul, Minnesota, came in late March of 1968, after many months of agonizing. Editorial comment in the Eugene and Portland and Salem newspapers and the *Oregon Daily Emerald* was uniformly in praise of Arthur's leadership during his seven-year incumbency, a time of great growth and also a time of unparalleled social ferment.

When the inevitable search committee to select a new president for the university was set up, the students decided to dramatize their own feelings on the subject. About fifty of them slept on the steps of Johnson Hall, the administration building, to call attention to their demand for a greater voice in the selection of the university's new president. They demanded an equal voice with the faculty. What they had been offered was a three-(students) to-seven (faculty) ratio.

The demonstrators moved into Johnson Hall itself and remained three days. "The students," according to a story by
Lucille Vaughan Payne, "knew what they wanted, and they went
straight to the power source to get it. What they wanted was
another Arthur Flemming." The students had made many gains
during Arthur's tenure: new courses outside the traditional curriculum, the university's blessing for community action programs and for more involvement in social programs generally, a
liberalized student conduct code, a measure of control over their
incidental fees, and limited but official representation at faculty
meetings. These gains would be lost if the state board hired a
"conservative" president, a step the students feared the faculty
would recommend.

Repeated conversations with Chancellor Lieuallen did not
resolve the impasse. Nor did an appearance before the State
Board of students to plead their case.

Meanwhile, public fury over the antics of the students was
mounting, with one irate Oregonian wiring Chancellor Lieuallen
to "use a horsewhip on the students."

In the end, a face-saving compromise was offered by Chancellor Lieuallen, to wit: instead of the seven or eight faculty
members originally planned, he would appoint only six. Three
would be teaching faculty, and three would be faculty with
administrative duties (as deans or heads of departments). And
with this, the students appeared relieved of the need for further
demonstrations, and the exodus from Johnson Hall followed.

Arthur was not, of course, directly involved in this decision,
but he spent many hours in consultation with Chancellor Lieuallen
urging patience and the need for compromise in dealing with the
protesting student activists.

A week later the nation was again plunged into a state of shock
and sorrow over the killing of Martin Luther King, Jr. The Black
Students' Union asked Arthur for permission to hold a memorial

service in Macarthur Court and that classes be canceled for the afternoon of the service. Arthur agreed. The Black Students' Union planning committee for the occasion asked Arthur if he would march with them from the Union Building to Macarthur Court and deliver a eulogy for Doctor King. He agreed to do this also. Under the circumstances, it was a great compliment the Black students paid Arthur in asking him to participate in this testimonial occasion for their slain leader.

Arthur also traveled to Atlanta to join the many thousands who gathered there for Doctor King's funeral. In his capacity as president of the National Council of Churches, he was assured a seat at the service at the church. He found, however, that the crowds were so dense that he actually couldn't get to his seat, so he simply joined the marching mourners as they walked from the church to Morehouse College—a truly ennobling experience.

By this time Arthur was solidly behind the report of the National Advisory Commission on Civil Disorders, known as the Kerner Report. The report, and his approval and support of it, especially as it leveled blame on "White racism," became his favorite speech topic. He insisted that a crash program to end race prejudice be started immediately by churches, schools, the mass media, government and politics, and business and labor. He even led his Sunday school class in Eugene in a study of the report.

One final administrative decision of Arthur's had consequences that were to mar the last months of our Oregon years. In mid-April, after the Black Students' Union had presented a list of grievances to Arthur and demanded action to eliminate alleged racism on the campus in the areas of athletics, dormitories, financial aid and admissions, curriculum, staff development, and community relations, Arthur announced the formation of a forty-member committee of both faculty and students to investigate the areas listed by the complaining students. This was divided into six subcommittees, four of which completed their study of the existing situation and filed reports in a few weeks. These reports contained a number of controversial recommendations designed to aid students from disadvantaged backgrounds attending the University of Oregon.

The professor of speech, Bower Aly, was highly vocal in his criticism of Arthur for setting up this committee, and at the final faculty meeting of the year, in early June, he introduced a "notice of motion." His resolution was harshly critical of Arthur in forming a committee on racism without, he said, "properly consulting the faculty." He also criticized Arthur for tardily announcing the committee, said the state law places responsibility for governing the university in the hands of both the president and the faculty, and pointed out that Arthur's actions in regard to the committee on racism were taken "after the announcement of his resignation and impending departure from the University of Oregon, and that therefore any actions taken by Arthur in response to the committee's recommendations should be subject to review by his successor." Mr. Aly therefore recommended censure by the faculty.

According to the existing rules governing faculty procedure, as a "notice of motion" the resolution was not offered for debate, but rather as an item of business that would be brought up at the next regular meeting of the faculty, which would not be until October. Immediately after Bower Aly introduced his "notice of motion," Thomas Hovet, professor of political science and head of that department, served notice that he would offer at the October meeting a motion commending Arthur for his response to the Black Students' Union grievances and endorsing the action he took in regard to the committee on racism.

What made Bower Aly's censure resolution particularly distasteful was that Arthur and I had enjoyed a very friendly relationship with Bower and Lucile Aly (also a university faculty member)—or so we thought. On numerous occasions when

Bower had made special requests in connection with leaves of absence and other matters, and when Bower's faculty associates advised against granting such requests, Arthur defended him and usually granted whatever it was Bower was petitioning for. Lucile Aly and I were "special" friends, often going out for dinner together when Bower and Arthur were busy or out of town.

Moreover, in October of 1965, the Alys had amended their wills to make Arthur the guardian, executor, and trustee for their youngest son, Stewart, in case they should predecease Stewart while he was still a minor. In the document drawn up and signed by Bower, Lucile, and Stewart, the final sentence reads, "It would be impossible to express in words how much each of the three of us appreciate your willingness to accept this obligation."

So it was indeed a considerable shock to us when Bower introduced his "notice of motion" for the faculty to vote on censuring Arthur for appointing the committee on racism—a committee that the president of the university certainly had every right to appoint. Bower's action cast a distinct pall over our last days in Oregon.

When the October faculty meeting rolled around we were eighteen hundred miles across the country in St. Paul, but Arthur got word from Eugene that Bower had withdrawn his motion. It was small comfort, however, and did little to erase the unhappiness he caused us the previous spring.

Our last official activity at the University of Oregon was to attend the Board of Higher Education meeting, held each at Ashland, Oregon, in July. Ashland was always the site of the summer board meeting because it allowed the state college and university presidents, board members, staff, and their families to attend the plays in the evening at the famous open-air Elizabethan theater there, a real treat for all of us. At that meeting the board adopted a resolution honoring Arthur for his service to the university and describing him in generous and laudatory terms.

And so our golden years at Oregon came to a close. In spite of the almost continuous periods of controversy and unrest, we both agree that we left a bit of our hearts in Oregon.

Close relationships with Eugene friends have continued to enrich my life. Four "special" friends and I, calling ourselves the Eugene Committee, have had an annual reunion most of the years since 1968. Our committee meetings have taken place mostly in San Francisco, but we have also met in Carmel; Seattle, Washington; and Toronto. We all look forward to these gatherings with keen anticipation.

There was one interruption to the normal work routine that is such a memorable event that it deserves inclusion in this story. It occurred toward the end of our Eugene years.

Since Arthur is a strict devotee of the so-called Christian work ethic, vacations for fun have never seemed to be either necessary or desirable. One cold winter day I decided it was high time Arthur and I took a trip "just for the heck of it." All of our previous traveling had been undertaken solely because of a speaking engagement, or a meeting of some kind—never simply for fun or relaxation.

So this exception to the work routine did not take place as a result of Arthur's planning or initiation, or because he felt any need for it. It happened because—at long last—I took matters in hand.

I was teaching at the time, so I had a bit of money of my own that allowed me to be adventurous. So, after consulting Mary Walker, Arthur's secretary, to check on the summer schedule as indicated at that point, I set out one February day for the travel agent's office. I had in mind taking the inland passage cruise from Vancouver, British Columbia, to Alaska.

I found out that one of these cruises was scheduled for mid-August, and I paid a deposit on two tickets for that particular cruise. I then telephoned Mary again and told her what I had done. I asked her to block out on Arthur's calendar the ten-day period for the trip and cautioned her not to tell him about it. I suggested she simply put my name on each of those days. Mary entered into the conspiracy with great glee.

I was absolutely ecstatic about what I had done. Never before had I dared to put my own desires for a vacation ahead of Arthur's business or speaking plans. So I felt a real sense of elation and power.

Well, it wasn't easy to preserve that block of time in August for the purpose I had in mind. Things kept cropping up to interfere, such as an invitation to dedicate the American Management Association's new building in Arizona the third week in August—an invitation that came to Arthur through his old friend Lawrence Appley. Arthur told me about this invitation when it was extended, saying that I could go along, too. When I told him he couldn't accept Larry's invitation to dedicate his building because we were going to be doing something else on that date, he became quite annoyed. But I "stuck to my guns," even writing to Larry myself to make the excuses.

Even President Johnson threatened to interfere with my vacation plan when he requested Arthur to go, as a representative of the National Council of Churches, with the official party to oversee the elections in Vietnam in August of 1967. I was really afraid my vacation plan would sink under this presidential request, but it didn't. By that time I think Arthur wanted to go on the cruise as much as I did.

Each time Arthur would press me for an explanation, all I told him was that we were going to be doing something very special, that it meant a great deal to me, and that I had invested a lot of money in it—so, please, would he, just this once, trust me and cooperate by keeping this segment of time sacred for my purpose, whatever it was! I didn't actually tell him what I had done until his birthday on June 12, when I presented him with two tickets for a cruise on the Canadian Pacific's *Prince George*, leaving Vancouver, British Columbia, on August 16.

It worked. We actually did go on that inland cruise, with Arthur loving every minute of it! Each day the ship docked for a few hours at points along the way, and we were free to take sightseeing tours around the area. We thus had an opportunity to become acquainted with Prince Rupert, Juneau, Skagway, and other points. One day we took a train trip on a narrow-gauge railway through the Klondike region up to Carcross. Somewhat scary, but beautiful.

Two weeks before we left Oregon for our new opportunity at Macalester College we acted in the role of parents for Mary Walker when she married Richard Williams. The wedding ceremony and reception took place at our house. With Mary's four children, and Dick's eight, their marriage created an instant family of fourteen. All of the children were present.

Sixteen years later, in June of 1984, Arthur returned to the University of Oregon to receive its distinguished Oregon citizen award.

13

M A C A L E S T E R

I cannot, even now, dwell on the Macalester years at any length without wincing. That we so badly miscalculated the extent of DeWitt Wallace's real interest in and commitment to innovation in higher education and his interest in expanding educational opportunities to disadvantaged persons seems inconceivable.

That Mr. Wallace so completely misjudged Arthur's dedication and commitment to expanding Macalester's involvement in both innovation and in creating new opportunities for education for minority people seems equally hard to understand. But, miscalculate we did. And he did. And the resulting pain still lingers.

So let's get on with the story.

I think the stellar role in our Macalester adventure must go to Paul Davis. At the time he entered our lives, Paul Davis was Mr. DeWitt Wallace's educational consultant and adviser. It was in the mid-1960s, and Paul was then about seventy years old.

He had spent his entire career in the field of education as far as I know. He had always occupied secondary roles, never the top administrative job. I believe his most important post was as vice-president at Columbia University during the time that General Eisenhower was president of that institution. In a footnote in *At Ease*, General Eisenhower refers to him thus: "In the management and raising of money respectively my chief counselors were Joseph Campbell and Paul Davis, two men who were masters in their fields. . . . Paul Davis was the most vigorous and informed exponent of voluntary giving for education I have ever encountered."

It was while he was at Columbia that Paul made the acquaintance of Mr. Wallace, and when General Eisenhower became president of the United States, Paul began his business association with Mr. Wallace. In spite of the fact that Paul had himself never been a top administrator of any college or university, he nevertheless looked on himself as a real expert in all areas of university administration, and Mr. Wallace so regarded him too.

One day he walked into Arthur's office at the University of Oregon and announced that he'd like to talk with him about certain things that were going on at the university. Arthur had never heard of Paul Davis until that day. Paul explained that he had spent several days just walking about the campus, chatting with various faculty members and students, visiting classes, and generally looking over the campus situation. Now he was ready to talk to the president of the university. He and Arthur, in the ensuing months, spent many hours discussing the problems and opportunities in the field of education.

Arthur invited him to dinner at our house, and subsequently, he became a frequent visitor to the campus and was often a dinner guest at our house. Later he brought his wife Helen to Eugene to live, and the four of us spent many happy hours together both in our Eugene home and at our McKenzie River cottage. We had about as pleasant and congenial relationship with Paul and Helen as we have ever had with any couple we have known throughout our lives. We invited them to many a special occasion and many a football game at the university, and they always accepted immediately any suggestion we made for entertainment.

Something else happened about this time that was also to have a far-reaching effect on our lives. This was the contribution that Lila Atchison Wallace made to the University of Oregon. In the covering letter she addressed to Arthur as president of the university, she said he could use the money wherever he thought it would help. I believe the amount was ten thousand dollars.

On finding out that Lila Atchison Wallace had once attended the University of Oregon, and knowing she was the co-founder and co-publisher of the *Reader's Digest*, Arthur decided to try to interest Mrs. Wallace in giving some additional support to the university.

Several trips to the Wallace's home in Mt. Kisco, New York, during which Arthur became acquainted with Mr. Wallace also, resulted in Mrs. Wallace's giving $500,000 to the university, and then, later, a million dollars to help found the university's new School of Community Service and Public Affairs. The school was named in her honor and bears the name of the Lila Atchison Wallace School of Community Affairs and Public Service.

With the coming of Paul Davis and DeWitt Wallace into our lives, Macalester College also became an important part of our interests.

Mr. Wallace's special educational project and the recipient of considerable financial support was Macalester College. His interest in and his affection for Macalester grew out of the fact that his father, James Wallace, had taught there for many years and had also served as Macalester's president. Though he was not a college graduate, DeWitt Wallace had himself attended Macalester for a year.

Paul Davis was a life trustee of Macalester and as Mr. Wallace's paid educational consultant was actually Mr. Wallace's "voice" on the board. Arthur's actual involvement with Macalester began when Paul, backed by Mr. Wallace, asked him to go on the board of that institution. Arthur agreed, and later he assumed the chairmanship of one of the board's committees and consequently was making several trips a year to St. Paul for meetings at the college.

I well remember the day that Macalester became considerably more than a name for me. It was a glorious Sunday afternoon in the spring of 1967. We picked up Paul and Helen after church and headed up the McKenzie River highway for dinner and a few

275

hours of relaxation at our cottage. It was on this outing that Paul tossed the idea of going to Macalester at me. We had hardly reached the outskirts of Eugene when Paul, from the back seat, threw this question in my direction:

"Bernice, how would you like to go to Macalester College?"

Arthur had already told me that Paul had approached him on this matter. Paul had told Arthur that Mr. Wallace was most anxious for Arthur to go to Macalester as president—in fact, so anxious was he that should this come about he (Mr. Wallace) would stand behind (Paul's phrase) a ten-year contract of $100,000 a year, or a total of $1,000,000. What neither Paul nor Mr. Wallace understood about Arthur was that he was not to be bought at any price!

"I'll think it over," I told Paul in answer to his question. "Is there a junior college in St. Paul where I could teach?" My interest in this, of course, grew out of the fact that I was at that time teaching part-time at the Lane Community College in Eugene.

"If there isn't, we'll build one," Paul answered instantly.

Then followed some banter about the proposal that had been made to Arthur, but no really serious consideration of Paul's (i.e., Mr. Wallace's) proposition took place at that time.

A couple of months later, after continued talks with Paul about the possibility of Arthur's going to Macalester, Arthur had a conference with Mr. Wallace at his home in Mt. Kisco. We were in Old Greenwich, Connecticut, anyway, for Art's marriage to Carolyn Sherwood.

At this time Arthur made it clear to Mr. Wallace that he was not interested in the million-dollar contract offer that had been suggested; in fact, he would only consider going to Macalester if he were convinced that it offered a really exceptional educational opportunity and, further, only if the invitation to assume the presidency came to him through the normal channels of trustee, faculty, and student search-and-selection procedures.

And still neither of us gave the idea much importance at that time. We were very happy at the University of Oregon and had expected to remain there until retirement.

But the wheels started grinding in the direction of Macalester. Conferences were held with various segments of the college constituency to explore the possibility of Arthur's assuming the leadership of Macalester. Arthur also prepared a detailed program of his hoped-for plans and dreams for Macalester if he should decide to go. He presented his plans to Mr. Wallace and to Paul Davis, and he was given every reason to believe that both of them supported his innovative ideas.

One Sunday morning the proposal to go to Macalester received considerable impetus through a telephone call to Arthur from Mrs. Wallace. I was still in bed when Arthur came into the bedroom to report the purpose of the call.

That dear, generous lady had offered some very thoughtful perquisites for me if we should go to Macalester: a retirement annuity for me equal to Arthur's if he should predecease me; a car and chauffeur for my personal use; a housekeeper; and a thorough re-planning and redecoration of the president's house to suit our needs and tastes, or, a brand new house of our own choice.

She had explained to Arthur that she wanted to have the fun of making life more comfortable for me, and this was her way of doing it. Many months later, when I actually met her for the first time, she further explained to me that her own mother, as the wife of a Presbyterian minister, had had a really difficult time with few of life's amenities, and that this mental picture of her own mother's difficulties prompted her to offer to insure that life for me would be free of some of these routine problems.

I was deeply touched by her thought of me, though realizing, of course, that her thoughtful offer had nothing at all to do with Arthur's eventual decision to go to Macalester College.

The next day Arthur was away, and Paul appeared at the house in the late afternoon. We sat on the sun porch while he explained that Mr. Wallace had telephoned him and repeated the gist of Mrs. Wallace's proposals to Arthur the day before. Then he took some paper and a pencil out of his coat pocket (a customary procedure of his during almost any conversation) and began asking questions about my age, and so on, and calculating on the paper an estimate of the cost of it all. Later he took me over to his apartment for dinner with him and Helen, all the while making joking references to me as "a rich widow."

Still, Arthur kept putting off a decision. He simply couldn't make up his mind that the opportunity at Macalester equaled the one at the University of Oregon; and, for Arthur, this was the only possible reason for going to Macalester.

Paul simply couldn't understand Arthur's method of decisionmaking. On a number of occasions, in my presence, he would click off the advantages for Arthur's deciding to go. He called it an unparalleled opportunity for innovation in higher education, what with Mr. Wallace's great interest in and his generosity to Macalester. Over the past years Mr. Wallace had given approximately $35 million for buildings and special programs, scholarships, and endowment. At this point Paul would roll his eyes and say, "And, of course, there are countless millions still to come to Macalester to make it the outstanding small, private college in the United States."

Then he would reiterate his conviction (i.e., Mr. Wallace's) that Arthur was the one to lead Macalester into this dreamed-of position at the top of the private higher educational institutions in the country. He would also stress the advantage of being in the middle of the country, where Arthur could fan out to New York, Washington, Chicago, or wherever, in order to keep up with his many and varied interests.

As the weeks went by, with Arthur still struggling with the decision, Paul showed increasing signs of impatience. He questioned Jerry Kieffer (Arthur's long-time associate at ODM, HEW, and then at the University of Oregon) as to whether making up his mind was a real difficulty with Arthur and whether this difficulty was an ingrained character trait. He asked Jerry whether there was anything else Mr. Wallace could offer Arthur to make the opportunity at Macalester more attractive. He obviously had very little understanding of the motivations of Arthur. Once he displayed his impatience to Arthur himself, revealing real annoyance at Arthur's hesitancy about jumping at the Macalester opportunity.

As far as Arthur was concerned, there was another factor lurking in the background. It was his approaching enforced retirement from the presidency of the University of Oregon at sixty-five, two years hence. The proposition at Macalester included no terminal date, no specter of retirement for a man simply not geared to any sort of low-key approach to the business of living. In fact, both Paul and Mr. Wallace had talked of the Macalester opportunity in terms of a ten-year incumbency. There was strong appeal in the idea that he could continue to be actively involved in higher education for the foreseeable future, and there was a growing conviction also that leadership in a private, well-financed college would provide a really exciting opportunity to do something worthwhile.

Along with these aspects of the decision making, there was still another factor. For a couple of years there were growing tensions on college campuses all over the country relating to the Vietnam War, the civil rights struggle, increasing pressure for the students to have a voice in policymaking in educational institutions, and so on. These tensions were all present at the University of Oregon. The taxpayers were by that time taking a "use the horsewhip on the students" approach, and so was the legislature. Decreased appropriations for higher education were the threatened result.

Considering all of these aspects of the two opportunities, Arthur finally, in February, 1968, told Mr. Archie Jackson, president of the board of trustees at Macalester, that he had decided to accept Macalester's offer of the presidency and would begin his duties the following summer.

August first found the moving van unloading in front of the Macalester president's house at 1644 Summit Avenue in St. Paul. We had decided to move into the house that had been occupied for this purpose for forty years. Only absolutely necessary redecorating had been done.

Neither did we take advantage of Mrs. Wallace's offer of a car, driver, and housekeeper, as we felt we should go to Macalester on the same terms as previous presidents had. Actually, Arthur never even discussed the question of his salary with Mr. Jackson until we were about ready to move to St. Paul.

As soon as the van was unloaded and the furniture put in place we left for Miami Beach for the Republican National Convention. Arthur had been invited to give the invocation at the first evening session, probably because he was at that time serving as president of the National Council of Churches. This was the convention that nominated Richard Nixon as the Republican candidate for president to run against Hubert Humphrey, the Democratic nominee.

Later, we went to Washington for Nixon's inauguration. Harry had worked hard in the Nixon campaign, had been involved in the transition activities from the Johnson administration to the new Nixon administration, and was to continue working as a full-time member of the White House staff after the inauguration. He provided us with the tickets.

The morning after the inauguration there was to be a swearing-in ceremony of the new White House staff by the new president. Harry wanted us to stay in Washington for this event, and we were to meet him in the Executive Office Building across from the White House. Arthur was very familiar with that building since his office had been housed there for the four years that he served as director of the Office of Defense Mobilization.

We arrived at the main entrance at the time specified by Harry. However, security had been tightened since the Eisenhower years, and there was a whole new staff of security officers in charge. They asked to see Arthur's identification. He didn't have any. It actually hadn't occurred to him that he would be in a situation where he had to prove who he was and that his intentions weren't suspect.

Arthur explained to the security officer that he was Arthur Flemming and that he desired admission to the building to meet our son Harry who was to be sworn in as a member of the new White House staff. At the mention of Harry's name, things took a turn for the better. The officer knew Harry, and decided to admit Harry's parents.

Suddenly we were aware that Arthur, a former Eisenhower cabinet member, had no status of his own, but accrued status only as Harry's father. We had a good laugh over this turn of events. Such experiences do help to keep one humble!

Back to St. Paul after the Republican Convention, Arthur plunged into his new job as president of Macalester College.

He declined to have any formal inauguration ceremony and instead chose to meet with the various segments of his new constituency—faculty, students, administrators, parents, alumni, and St. Paul neighbors—in the college gymnasium in what the newspapers called an informal inauguration. He was introduced by Doctor Thomas Hill, then head of the philosophy department.

Arthur's speech on this occasion warned of change. He said that colleges and universities need to redefine their goals continually and called on all segments of the Macalester community to participate in defining and redefining objectives to make the college program more relevant to present-day living.

On taking office he said he would open many doors to Macalester. One editorial said: "Innovation and experiment are his watchwords, and he intends to thrust the college, faculty, and students into the community's more difficult problem areas."

At his first press conference Arthur said that his major task would be to help Macalester become more involved in a meaningful way in the issues confronting American society. His favorite theme song at this period was constant reference to the Kerner Commission Report on Civil Disorders. He agreed completely with the report's conclusion that White racism is the root cause of discrimination and accompanying disorders among Black citizens. He said Congress and the people generally are ducking the indictment against White racism. He said colleges and churches are doing all they can to correct problems emphasized in the Kerner Report.

The crusader was clearly present when Arthur further stated that he planned to have Macalester get involved in urban affairs programs that bring community and college together for actual benefit. He added he wanted Macalester students to be involved in public affairs and community service projects while attending college.

Speaking at a symposium at Macalester in November of 1968 on International Student Militancy, he used as his thesis that the gap between the ideal of individual worth and dignity and the actual reality had created student militancy. He cited racism, the Vietnam War, the selective service, and irrelevant education as instances of this gap. "Student activism has been a protest; it must now begin to develop programs to close the gap. But I am encouraged by student activism. I believe your generation will stay with the issues until the gap is closed."

His listeners could hardly believe their ears. One of the panelists began his statement by peering at the student audience and demanding, "My God, what kind of school is this where the college president has to tell the students to get off their asses and be activists?"

And so, in the very first weeks of Macalester's president's arrival, he set a different tone on the campus. He worked with a student-faculty committee to relax social conduct rules, laid plans to expand enrollment of disadvantaged students, and brought students into every level of decisionmaking.

He was off and running—full of ideas and dreams of leading Macalester to what Paul Davis had repeatedly said would be "the top private college in the United States, with DeWitt Wallace's financial support to help bring this about."

Concurrent with the announcement of Arthur's selection as president of Macalester was the announcement, as a result of a generous pledge from Mr. Wallace and other donors, of the establishment of the Macalester Foundation for the Advancement of Higher Education. It was to have as its primary objective the conduct of studies dealing with problems in administration that are shared by all of the nation's colleges and universities.

Special attention was to be given to administrative and experimental approaches to such issues as student involvement in the life of the educational community, development of a faculty personnel policy designed to provide maximum opportunities for keeping abreast of developments in the various fields of learning, the establishment of individualized learning programs, clarification of the role of institutions of higher learning in the area of service to society, and the effective use of technological developments in the learning process. The foundation appeared to be an exciting companion to the presidency of Macalester. To administer its program Arthur again called on his old friend Jarrold Kieffer, who came to Macalester the year after we did.

From the beginning of our St. Paul residency, a frequent visitor at our house was Paul Davis. He made a trip from the West Coast about every two months to check on how things were going. Always we would invite him to dinner, and he and Arthur would talk for hours about plans for Macalester and the new foundation. Paul never missed the opportunity to make some remark about Arthur's being the only man he'd ever offered a million dollars to, and he turned it down!

Paul never did understand what manner of man Arthur was. Nor, apparently did Mr. Wallace, whose influence, based on the power of the purse, was always lurking in the background. Paul's entire experience had been in the field of education. He had little interest, and no involvement whatever, in the world outside this field. Often, in conversation with him, I was surprised at his lack of background knowledge and understanding of current issues and problems and personalities in the public arena.

Both Paul and DeWitt Wallace, finding themselves linked with a man who was known to be deeply involved in virtually all of the issues that were producing ferment in the country, ultimately found themselves to be at odds with much of what Arthur was trying to do as far as change at Macalester College was concerned.

Others saw Arthur clearly, however, as the various editorial comments about him showed. Following are excerpts from some of the editorial columns that appeared at the time of his appointment:

> Flemming is, to an unusual degree, in touch with the great social problems, changes, and needs in America today. And as an announcement of the new Macalester Foundation for the Advancement of Higher Education indicates, he has a deep interest in understanding and improving forms of education.
>
> *The Minneapolis Tribune*

> Arthur Flemming is definitely within the mainstream of today's progressive and forward looking trends in the nation's intellectual community.
>
> Student activism generates no fear in Flemming. He welcomes campus involvement in social, political, and educational issues.

He is proud that "there has never been a time in the nation's history when the undergraduate has been so strongly involved in service activities." This, he believes, is an encouraging sign for America's future.

St. Paul Pioneer Press

Dr. Flemming has performed extraordinary services as president of the University of Oregon. All of Oregon is in his debt. His sustained energy, both intellectual and physical, has been a marvel to his associates. Dr. Flemming can look forward to many years of active leadership at Macalester.

Portland Oregonian

If there ever was a job designed for a man or a man made to perform a job, Macalester and Flemming were it. Macalester is setting out to do many of the things President Flemming has fought for in his almost seven years at the University.... For though the University will lose a remarkable president, we also realize the University's loss is education's gain. We applaud Mr. Flemming's decision because now, as possibly never before, he will be in a position to use his background, insight, and energy for the betterment of the entire educational society.

Oregon Daily Emerald
(University of Oregon student newspaper)

Arthur was hardly unpacked in St. Paul when violent civil disorders occurred after a dance at the city auditorium and the following night in the Selby-Dale area of the city, the ghetto neighborhood. Four policemen were wounded, at least fifteen persons were arrested, an estimated fifty-two persons were injured, and considerable damage was caused by fire bombings of at least four buildings.

The St. Paul Urban Coalition decided to appoint a special committee to study the disorders, and Arthur, who had been on his new job one month, was asked to head it. I well remember the day Arthur came bounding into the house to tell of this. He really welcomed this opportunity to become involved in community activity. Right off he accepted the assignment and asked only that he be assured of a high-level committee to work with him. Thus he plunged immediately into a touchy civic problem, and he attacked it with his customary vigor.

A few weeks after this, Governor LeVander announced his appointment of a governor's commission to prepare a state crime control plan and distribute grants under the federal Safe Streets and Crime Control Act. Arthur was asked to be a member of this commission.

So he very early established himself as a concerned citizen of St. Paul and of the state of Minnesota—one who could never sit by and remain in his ivory tower at Macalester while the great social issues and problems of the time fell into other hands.

It was a national election year, too, and Arthur publicly supported the election of Richard Nixon, the Republican nominee. He accepted appointment as vice-chairman of the Eisenhower Team for Nixon.

He based his support of Mr. Nixon on his association with the former vice-president during his four years as director of the Office of Defense Mobilization and his two and a-half years as secretary of Health, Education, and Welfare. It was particularly during the cabinet years that Arthur had experienced Nixon's support of his liberal proposals for new welfare and education legislation, as well as in the area of health.

Also, in an address to the final session of the Governor's Conference on Education in Minnesota, Arthur called for an educational bill of rights for ghetto children, using the education recommendations of the National Advisory Commission on Civil Disorders as his model.

On the Macalester front he was deep in plans for a new Expanded Educational Opportunity Program which would make it possible for seventy-five minority students to pursue a college education financed by funds appropriated for this purpose. He found the climate among most of the faculty and the students very receptive to the idea, and the majority of the board of trustees were in support of it, too.

At the same time, he was moving forward in his reappraisal of the student rules and conduct area.

A bit of special excitement occurred after the election. Arthur decided to approach Doctor Malcolm Moos, the president of the University of Minnesota, to see if they could work cooperatively on a proposal to invite the defeated presidential candidate, Hubert Humphrey, to return to Minnesota to teach political science classes at Macalester and at the University of Minnesota. The details were worked out, and the invitation extended. After some juggling back and forth, the then vice-president agreed to become a college teacher again. He had taught at Macalester before he was elected mayor of Minneapolis, his first political office.

It was decided to make the announcement of Mr. Humphrey's new role at a public meeting in the concert hall of the Janet Wallace Fine Arts Center on the Macalester campus on Sunday, December 15. Students, faculty, administrative officers of both institutions, friends, and members of the communications media were invited.

The day of this important announcement happened to coincide with our annual faculty reception scheduled for the hours of three to five in the afternoon. Arthur therefore invited his new faculty member and Mrs. Humphrey to join us in the receiving line at our house and to greet Macalester faculty members and their wives (or husbands) following the formal announcement of the appointment. He received an acceptance through Mr. Humphrey's office, but, as often happens in matters of this kind, he forgot to tell me about it.

My information came through the secret service representative who telephoned me on Friday afternoon to ask if he could come out and "case the house and surroundings." It was a bit of a jolt to be told that the vice-president of the United States would be coming to one's home and that proper safety precautions must be taken. Anyway, the preliminary investigation of the house and the streets immediately surrounding it was forthwith made and plans made to protect the vice-president during his time on the Macalester campus and at our house.

I was also told at that time that I must have one telephone where the vice-president could talk privately, if necessary. We had four telephones in the house: one in the kitchen, one in the library, one in the master bedroom, and one in the laundry. Since the first three would obviously be pretty much in the main lines of travel during the hours of the party, it was decided that, in case of urgency, the vice-president would have to use the phone in the laundry room. This didn't quite fit in with my ideas of decorum in such situations. Since it was Friday, however, and the party was on Sunday, there was nothing I could do about it. Fortunately, no crisis arose that required the use of our laundry room telephone plan.

It was truly a great day for Macalester and a real joy and privilege to have Vice-President and Mrs. Humphrey at our faculty party. There are few things that can spice up a routine social event such as a faculty reception any more effectively than the surprise appearance of the vice-president and his wife in the receiving line. They are two very lovable people and delighted everyone with their obvious enjoyment of the occasion.

The vice-president gave ample evidence of his pleasure over his new appointment by joining wholeheartedly in the festivities, even going out to the kitchen and personally greeting the Macalester co-eds who were helping there.

The year that Professor Humphrey spent at Macalester was a time of special ferment on all college campuses, and he was in the thick of it. One incident in which he firmly supported Arthur and the students was when a St. Paul landlord refused to rent an apartment to a Black student. The Black student charged the landlord with discrimination.

A group of Macalester students decided to picket the building where the apartment was, and both Arthur and Mr. Humphrey agreed to march with them. Just prior to the march, however, the landlord announced that he had changed his mind and would rent to the Black student.

Mr. Humphrey was the subject of some criticism on the part of a group of students who claimed he was using Macalester as a forum to promote his political ambitions. One of them became so irate that he erected a barricade around Mr. Humphrey's office to prevent him from entering. Arthur decided not to interfere, and the barricade was removed shortly by some of the more sympathetic students.

The excitement and the glamour of having a former vice-president on the faculty ended when Mr. Humphrey decided to run for the United States Senate seat to be vacated by Minnesota Senator Eugene McCarthy.

Problems began to mount the second year that we were at the Macalester campus. A particularly unfortunate development was the appointment as editor of *The Mac Weekly* of a sophomore student whose vitriolic personality, immaturity, and poor judgment spilled over into each issue of the paper, causing considerable comment and distress both on and off the campus. Repercussions even came from Mr. Wallace, who simply couldn't understand how such a character should be allowed to continue in this important post. Arthur's attitude was to defend the freedom of the press and to give the student attitudes time to work their way toward a change. To virtually everyone's great relief, this young man served only one term, but the damage he did in that short term was enormous.

He was replaced by a very capable girl as editor, who took pains to upgrade *The Mac Weekly* and really succeeded in doing so.

Then, in the spring of 1970, came the decision of President Nixon to invade Cambodia, followed by a period of tremendous turmoil on the college campuses around the country. The worst was the killing of four students at Kent State University in Ohio. Macalester had its own set of demonstrations during this period. One was a "sit in" in the business offices of the college. A group of seventy-five students occupied the building for one evening, and Arthur again insisted on "waiting it out," instead of calling the police as some of his advisers counseled and which was done in similar situations on many other campuses. After one night, the students left the building peacefully, and the damage was minimal, amounting to about $500.

The administrative staff, in a meeting to discuss the matter, was presented with a bill for $500 by the business manager, who demanded that the students involved in the "sit in" be required to pay it. Arthur said that would not be the way to deal with the matter.

"Who is going to pay for it then?" demanded the business manager. "We don't have funds for this kind of thing."

Arthur, in a rare display of anger and impatience, banged his fist on the table and said, "Give me the bill. I'll pay it." As far as I know, that is the last that was heard of that bill. Arthur never told me about this incident, but one of the staff people present did.

The Cambodian decision gave rise to other imaginative activities by the Macalester students, none of which resulted in any violence, damage, or loss of life. One was the raising of the flag up-side-down. Another was a "sit down" of about 150 students on Grand Avenue, a main thoroughfare in St. Paul which cut right through the campus. The police arrived, but instead of forcing the students to abandon their protest, they took a more tolerant approach and simply rerouted the traffic around the block. This "sit down" lasted four hours and then was peacefully abandoned.

One more instance of student activism took the form of pressure on the trustees to let the students have a voice in determining how Macalester's votes, based on stock holdings, would be cast at annual stockholders' meetings. This drive was of course aimed at expressing student views toward corporations manufacturing war materials of all kinds.

During this period there were ominous rumblings from Paul Davis. Safe in the security and comfort of his Los Angeles penthouse apartment, he freely criticized Arthur's handling of all of these incidents of student unrest. He also voiced criticism of Arthur's administration in other areas at Macalester, from the Expanded Educational Opportunity Program to the liberalized student conduct code—in fact, practically everything.

For a long time I had been feeling the growing antagonism of Paul, based on a few remarks other people had made to me, and also on a couple of incidents I was a party to. Arthur himself never discussed his own apprehensions about Paul because he never thinks or talks in negative terms about his fellow beings.

But a couple of recent visits of Paul to our house pointed out clearly to me that something was amiss. Arthur continued to invite him to dinner whenever he was in St. Paul, which was about once every two months. And Paul always accepted.

On one such occasion, after dinner, we were sitting in the living room, and this period that was normally a relaxed, friendly discussion for us all became, for Paul, an opportunity to deliver a lecture to Arthur on how he should deal with Mr. Wallace. He told Arthur he should consult Mr. Wallace more often to get Mr. Wallace's educational ideas and should take pains to implement these ideas. He took about an hour to cover all of the points in his tirade, referring all the while to the list on the paper he had taken from his coat pocket. Arthur said little. He just listened, neither arguing nor defending himself. But the atmosphere was certainly tense. I was acutely uncomfortable and really shocked that a supposedly good friend, who had accepted an invitation for dinner, would take advantage of the situation in this really unpleasant sort of way.

Later, when he was standing in the hall with his coat on and hat in hand, Paul said, "Arthur, if anyone had treated me as badly as I have treated you tonight, I certainly wouldn't invite him to dinner." Speaking out of a deep sense of outrage and hurt, I said, "Neither would I." Arthur made no reply.

On Paul's next visit to the Macalester campus, Arthur again invited him to dinner, and he accepted. And, in the living room afterward, Paul plunged in again, all the while referring to the list he took from his coat pocket. "Arthur," he began, "when I was here the last time, I gave you a lecture. I 'got by' with it, so now I'm going to give you another one."

"Shall I leave?" I asked.

"No. You stay right here," said Arthur.

So Paul launched into another hour-long lecture, this one being on Arthur as a consultative administrator. The gist of it was that, in Paul's view, Arthur was not nearly so good an exponent of consultative management as he thought he was.

Again I was rendered well-nigh speechless with shock and resentment at Paul's outspoken criticism of Arthur. That night, when he left, I suggested to Arthur that I would feel a great deal more comfortable if he ceased to invite Paul to dinner at our house.

But Arthur was still trying to figure out his motives, still not accepting my conviction that Paul was bent on "doing him in." Once, later, Arthur, who was still trying to work with Paul over resolving Macalester's various problems, asked me to have Paul at the house for dinner. I did not agree. I had had my fill of Paul Davis and had no intention of listening to another one of his hour-long lectures about Arthur's shortcomings, as seen by Paul.

Paul's criticisms of Arthur were not confined to our living

room. He was sowing discord throughout the Macalester community, pitting person against person, and group against group. Many persons told me later that this had been a technique of his used over and over through the years of his association with the college. As a result, considerable ill feeling was generated among faculty and students whom Paul had sought out and talked with.

A story in the newspapers appeared in May of 1970 that indicated that Mr. Wallace had asked Paul to reappraise his giving in education, particularly his giving to Macalester. In it Paul was quoted as saying that "the review was a perfectly normal one," but added that higher education "is under scrutiny and surveillance by donors as never before."

In the same story Mr. Wallace was quoted as saying that "he had been displeased about a few things at the college" (i.e., Macalester) but added "there is no basis whatever for reports that he is thinking of cutting his endowments to Macalester College." There is likewise no question that Mr. Wallace had become increasingly unable to understand student activism at Macalester.

Other stories similar to the one quoted above appeared, and as a result, campus gossip and unrest as to the future was rampant. When I read these stories I asked Arthur if he wanted to leave Macalester. He said, "No," but I told him I was ready and anxious to go the minute he said the word.

In December Arthur told me he was going to leave Macalester. The only question was when. I was delighted.

There was a meeting of the board of trustees scheduled for late January. Arthur was in Washington a couple of days before it. He telephoned me and read the statement he had prepared. It was a simple request to be retired as president of Macalester at the end of the current academic year.

That night I was scheduled to speak at the mid-winter meeting of the Macalester Faculty Women's Club and had been invited to be the guest of the board for dinner prior to the meeting. I had little heart for the occasion, but I think I managed to conduct myself so that my heavy heartedness did not show. I talked about the junior college development in the field of education, and it apparently went over well.

Paul Davis was in St. Paul during that entire week. Prior to the college's board meeting, he gave the newspapers a story about Mr. Wallace's decision to cut off all giving to Macalester. He also gave a televised interview about the matter and appeared to relish his role as the spokesman for Macalester's great benefactor. On Paul's recommendation, Mr. Wallace had also decided to abolish the Macalester Foundation, thus smashing the dreams of those participating in that program, particularly Jerry Kieffer.

Arthur's resignation and the cutting off of Mr. Wallace's giving were inevitably linked, with the newspapers speculating wildly about the whys of both.

I was driving home after my classes at the Normandale Junior College the afternoon that Arthur's statement of his request for retirement became public. I had the car radio tuned in to the Twin Cities' talk station. Listening to it was my customary diversion during my half-hour drive home. I grew more and more depressed as I listened to caller after caller tell the WOL communicator how glad they were that Arthur was leaving Macalester. It comforted me very little to reflect on the fact that many callers who air their hates on talk shows are, for the most part, unstable people. I later learned that the station had devoted the better part of the day airing the views of irate callers complaining about sex and permissiveness at Macalester, about which they had no factual information whatsoever.

When I got home and turned on editorialist Moore's evening newscast, I again had to listen to (no, I didn't have to— I just did) distortions and innuendos about the developments at Macalester. The editorialist used his time to make one unkind (and untrue) statement after another about Arthur.

Arthur refused to clarify or add to his original statement of his retirement request. Moreover, he didn't at that time know what he would do when we left Macalester, though several ideas had been presented to him, all in the field of government.

The day of the board meeting at which Arthur's request to be retired was presented, Decker Anstrom, the president of the Macalester College Council, the student government organization, asked to be recognized. Mr. Jackson, the board chairman, granted him the floor.

Decker read a lengthy statement dealing with many things: he told of the many constructive aspects of student activism at Macalester, including the improvement in Black-White relationships; he expressed gratitude for the many programs that Mr. Wallace had provided support for in the past; and then he launched into a critical appraisal of Mr. Davis's role at Macalester College. He made reference to Mr. Davis's statement to the press that Macalester was spreading itself too thin trying to educate top students and bottom students, many of whom he said "would end up as gas pumpers and secretaries."

Mr. Davis had also told the press that he doubted that Macalester was the place to offer educational opportunities to disadvantaged students.

Decker pointed out that Mr. Davis's statements were at variance with the actual facts and indicated that he (i.e., Mr. Davis) really didn't understand what Macalester was. He wound up his remarks by suggesting that Mr. Davis should terminate his association with Macalester College.

This was an act of real courage on Decker's part. Many people in the college community expressed similar views in private, but Decker's was the only voice raised in public against Paul Davis.

Because of his position as the president of the Macalester College Council, Decker Anstrom and Arthur became well acquainted. Decker had many one-to-one conferences with Arthur, and he was also present at many meetings of the board of trustees, as well as faculty sessions where Macalester problems were discussed. He was a well-informed participant in discussions of college business during that last year we were at Macalester.

Later, when Arthur became the full-time chairman of the White House Conference on Aging, he set up a special youth delegate group to assist him with the planning of the conference. Decker was one of those selected to work in that capacity. Decker was therefore in a unique position to observe Arthur in two distinct roles: that of a college president during very troubled times, and as a bureaucrat planning and presiding over a high-level national conference. He formed some, I think, quite valid impressions growing out of these intimate contacts. The following is quoted from a letter Decker wrote me after his graduation from Macalester:

> He [i.e., Arthur] has always shown the inclination to treat younger people, with much less experience and knowledge than himself, as his peers. As such he shows an unlimited ability to accept new interpretations, ideas, and suggestions. I think that this is the one thing that keeps him so young himself. Given his knowledge, experience, etc., it would be very easy for him to be patronizing to younger people, but I have never noticed this. Throughout my experience at Macalester he was completely open to all students and their ideas, and I've seen the same thing with the young people involved with the Conference on Aging. Young people, I think, immediately sense this about him, and this is perhaps the major reason he has such outstanding rapport with them. They know that he respects them as human beings, not young human beings, but human beings.
>
> I might add that he shows this with all people, especially with minority groups. In a very real sense this is the way he demonstrates his belief in the potential of every human being— he hears them and their concerns, not just listens to them. (I hope you understand the difference; it is important in my mind.) As a result,

he is one of the few people completely free from prejudice that I know.

He always seems to have an optimistic view of life. While I know there have to be times when he is not happy (at least I think so) I've never really seen one. Put simply, his actions seem to follow a love of life and a joy in living it that is contagious to others, because he reveals the infinite possibilities before people, and keeps his eye on these, rather than the things that would lead one to despair.

He is a man who insists on action now . . . not that he down-grades planning or philosophy, but rather he has the vision and courage (I'd especially emphasize that) to do things now! As examples: (a) he could have gone slower on the EEO program at Macalester, but he moved quickly and forcefully. He must have known the risks and possible reactions from more conservative voices who would caution slower, slower, but he went ahead, with courage.

(b) On the Rights and Freedoms Document at Mac, he could have placated faculty opposition by slowing down the drafting of the document, or after it was passed, he could have downplayed it with trustees, instead of always defending it to them, and probably could have avoided student reaction on both counts. But he did not —he saw a need and moved to correct it.

(c) He could have kept his opposition to the war in lower profile, and thus placated some trustees and the St. Paul community, but he did not.

(d) He could have, after Paul took care of things (i.e., recom-mended to Mr. Wallace that he discontinue his giving to Macalester, and Mr. Wallace's subsequent action to do that), avoided the difficult job of cutting 20% of Mac's budget for last year, and passed that horrible job on to his successor, but he did not. He knew that it had to be done, he did it, and though not becoming popular for taking on such a thankless task, performed a real service for the college.

I think this is really the real key—he is no doubt a mystery to most of his friends, I think, in a lot of ways, but I think that underlying everything he does is an impatience with those who caution to go slowly, don't risk anything, or at least not too much, and even more, a full and deep intolerance for injustice. Seeing so much injustice, and feeling it so deeply, he can't go slowly, but must act now, not tomorrow! As such, there is a little bit of the old revival preacher in him, and that I like a lot!

The "preacher" in him, plus a lot of other things, leads to a kindness, a gentleness, a compassion, a concern for people, that transcends all of his activities. His passion and concern strikes everyone he comes into contact with, and I guess all I can do is state that—but I've seen it in thousands of cases, with thousands of people.

I have quoted Decker's letter to me at such length because I consider it a very perceptive appraisal. I am indebted to him for sharing his insights with me.

To return to that famous January board meeting at Macalester, Arthur's request for retirement was approved, and a committee was appointed to search for a new president of the college.

A couple of days later the Black students reacted by calling a press conference of their own. They charged that the Expanded Educational Opportunity Program resulted in the "forced and untimely resignation of President Flemming because of his strong support of the EEO program." They appealed to the board of trustees to rescind their action of approving Arthur's resignation. But it was obviously too late for that.

One of Macalester's administrative officers, Fred Kramer, the dean of students, also went to bat for Arthur. He drew up a detailed statement for the Student Life Committee of the board of trustees. He spoke of his own anger and frustration over the recent events on the Macalester campus and included these paragraphs:

> To many, President Flemming's leaving is a verification of the futility of working for and advocating reform and ordered change. When a man of commitment, moral courage, and vision, and rare insight into student concerns can be cut down, it is hard for students to be encouraged about any efforts or leadership for productive

change that they can offer.

It is ironic that some came to equate President Flemming with radical change and a threat to the established order when he along with men like John Gardner are so totally committed to the reform of our established institutions so that these institutions can be preserved. President Flemming has worked tirelessly with students to help them find ways to channel their deeply felt concerns through established structures both in the college and in society.

It was not until late April that we knew for sure what new direction our lives would take. For a year Arthur had been serving as chairman of the planning committee for the upcoming White House Conference on Aging. (He had been chairman of the first White House Conference on Aging ten years earlier when he was secretary of Health, Education, and Welfare.)

There was a general feeling among interested groups that the plans being made for the second conference were getting bogged down in political maneuverings, and some powerful groups were actually threatening to boycott.

The president took note of this and decided to ask Arthur to assume the chairmanship of the conference on a full-time basis in an effort to turn it around to a really important and constructive conference. Thus it came about that once more we headed for Washington.

The rest of that academic year was uneventful. As soon as the decision to return to Washington had been made, I tended to have a somewhat detached feeling about the goings-on at Macalester, and instead turned my thoughts to finding a house for us in the capital city area.

As the college year drew to a close, a particularly heart-warming development was the invitation extended to Arthur by the seniors to be their commencement speaker. The two previous graduating classes had voted not to have any speaker at all.

Arthur was introduced by Jeff Goltz, the chairman of the senior commencement committee. In telling of the reasons why the seniors had voted for Arthur as their speaker, Jeff said:

> We have selected him because he has meant a lot to us and has
> done a lot for us in the last three years. I am not speaking of any
> particular program or set of programs or of any procedure or set of
> procedures that he helped to institute at Macalester, although these
> have been important to us. I am speaking rather of an attitude he
> has conveyed to us—a feeling, a style. It is a style that is always
> optimistic, always forward-looking, always positive. If we have
> picked up just a little of this, then we have profited greatly from his
> presence. It is this positive forward-looking style, coupled with his
> creativeness in education, that has made Doctor Flemming mean-
> ingful to us.
>
> The class of 1971 is proud to present as its commencement
> speaker one of our greatest teachers, one of our most innovative
> educators, and one of our best friends, Doctor Arthur Flemming.

Sitting down in the audience, I am sure I clapped louder and
longer than anyone else there!

Announcement was also made at the commencement of the
establishment of an endowed scholarship honoring Arthur, to be
awarded to a minority student from a Minnesota high school.
This was a complete surprise to Arthur, though Decker had told
me about it earlier. In announcing the scholarship, Kathy Cooper,
a Black student from Richmond, Virginia, cited Arthur's "Christian concern for and life-long advocacy of equal opportunity for
all people." The students could not have chosen to honor him in
any more appropriate way or in any way more pleasing to him.

And so, out of our lives went Macalester College, Paul Davis,
and Mr. Wallace. I still find it hard to understand how Mr.
Wallace, who was so anxious to have Arthur at Macalester that
he offered to support a million-dollar salary offer, plus extensive
additional perquisites, and then, a couple of years later, could
willingly conspire to "pull the rug" from under him without so
much as a single word of explanation or apology. Not a single
word. But he did.

I should add that Arthur contends, and always will, that Macalester's faculty, students, and alumni constitute one of the nation's strongest liberal arts colleges. He had some problems, but he also had the benefit of some outstanding associations.

The last time Arthur saw the Wallaces was a chance encounter at Whitney Young's funeral. As a member of the board of the National Urban league, as well as a good personal friend of Whitney's, Arthur was invited to his funeral in the spring of 1971 and to sit in the front of the church with the members of the league's board. At the conclusion of the service, the members of the board walked down the aisle behind the family. As he neared the rear of the church, Arthur noticed Mr. and Mrs. Wallace sitting close to the aisle. He stopped, leaned over, and shook hands with them both. Didn't I say before that Arthur never held a grudge against anybody?

Before I leave the Macalester years, I must include in my recital of events Arthur's extracurricular activities on the national level. His third and final year as president of the National Council of Churches was after we went to Macalester, with Arthur continuing to push for social action by the council and its member denominations. One of his more colorful experiences was when James Forman, one of the most vocal Black civil rights leaders, made his demands, using the politics of confrontation as his vehicle, for reparations from the churches for years of neglect of the problems of the Negro citizens. Much division among church leaders followed Forman's seemingly unreasonable demands, but Arthur took the view that, in spite of Forman's tactics, his demands deserved attention and consideration. The council, urged by Arthur, made substantial appropriations for people in the ghettos, and one denomination after another followed suit.

His term came to an end in Detroit, in December, 1969. The air was charged with controversy over issues and also over who should be elected as the council's new president. The nominating committee had agreed to support Doctor Cynthia Wedel, a prominent Episcopal lay woman and long an active leader in the work of the council. Black militants were there in force and threw the assembly into temporary confusion by trying to take over the business proceedings. Their demand was to present a resolution that would pledge the council never again (as had happened previously in connection with advocates of the Black Manifesto) to use police force to intervene in matters regarding use of church money for the poor.

One emotionally disturbed participant at one session threw some red paint, spotting Arthur's dark blue suit, but Arthur paid no attention whatsoever.

I felt an immense sense of relief when Arthur turned over the gavel to Cynthia Wedel at the conclusion of the tri-annual meeting.

The National Conference on Social Welfare had elected him to be its president while we were still at the University of Oregon, but his term did not actually begin until after we were in St. Paul. This organization, which at that time was composed of some eight thousand members of professional social worker organizations, had traditionally been simply a sort of forum to discuss broad issues and problems in the field of social welfare. For the ninety-five years of its existence it had in no sense ever been an activist group of people.

But ferment was taking place in that body, too, just as it was in most other interest groups around the country. So, concurrent with Arthur's election, change in the emphasis of the National Conference on Social Welfare became the watchword of the more activist elements.

The big organized push was for change as far as welfare recipients was concerned, with a newly organized group called the Welfare Rights Organization leading the way.

During the months preceding the 1969 conference Arthur

made many trips to Columbus to confer with the executive secretary, Joe Hoffer, and the executive board, and to plan the agenda for the conference. And when the time for the annual meeting came around, a forward-looking program had been agreed on.

The conference was held late in May at the Hilton Hotel in New York City. We arrived at the hotel around noon on Sunday, with the opening session scheduled for that evening. Mr. Hoffer immediately told Arthur about the warnings he had received that serious trouble was brewing. The air was literally charged with threats from minority groups pushing for special consideration. The New York police had been alerted to stand by in case of trouble. In an era of confrontation politics, anything might happen.

Our Tom was a delegate to the conference, and he and I went to the ballroom together for the opening session. It was plain that trouble was in the air when we saw that the podium was completely surrounded by a ring of people three deep—mostly young, both Black and White.

We took a seat near the front, but as the seven-thirty opening hour approached, it was clear that the orderly process of convention opening, with the president's keynote speech, was not likely to proceed.

The several hundred angry young militants milling about were out to break up the convention. The group included students, new organizations of militant social workers, and a large number from the newly organized Welfare Rights Organization, made up of welfare mothers. This group was under the direction of dashiki-clad Doctor George Wiley, a former chemistry professor of Syracuse University, who had left his teaching job to lead this new group.

They proceeded to hold the delegates captive for about three hours while they shouted from the microphone a list of demands and then solicited contributions. They said that nobody was going to leave the ballroom until thousands of dollars had been collected so that more of the poor could attend such conventions. They blocked off all of the exits so that none of the delegates could leave. And then women welfare recipients marched up and down the aisles passing plastic ice buckets for contributions.

They also demanded $25,000 from the convention registration fees to help organize welfare recipients.

Finally, hotel personnel removed the temporary dividing wall around the part of the ballroom where the people were seated, and this made it possible for the captive delegates to move about.

During all of this time Arthur was nowhere to be seen. Tom and I imagined that he was probably being held captive back stage somewhere. He and the other members of the board had made no attempt whatever to mount the platform. We had no way of knowing that he was seated in the rear of the ballroom.

About ten-thirty, after Arthur and the board members had agreed to listen to the demands of the militants, the ninety-sixth annual forum of the National Conference on Social Welfare got under way, with Arthur mounting the podium to deliver his keynote speech. His title was "An Action Platform for Human Welfare."

The chaos was not over with this confrontation staged by Wiley and his welfare mothers. They set the stage for others to do likewise, and a veritable procession of protestors followed during the ensuing four days of the conference—Black social workers, Spanish-speaking people, militant students, and even a Native American shouted various complaints. One after another they grabbed the microphone and made their demands insistently. It was a time of almost continuous confrontations and then conciliations.

The Washington Post described the failure to silence the militants as a conscious strategy of Flemming. It said that "despite contrary advice from some of his board, he wanted to keep the avenues of communication wide open, and by not stopping anyone from speaking, prevent the possibility of violence."

He actually was really proud of the fact that he managed, by keeping the convention open, to avoid resorting to police interference. It was "touch-and-go" every step of the way.

Again, as with the completion of his term as president of the National Council of Churches, I felt a great sense of relief when Arthur turned the gavel over to the newly elected president, the ex-secretary of Health, Education, and Welfare, Wilbur Cohen.

The next day, Friday, Arthur and I went up to Mt. Kisco for luncheon with the Wallaces. It was pure delight for both of us to spend a few hours in relaxed association with these two citizens who have given so much generous support to good causes. We had absolutely no inkling at that time of what was ahead at Macalester that would completely alter this relationship.

The third national organization Arthur was to lead during this period was the American Council on Education. This organization, too, was in the middle of ferment, and its fifty-second annual meeting, which was the one that elected Arthur chairman, had as its theme, "The Campus and Racial Crisis."

The council includes among its 1,600 members some 1,345 accredited private and public colleges and universities, plus organizations and associations in the higher education field. It acts as a coordinating agency for higher education.

The program of the 1970 meeting, over which Arthur presided, had as its theme "Higher Education for Everybody? Issues and Implications." This grew out of a recognition of the necessity to remove all barriers to equality of opportunity in the United States and that this goal must include steps to make post-secondary education accessible to anyone who might profit by it. Again Arthur was in the forefront of change, though the council convention produced no militancy or confrontations such had been the daily diet at the National Conference on Social Welfare.

Two of Arthur's other extracurricular activities during the Macalester years deserve mention: his election to the board of the National Urban League, and his chairmanship of a commission to study the operation of the Social Security system (provided by the Congress every four years) and to make recommendations for change that are deemed desirable by the commission.

The church was not forgotten either. When the National Council of Churches' presidency was over, he was able to turn his attention to a project being developed in Minnesota—that of chairing a group of top-level leaders of all faiths who were trying to develop plans for church unity in that state.

The last days in St. Paul were devoted to the Macalester commencement activities. On our final evening in the Macalester president's house we had two callers. One was Archie Jackson, the president of the board of trustees, who came simply to say goodbye and to wish us well in our new venture.

The other was Robert Rose, the president of the Macalester Alumni Association. Bob brought a gift for Arthur—an iron turtle. Accompanying the turtle was a card on which Bob had written, "The only way a turtle makes progress is to stick his neck out." That turtle has been on the floor of our living room ever since. I am not likely to forget Bob Rose.

Arthur began his new responsibilities with the White House Conference on Aging on a full-time basis immediately. Mid-June found us moving into our new home in Alexandria, Virginia.

We had been living in "public" buildings for ten years. We were really delighted to be in a home of our own again.

14

A NEW CRUSADE: THE OLD FOLKS

T hose ten years of living in so-called "public" houses (i. e., houses provided for us by the institution Arthur was serving as president) were not without their compensations. The house the state of Oregon provided for the president of the university was a really beautiful home, situated on a magnificently land-scaped site a short distance from the university. Outside it was cared for by a full-time gardener, and inside I had the help of a full-time housekeeper. Oregon's long rainy season guarantees that all growing things are lush and abundant.

In the spring, a look outside our bedroom window provided a view of a huge, shapely, pink hawthorne tree, one of the most glorious sights I've ever seen. In the winter, a giant holly tree laden with red berries was another annual treat. In January, the daphne bushes along the rear of the house provided another special experience. We would cut some of the branches and bring them into the house as buds, and as the buds opened the house was filled with a heavenly aroma. Treats like these are not found many places.

In St. Paul we were also provided with a handsome house to live in, but the surrounding grounds in no way compared with our Eugene home. Nor did we have a gardener and housekeeper. One of the college maintenance men cut the grass, but that was all.

So, when President Nixon asked Arthur to come to Washington to assume the full-time chairmanship of the upcoming White House Conference on Aging, finding a house to live in required thorough investigation. Harry lived in Alexandria, and he insisted that Alexandria was by all odds the most desirable of the suburban areas. I made a number of trips from St. Paul to look for a suitable house. Arthur was determined that we must have a house large enough for our children, grandchildren, and their friends to visit us. A five-bedroom house in the west end of the city was our eventual choice, and we moved back to the capital city area in June of 1971.

Arthur began his new duties as chairman of the White House Conference the first of June. That same month President Nixon made a speech in which he said:

> What we must build in this country—among all our people—is a new attitude toward old age; an attitude which insists that there can be no retirement from living, no retirement from responsibility, and no retirement from citizenship.

Arthur agreed wholeheartedly with the president, and this became his new crusade. He took as his theme song that today's older Americans want and deserve what younger Americans simply take for granted. In speech after speech he said, "They want to be involved in life in a meaningful way. They want to be part of the mainstream."

Arthur had chaired the first White House Conference on Aging in 1961 when he was secretary of Health, Education, and Welfare ten years earlier under President Eisenhower. Some six hundred recommendations came out of that conference, and some of them led to major changes. These included Medicare, Medicaid, and the Older Americans Act of 1965, which set up the Administration on Aging to coordinate federal old-age programs. But, still, the conference fell short of expectations, with many of the six hundred recommendations forgotten.

Arthur saw in the new chairmanship of the second White House Conference on Aging an opportunity to try again to help stem the depressing human erosion so apparent among the aging. His hope for the conference was to help put more money in the hands of older citizens, and pay more attention to their needs. He also saw in it an opportunity to restore the faith of older Americans in their society, instead of simply alienating and frustrating them.

He undertook his new assignment in a climate of deep discouragement on the part of many people working on the plans for the conference.

One problem was a row over gubernatorial choice of people to make the expense-paid trip to Washington. Originally, the governors were asked to suggest a specific number of official delegates to the conference, ranging from fourteen from smaller states to 125 from New York and California. Then they were told to raise their state totals by 50 percent.

National organizations with an interest in older people were also naming some 780 delegates.

This led to charges that Washington officials were going to rig the conference voting by selecting state delegations unlikely to disagree with the Nixon administration.

Arthur attacked this by addressing a special letter to the governors explaining the reason for the request for extra names. He told the governors that the request for additional names was made because of the possibility that some people would be named by both their governor *and* a national organization to which they belong, in which case the governor could select another delegate. To combat charges that the conference agenda was rigged, Arthur decided to have an Open Forum Night on the twenty-ninth of November. "We must make certain that the information available to the delegates is as complete as possible. We must not overlook any group or any organization that wants to be heard, or any point of view that needs to be expressed," he said. And he promised that the meeting would "run as long as necessary so that all may be heard."

To chair the Open Forum he invited one of the country's most distinguished elder citizens, former Chief Justice of the United States Earl Warren who agreed to act as chairman. Both Arthur and Mr. Warren agreed that the older people must have a chance to air their ideas and needs, whatever they were—better health care programs, nutrition, transportation, job opportunities, or anything else.

Arthur also visited during the summer and fall many of the state Conferences on Aging, and he also set up regional meetings throughout the country. Another idea of his was to involve the young people in the planning process and in the upcoming conference itself. Accordingly, more than one hundred people between the ages of seventeen and twenty-four were invited to the regional meetings to prepare for the conference, two from each state and territory. At each meeting, Arthur undertook to orient the youth delegates to the purposes of the conference. He described their special role during the conference as one to help bridge the gap between their generation and the twenty million older Americans.

In October, he sought the help of nearly four hundred voluntary agencies dealing with problems of the aging and invited them to participate in the planning. At a pre-conference meeting in Washington, more than 250 representatives of 175 national organizations responded to his invitation and agreed to launch a program with the ultimate goal of making all needed home services available and accessible to older people wherever they may live.

The 1971 conference began on Sunday, November 28, and was quite definitely a working conference. Its job was to build, in three and a half days, the framework for a national policy on aging to guide programs for older people during the decade to follow.

It was organized into fourteen sections, one for each of the major conference subject areas, and included such topics as

Aging and Blindness, Mental Health Care Strategies and Aging, Aging and Aged Blacks, Aging Migrants, The Poor Elderly, Rural Older People, Youth and Age, The Religious Community and the Aging, and Volunteer Roles for Older People.

Arthur opened the conference by calling on the delegates to make personal commitments to effect change in society's attitudes toward the elderly, and he called for action instead of rhetoric, on the problems of the elderly.

"Policy proposals in the field of aging that are not backed up by sound programs for action," he told the thirty-five hundred delegates, "are nothing more than 'sounding brass.'"

Arthur had stressed the need for action earlier the same day during an appearance on "Meet the Press."

In addition to the working sessions each day, cabinet members and top executive officials in the federal government spoke at luncheon meetings.

The president himself came to the conference on the last day and outlined the program he intended to press for that would help the nation's elderly citizens to have a better life. Nixon pledged vigorous action to secure adequate income for older Americans through tax relief, pension reforms, and other efforts. He urged support of his welfare reform bill (HR 1), which would establish a national floor under the income of all older persons. He said he was going to recommend an appropriation of $100 million for nutrition programs.

During his talk he also made a public announcement that he intended to have Arthur, after the conference, join the White House staff as his personal consultant on aging.

And, on this note, the 1971 White House Conference on Aging ended, and the job of implementation of its recommendations began.

A few days later Arthur received a personal letter from the president thanking him for his "outstanding leadership in connection with the White House Conference on Aging" and adding "I think the overall impact of the conference was positive and encouraging, and your efforts in spearheading this unique meeting deserves the gratitude of all our fellow Americans."

It was decided to hold a formal "swearing in" ceremony for Arthur as the White House consultant on aging on January 11, 1972. Harry, Sue and John, and our Parker grandchildren, Charlie, Beth, and John, joined us in the president's office for this occasion.

The president began the ceremony by making a heart-warming speech about why he wanted Arthur to be his special consultant on aging. He spoke of Arthur's experience in other top government positions, and his experience in the field of education. He talked about his commitment in the field of helping older people, and he pointed to the fact that Arthur was one of the most tenacious people he knew in pursuing the goals he set for improving the lot of these citizens. He said:

> I am delighted to be gaining the services of this distinguished public servant. No one in the United States today is more qualified to raise the voice [i.e., of older Americans] forcefully and persuasively than Arthur Flemming. He will advise us on the whole range of concerns relating to older persons; he will pursue aggressively, as my representative, the goals of better implementation and tighter coordination of all federal activities in the field of aging. He will continue as a member of our cabinet-level domestic council committee on aging, and he will also continue as chairman of the White House Conference on Aging during the crucial post-conference year—the year of action.

For me, the "swearing-in" ceremony was especially noteworthy because, for the first time in four such occasions (the Civil Service Commission, the Office of Defense Mobilization, and the Department of Health, Education, and Welfare) the president asked me to hold the Bible when Arthur repeated the oath of office, which was administered by Judge Thomas A. Flannery, of the United States District Court for the District of Columbia.

Then, afterward, the president gave me the Bible that was used. He had previously inscribed that same Bible to Arthur. He gave each one of the adults and children a momento too. It was an impressive occasion indeed. And when he went to bed that night Charlie (nine at the time) told his mother that it had been the greatest day of his life!

One more thoughtful gesture to me was that I later received through the mail a picture of the "swearing-in" ceremony personally inscribed by the president.

We left the White House and walked through Lafayette Square to the Hay-Adams House for lunch. We had a good time talking it all over with the Parker children.

Later Arthur and I walked downtown together—he to his office, and I to pick up the car and go home. He was deep in thought.

Then he said, "This January is better than last January."

And it certainly was!

One of the major programs conceived and carried out by Arthur during the post-conference year was called Project Find. This program was under the personal sponsorship of Mrs. Nixon and was a nationwide government project to seek out elderly Americans who were eligible for, but unaware of the food stamp program.

The American Red Cross accepted Arthur's invitation to become the lead agency in the private sector. Many other national organizations joined the Red Cross in enlisting volunteers for this program. Arthur was delighted at the success of this joint public sector-private sector effort. Project Find was the forerunner of SSI-Alert, which was launched by Arthur as commissioner on aging after the passage of the Supplementary Security Insurance Program in 1972 in order to find the aged, blind, and disabled who had been made eligible for the program by the Congress.

A special treat for us that year, too, was the privilege of acting as host and hostess for Mrs. Nixon on one of her cruises for special groups down the Potomac River on the presidential yacht, the *Sequoia*. A group of older Americans from the American Association of Retired Persons and the National Association of Retired Teachers participated in the inaugural cruise on June 5, 1972. Luncheon was served on the *Sequoia*, there was musical entertainment, artists drawing sketches of participants, and a Polaroid souvenir photograph given as a momento to each person. It was a beautiful day and a delightful experience for us all.

Soon after President Nixon's election for his second term, all presidential appointees (excluding those appointed for specified terms) were summoned to the White House and advised that they should submit their *pro forma* resignations. From then on there were rumors about high-ranking public officials whose resignations were being accepted, and other rumors about who would replace them.

As the weeks passed, and Arthur had no word that his letter of resignation had been accepted, we began to think that—maybe—he would be continued in his post as White House consultant on aging.

Then, word came to him that the president had accepted the resignation of John B. Martin, the commissioner on aging, and that he was going to appoint Arthur to that spot.

Finally, on April 12, 1973, the White House announced Arthur's nomination to be the United States commissioner on aging.

On the day of the announcement, Health, Education, and Welfare Secretary Weinberger issued a statement expressing pleasure over Arthur's nomination. "I warmly welcome the president's action to bring Arthur Flemming back to HEW,"

Secretary Weinberger said. "His long and valuable service in the top councils of government, plus his warm, humanitarian instincts, make certain that he will give valuable service to our older people in particular and to our country in general. No better man could be found in or out of public life to head up the aging program then Arthur Flemming."

Arthur's name was sent to the Committee on Labor and Public Welfare of the Senate, but they did not get around to considering it until May 10. The chairman, Senator Harrison Williams of New Jersey, asked Arthur if he would like to make an opening statement, and Arthur responded by reviewing his recent experience as chairman of the White House Conference on Aging, as White House consultant on aging, and expressing his deep interest in the opportunity the appointment to be commissioner on aging afforded to help this large segment of American citizens.

The chairman asked a question or two, which Arthur answered briefly. Then, beginning with Senator Javits, each member of the investigating committee, in turn, made a complimentary statement about Arthur's fitness for the appointment and expressed their confidence in him. Even Senator Jennings Randolph, who was not present at the hearing, had sent a statement lauding Arthur's appointment.

The committee, and later the full Senate, approved his nomination without a dissenting vote.

On June 19, 1973, he was sworn in as United States commissioner on aging at ceremonies in the reception room of Secretary Weinberger. And then he moved back to the HEW building to begin his new duties. Apparently it troubled him not at all to return there to serve in a considerably lesser capacity than he had served in during President Eisenhower's administration.

Congress had amended the Older Americans Act in such a manner as to bring a National Aging Network into existence consisting of state and area agencies on aging. Both the state and area agencies had the responsibility of developing plans, under guidelines, for comprehensive programs in the field of aging.

Congress not only created this National Aging Network, but it also provided for increased financial support for the needs of older Americans. In addition, the network worked with a wide range of senior and professional advocacy organizations across the country, and a large group of citizens were drawn into active participation in policy and decision making.

Momentum in the field of aging continued to speed up when Arthur began his job as administrator of the Office on Aging. With twenty-nine million people sixty years of age and older in the nation, Arthur kept pushing for more help for those older persons whose incomes were below the poverty guidelines.

By mid-summer of 1974 the government's new $100 million nutrition program was serving over two hundred thousand meals five days a week at forty-seven hundred sites. This compared with twenty thousand the previous year.

Arthur also supported volunteer programs for the elderly and pressed for new programs to teach new careers to older people in community service areas. More adequate health service for the elderly was another of his concerns, and he supported a proposal for a national health insurance program for all age groups.

Because of his status as a former HEW secretary, plus his personal experience and expertise, Arthur was an outstanding advocate for older persons. Many of the professionals in the field of aging gave Arthur credit for high achievement in improving life for the elderly.

Arthur reached the mandatory retirement age of seventy during President Ford's administration. Both President Ford, and later President Carter, issued waivers to permit him to continue his public responsibility beyond that age.

With the new administration of President Carter in early 1977, the job of commissioner on aging was a so-called political plum to be awarded to a "deserving" Democrat. Finally, after a year of searching for a replacement for Arthur, the choice was duly announced, and confirmation proceedings concluded. On February 16, 1978, Robert C. Benedict, former commissioner of the Pennsylvania Office for the Aging, was sworn in with appropriate ceremony.

Secretary Califano used the occasion to honor Arthur with a distinguished public service award, the HEW Department's highest accolade. Secretary Califano praised Arthur for representing "the nation's elderly with uncommon zeal, dedication, and wisdom."

Bob Benedict was young enough to be Arthur's grandson (well, almost, anyway), and he frequently got in touch with Arthur for advice in dealing with various agency problems. At the end of his three years of service as commissioner on aging, Bob wrote Arthur a letter expressing in the highest terms his appreciation for all the advice and help Arthur had given him. This, I submit, is a really unusual relationship to exist between two high-level bureaucrats, one the replacement for the other, and of different political parties.

One more honor came to Arthur during Secretary Califano's term. The Department of Health, Education, and Welfare inaugurated a Distinguished Speaker Series in January of 1978 and named the series in honor of Arthur and Wilbur J. Cohen, a former Democratic incumbent in the office of secretary the latter part of the Johnson administration.

Tom went with me to the opening lecture by Congresswoman Shirley Chisholm, of New York. It was a real thrill to sit in the HEW auditorium on this occasion facing the giant banner in HEW colors with "FLEMMING-COHEN DISTINGUISHED LECTURE SERIES" as the backdrop for the platform guests.

With his formal responsibilities as commissioner on aging

over, Arthur immediately plunged into work on an idea he had about careers for older people. Aided by support from the Clark Foundation, obtained by Merrill Clark, vice-president of the Academy for Educational Development, he formed a National Committee on Careers for Older Americans. The Foundation enabled him to hire top-level experts to prepare a report. He was assisted by his long-time associate, Jarold Kieffer, as staff director. A committee of non-paid members representing leaders in industry, labor, education, and government helped him.

The report that resulted was entitled, "Jobs for Older Americans: An Untapped Resource," and includes this statement: "Employers— both private and public—can judge older people not on the basis of their age, but on their merits as individuals. If they do, many will be encouraged to remain on the job. Others will be encouraged to become workers again on a full- or part-time basis. Approximately four million non-working older people have indicated an interest in such possibilities.''

Early in 1980, attention began to focus on the third decennial White House Conference on Aging, scheduled to be held in late November-early December. A reception to launch the plans was held on March 26, 1980, and at that time President Carter announced that he was appointing Sadie Alexander, an eighty-year-old Black woman from Philadelphia, to chair the conference. Doctor Alexander had many accomplishments to her credit, one of which was that she was the first Black woman in the nation ever to have earned a PhD.

Then the president said: "Dr. Arthur Flemming, who is not here this afternoon—I think you have probably guessed where he is. He is on the Hill meeting the appropriation committees to be sure that our programs are protected. He has participated in all of the White House Conferences on Aging. He will be the co-chair, and his accomplishments and his idealism, his commitment, and his wisdom, are unparalleled, I think, in government.

I am very grateful to him."

Shortly thereafter the work of organizing the conference began, with Arthur attending many long meetings—often on Sunday afternoons—with former Representative Jerome Waldie, whom President Carter had chosen to be the over-all executive director of the conference.

With the election of President Reagan, a new chairman and a new staff director were chosen from the Republican ranks. All of President Carter's choices were asked to submit their resignations, including Arthur. Arthur was invited to indicate whether he wished to be retained, and he signified his willingness to do so. Subsequently, he was formally notified by the new HEW secretary, Richard Schweiker, that he was to be continued as a deputy chairman of the conference and as a member of the advisory committee.

There was a great deal of political jockeying. Secretary of Health and Human Services (as HEW was renamed) Schweiker was accused of having a hand in this because he furnished the Republican party chairman, Mr. Richard Richards, with a list of the delegates, and Mr. Richards thereupon polled the delegates to find out what their attitudes were on Reagan policies. Suspicion was rampant that the White House was bent on controlling the upcoming conference. At the very least, the White House certainly didn't want the conference to turn into a free-for-all arena for criticism of the Reagan administration and its policies.

Elizabeth Dole, the White House staff person in charge of public liaison, became greatly concerned about this. She contacted Arthur and sought his advice and help in counteracting this feeling of suspicion against the administration.

It is particularly interesting to note that Mrs. Dole sought Arthur's help with the upcoming White House Conference at precisely the same time that the White House was busy firing him as chairman of the United States Commission on Civil Rights.

319

Arthur suggested to Mrs. Dole that the place to start producing a better climate would be for Secretary Schweicker to call a meeting of the Advisory Committee to discuss the matter and to try to get the conference headed in a positive direction. On Friday, November 20, ten days before the conference was to open, such a meeting of the leaders of the committee was held in the secretary's office.

When the White House Conference actually convened on November 30, 1981, there was still considerable dissatisfaction among the delegates. There were charges floating around that the membership of the various committees had been "stacked" by the administration.

Early on Tuesday morning, Arthur got a telephone call from Jack Ossofsky, of the Leadership Council on Aging Organizations, asking him to chair an open meeting of the delegates on Tuesday evening so that they might have an opportunity to air their grievances. (This was, of course, an echo of the Open Forum Arthur had provided in the 1971 conference and at which former Chief Justice Warren presided.) No such open meeting had been planned for the 1981 conference.

Arthur was in complete sympathy with the idea and agreed to chair the meeting. It was hurriedly set up for seven o'clock that same evening, and approximately seven hundred of the delegates turned out. It went on until after eleven o'clock, with a continuous stream of delegates taking the mike to vocalize their complaints about how the conference was being run. Congressman Claude Pepper, chairman of the House Select Committee on Aging, came to the meeting and promised his complete support for the delegates' demands for more open participation in the deliberations of the fourteen committees working in the various areas of concern. He was wildly cheered.

That same Tuesday Arthur was scheduled to preside at a luncheon for the delegates at the Washington Sheraton Hotel.

When he arrived at the ballroom where the luncheon was to be held, he noticed that there were secret service men all over the place. Secretary Schweicker told him that the president was expected at 12:29 PM. The secretary asked Arthur to start the proceedings by leading in a salute to the flag, and that he would then introduce the president. This the secretary did, in the usual manner, simply saying, "The President of the United States."

It was a surprise appearance on the part of the president, and he used the occasion to defend his efforts to solve the Social Security problems. He also denied that he was "somehow an enemy of my own generation."

According to *The Washington Post* the next day, "[President] Reagan received a warm reception from the delegates, but not nearly as enthusiastic as that given Monday to Pepper, an honorary chairman of the Conference, or to Arthur Flemming, a member of the Conference Advisory Committee, and the man whom Reagan recently fired as head of the U.S. Civil Rights Commission. Flemming was seated on the dais while Reagan spoke."

Three of the special groups of delegates—the Hispanic-Americans, the California delegation, and the Hispanics—held parties during the conference and each group gave Arthur a special award in recognition of his work with the elderly.

One particularly warm letter had come to Arthur from one of his Hispanic friends who worked with the older people. It was written on the day of the firing from the Civil Rights Commission. It follows:

Dearest Dr. Flemming:
I just heard the bad news, and I am sick. I cannot conceive that this community could produce a President so insensitive and so unethical with the rights of the people as to play Hollywood games with a person of your stature. I want you to know that if there ever was a hero in my life, that hero is you.
To stand up for the rights of all people, in particular the

321

"nobodies" of this land, takes more than courage. It takes guts, and we admire you very much. I am sure I speak for many— the school children, the battered women, the underpaid, the unemployed, the homeless, the citizens brutalized by unsympathetic police systems, the young, the old, etc. I am also very grateful for all you have done for all of us Hispanics, but for me in particular by giving me a chance to do volunteer work for you and with you.

I am terribly sad at the thought that you will not be there to guide us any more.

Please take good care of yourself, enjoy your days off, which are very well deserved, and don't give up. We love you too much.

[Signature omitted for obvious reasons.]

That letter really came from the heart.

Actually the White House Conference ended on a quite positive note. As Maggie Kuhn, head of the Gray Panthers, who led a march of approximately two hundred older persons to the White House during the conference, said, "The president got the political message."

A great many special awards and honors came to Arthur for his work on behalf of the elderly, including the prestigious Andrus Award given by the American Association of Retired Persons and the Ollie Randle Award of the National Council on Aging.

On the personal side, there were some developments worth including here. After six years in our big, five-bedroom house and a fairly steady procession of guests, I began an aggressive campaign to convince Arthur that it was time for us to consider a change in lifestyle. Smaller, more manageable quarters was the goal I hoped to achieve.

At first he protested loudly that he had to have "room," that he liked a yard to walk around in, and so on. Actually, he never walked in the yard except once in the spring and once in the fall to note the condition of the trees, grass, and shrubbery around the house. Then, he would point out to me what needed to be done and direct me to call a yard service and landscape men to do the work he thought necessary to keep the property in good shape. In between, the yard was my complete responsibility, of course.

I had concluded long before that it was the idea of the yard that he liked, since his parents' home in Kingston was always kept in "showplace" condition. He certainly didn't want any responsibility for keeping our yard up.

Actually, I didn't like yard work either, nor did I have any liking for gardening, flower bed development, or any other outside work in the dirt. And the annual leaf-raking season was a nightmare for me, since nearly all of the houses we have lived in were surrounded by trees.

So I kept working on the idea of a move. A lovely little townhouse just a half-block from the Potomac River in Old Town, Alexandria, came on the market shortly after I got my "let's-move-to-smaller-quarters" campaign under way. I looked at it, liked it, and persuaded Arthur to examine it too. Within a couple of days we signed an agreement to buy it.

From the beginning I loved our new home, and so did Arthur. This was our thirteenth move, and I fervently hoped it would be the last. (It wasn't.) Arthur took early morning walks along the Potomac when the weather was pleasant. I developed the habit of taking a book under my arm in the late afternoon, walking down to the river, and finding a quiet bench. I loved watching the boats on the river, and watching the people walking their dogs or their small children, or the lovers strolling hand in hand or lying on the grass. Every once in a while I'd read a paragraph or two.

Arthur was involved in an unusual way in a special event that took place in April of 1977. That was the wedding of Decker Anstrom and Sherron Heimstra.

Decker was the student body president at Macalester College during our last year there. He and Arthur became good friends, and when Arthur returned to Washington in 1971 to work on the second White House Conference on Aging, he made it possible for Decker to become involved in the work of that conference as one of the younger delegates. Later Decker joined Arthur's staff at the Administration on Aging as his full-time assistant.

There Decker met and was attracted to a really delightful young fellow employee, known to friends as Sherry. We made a foursome for dinner occasionally. In due time Decker and Sherry decided on April 15, 1977, as their wedding date.

When Decker confided these plans to Arthur, he told him that he and Sherry wanted him to participate in the ceremony. They were writing the order of service themselves and planned to have a classmate of Decker's from Macalester, by then an ordained minister, officiate, with Arthur assisting. The young minister's name was Susan Halse. She was married to an attorney, Bob Stumberg, another Macalester classmate.

We invited Decker and Sherry and Susan and Bob to dinner at our house for the purpose of making plans for the ceremony. Susan was by this time obviously very large with child. Later I asked whether she and Arthur were going to wear clerical robes at the wedding. She answered immediately, and with feeling, "I am." So they both wore robes.

The wedding was in the chapel at Ft. McNair, in Washington, with a reception following at the Officers' Club. It was a beautiful day and a very special wedding—lovely in every respect.

I don't imagine there are very many formal weddings where the ritual is shared by an obviously pregnant woman minister, assisted by a seventy-two-year-old man. I love to recall that day and that mental picture. (A son born later to Decker and Sherry was named Thomas Arthur Anstrom, giving Arthur, to date, five namesakes.)

Another special event took place when Arthur reached a milestone in June of 1980, his seventy-fifth birthday. To Lib and

Sue it seemed an appropriate occasion for a real family celebration, and as early as February they began talking with me about this possibility. We set the date for the party (a dinner to be held at Sue's and John's home) for Sunday, May 25, the Memorial Day weekend, to make it easier for the out-of-town family members to be present.

The theme we decided on was "Half-Way to 150," since Arthur's usual birthday gimmick was always to say to each celebrant, "Now you're half-way to. . . ." I made place cards carrying this "Half-way to 150" message, and we had large banners floating out of the table bouquets proclaiming the same. And everybody came—all twenty-three Flemmings, that is, plus John's parents Ralph and Elsie Parker, Decker and Sherry Anstrom, and Ed's friend Cindy. We had a professional photographer come to take a formal picture of the family. It was the first occasion in ten years when absolutely everybody was present at the same time.

It was a smashing success. After dinner, Harry, by pre-arrangement, assumed the role of master of ceremonies, and he filled this role in truly professional style. We had prepared speeches by George Arthur Speese, representing the grandchildren; John Parker, representing the in-law children; Lib, representing the children; and I, representing myself.

The surprise was complete as far as Arthur was concerned. He was totally amazed to find all of his children, their spouses, and the grandchildren gathered to honor him. The speeches were full of heart-warming recollections of Arthur's contributions to all of our lives.

Lib, assisted by her husband George, decided to make her tribute to her father a bit different from the rest, and chose to do a parody on "The Night Before Christmas." It captured the spirit of the celebration so well that I am including it here.

325

To Dad, on his Seventy-fifth Birthday

'Twas the *day* before Christmas, and all over town
Most merchants approached the day with a frown.
A few, however, looked forward with glee,
Having heard about Flemming, and his Christmas Eve spree.

Beginning with jewelry, and ending with books
No department he misses, despite the strange looks.
Toys, appliances, clothing, and such—
Has he purchased too little? More likely, too much!

That evening the stockings are hung up with care;
St. Nicholas, of course, more likely's not there.
He's gone after *more* presents, paper and bows,
And he won't be home till the last store's closed!

Early on Christmas, Santa surveys with pride;
From youngest to oldest, no one's been denied.
He distributes the gifts, and is then heard to say
"Merry Christmas to all, and to all a good day!"

Now, should you conclude that our story is o'er,
Of the life of our hero, we'd like to share more.
A busier person, you're not likely to find;
To list his activities boggles one's mind.

Civil Service Commission, college prexy, and then—
The opportunity arose to be one of Ike's men.
If you think *this* position was a "big bowl of cherries,"
You've forgotten the year that he banned the cranberries.

Onward and upward, the challenges came;
We won't whistle and shout, but we'll call them by name—
Macalester, Oregon, the oppressed, and the lame,
Once Flemming had been there, they just weren't the same!

Dad's travels have carried him miles from his home.
His idea of heaven is a jet with a phone!
All will acknowledge he's gone pretty far
For a fellow who's never driven a car.

One wonders if Wood and Tom Tate can still smile
When they hear the phrase "Second sacrificial mile!"
And perhaps Bunny felt somewhat the same
As she stood looking down from the wing of a plane!

There's no such thing as "Impossible Dream."
Our hero would say, "It just needs a new scheme!"
Recall Minshall, the "monster"—running, digging, and straining
All who saw him agreed: this dog needed much training!

Stymied? Defeated? Not *our* man of the ages;
Grabbing the phone book he turned to the yellow pages.
"Here's a trainer in Maryland." Bunny said, "Are you mad?"
"Of course not," said Grandad. "We'll send him by cab."

His life—it has been a most positive one;
Accepting the negative just isn't done.
"Can't," Won't," and "No" aren't part of his life;
Ask the kids, or the grandkids; *especially* his wife.

Retirement? *Never! Certainly not* when he dies;
A *new* opportunity waits in the skies.
All those who know him are *sure* he will be
Helping God and the angels "reach higher possibilities."

This 'ode' in Dad's honor is the means that we chose;
With these lines we, lovingly, come to a close.
A teacher, a preacher, a leader of men—
Father and grandfather—Most of all, *Friend.*

Elizabeth Anne and George
May 25, 1980

A few days after the seventy-fifth birthday party, we left on a
two-week holiday in Europe. Without Arthur's knowledge, I had
planned and scheduled this trip, which included a Norwegian
Fjords cruise and visits to London, Scotland, and Ireland. This
break, along with our 1967 trip to Alaska, constitute the only
vacations we have ever had.

15

THE UNITED STATES COMMISSION ON CIVIL RIGHTS

Reagan Dismisses Civil Rights Chief, Busing Supporter
The New York Times, November 17, 1981

President to Push Flemming Off Civil Rights Commission
The Washington Post, November 17, 1981

Reagan Fires Rights Chief Who Fires Back Parting Shot
The Baltimore Sun, November 17, 1981

Rights Chief Gets the Ax, Decries Ouster
The Kansas City Times, November 17, 1981

P USH—FIRE—DISMISS—OUST: Strong words!
These sample headlines from leading newspapers, all from front-page stories bearing the same date, sent a clear message that something fairly dramatic was happening to Arthur. Countless other newspapers blared forth the same story. They signaled that Arthur's eight-year tenure as chairman of the United States Commission on Civil Rights through Presidents Nixon, Ford, and Carter years, was coming to an end.

Only once before in the twenty-four year history of the commission had a president dismissed a chairman from the commission. That was in 1973, and in that case the president did not remove Father Hesburgh from the commission. Father Hesburgh's resignation from the commission was voluntary, not involuntary. It was duly accepted in the customary polite exchange between the president and the resigning official.

Not so this time. There was no polite exchange. There was no request for Arthur to submit his resignation. If there had been, Arthur would, of course, have acquiesced, since his commission read that he was to serve "at the pleasure of the president." And, as a result, the story would probably have landed deep in some inconspicuous spot in the body of the paper instead of being featured on page one.

The Civil Rights Commission is in a slightly different category from most executive commissions set up by the Congress. It is sometimes referred to as the "conscience" of the government in the field of civil rights. Arthur often says it has the responsibility of staying on the "cutting edge" of all issues in the field of civil rights and should always be willing to call the shots as it sees them.

The commission has two major roles: first of all, it has the responsibility of identifying major issues in the field of civil rights, conducting field studies, holding public hearings, evaluating the evidence, and then making recommendations to the president and to the Congress; and, in addition, the commission has the responsibility of monitoring the activities of all of the federal agencies whose job it is to enforce civil rights laws. Here again, it conducts field studies, holds public hearings, evaluates the evidence, and makes recommendations to the Congress and to the president. When the commission holds public hearings it has the authority to subpoena witnesses and place them under oath.

It is a bipartisan panel, and at the time of Arthur's incumbency it had six members appointed by the president and confirmed by the Senate, with three members from each major political party.

Also at that time, the members served "at the pleasure of the president," that is, they did not have specified terms of office. All of the members had other full-time occupations and cut across ethnic, religious, and professional lines. For example, the commission has lawyers, college presidents, clergymen, and so on, as members.

Arthur was the full-time United States commissioner on aging when President Nixon asked him to assume the chairmanship of the United States Commission on Civil Rights in 1974. In announcing Arthur's appointment, the president said that he had waited a whole year to find just "the right person" for the job. Again, as he had four times before, Arthur sailed through the confirmation proceedings without a dissenting vote.

Being chairman of the Commission on Civil Rights gave Arthur's crusading instincts full play. His commitment to justice for all people made him a natural in such a position of responsibility. It is my belief that he enjoyed being in this post as much as any he had ever undertaken, and probably more. He had tremendous respect for his fellow commissioners, and I don't believe he ever missed a meeting or a commission hearing during the eight years he served as chairman.

The commission took on all manner of unpopular questions of public policy and sought to ferret out the actual facts about how the civil rights laws were being enforced in various parts of the country. Desegregation became one of their most hotly discussed subjects. This was a highly emotional issue. Hearings were held in Boston, Miami, Tampa, Louisville, and Denver to find out how these communities were complying with the Supreme Court's decision in *Brown versus Board of Education*. In fact, the day of Arthur's firing, the commission held a press conference to publicize its latest findings on school desegregation.

Arthur felt that the opponents of busing as a tool to achieve desegregation in public schools were not really opposed to busing per se; they were opposed to desegregation and used busing as the focus of opposition. They did not, in other words, take into account that the majority of school children over the country are bused daily to school, and only a very small percentage of them are bused for the purpose of implementing desegre-

331

gation in particular districts.

Sex discrimination and age discrimination were other areas of examination by the commission. For the most part, there were enough legal tools to improve inequities substantially, but the Civil Rights Commission Report in 1976 found that there had been little improvement in the plight of women and minorities seeking better jobs during the previous twenty years. Arthur kept pressing for the development and implementation of affirmative action plans by employers to deal with the problems of employment.

The commission got solidly behind the Equal Rights Amendment and said it believed ratification "is essential to assure equal justice for women and men under the law." Furthermore, it stated that although state, local, and federal governments may act to promote sexual equality without ratification of the amendment, "the reality is that without the amendment governments at all of these levels have not taken—and most likely will not take—the steps necessary to rid their laws, policies, and practices of the sex bias that continues to intrude upon the lives of women and men in this country."

One of the commission reports was titled, "Window Dressing on the Set: Women and Minorities in Television." It criticized the continual stereotyping of women and minorities and pointed out that this practice helped to perpetuate prejudices which constituted a serious roadblock to the achievement of the equal opportunities guaranteed by the Constitution in such areas as employment, housing, and education. In a letter to the editor of *The Evening Star*, which he wrote in answer to an editorial in *The Star* criticizing the report, Arthur concluded:

> Television plays a dominant role in the mass communication of ideas in the United States. Minorities and women must be fairly and equitably represented in the exercise of this awesome power. The nation must do everything possible, consistent with the First

Amendment, to ensure that the power is not exercised in such a manner as to do irreparable harm to minorities and women. Government and the private sector should and must work together to achieve these objectives.

The Commission on Civil Rights became highly vocal and disturbed over what it termed a "back-door method" of diluting civil rights progress in various fields. It charged that the practice of attaching restrictive amendments to money bills pending in Congress would virtually cripple civil rights enforcement by the federal government. Speaking to a group of civil rights officials convening in Washington in October of 1980, Arthur said: "Nobody would introduce a bill to repeal the Civil Rights Act of 1964. The strategy is now to put riders on appropriation bills which, when added together, can lead to virtual repeal of the Civil Rights Act."

He went on to say that one amendment, already approved in the House, would prevent the Education and Justice Departments from doing anything to require school busing; prevent federal spending on programs that use numerical goals for hiring women and minorities; restrict spending for bilingual education; frustrate enforcement of rules guaranteeing women equal opportunity in school sports; and prevent the Internal Revenue Service from revoking the tax-exempt status of private schools that discriminate against minorities. He called the appropriation riders a very insidious way of trying to effect a change in policy because there are usually no committee hearings and no floor debate. Legislators who use this tactic know that Congress is loath to jeopardize the funds for an entire agency by extended debate on controversial amendments.

Another area in which the commission received almost continuous complaints was with regard to police brutality. Responding to widespread concern that police were depriving individuals of their constitutional rights, the commission held hearings and

333

heard witnesses tell of incidents of brutality against Mexican-Americans, homosexuals, Blacks, and other minorities. In fact, police brutality was identified as the number-one concern of Blacks in Philadelphia and other cities.

The issue was still a vital one in 1980, when the Commission on Civil Rights called for immediate measures to protect individuals from what it called the potentially explosive issue of police abuse. The commission's concern grew out of complaints from cities such as Philadelphia and Houston and riots in Miami in which fifteen persons died and twenty-five hundred were left homeless after five Dade county policemen were acquitted of charges that they beat to death a thirty-three year old Black man. The Miami Black community looked on this case as a miscarriage of justice.

The commission held public hearings in Miami as well as Houston and Philadelphia, and, as an outgrowth of these hearings, the commission made detailed recommendations, which they hoped would lead to better police-citizen relations in the disturbed cities.

The commission also took notice of the fact that the Voting Rights Act of 1965 was due for a review and renewal. In its report entitled, "The Voting Rights Act: Unfulfilled Goals" there were details of many specific cases in which citizens in the South and other regions said that their voting rights had been compromised by the actions of state or local governments. In transmitting its report to President Reagan and to the Congress, the commission pointed out that, "Minorities continue to face a variety of problems which the act was designed to overcome. This report has documented cases in which there was resistance and hostility by some state and local officials to increased minority participation in virtually every aspect of the electoral process."

Perhaps the most volatile issue of all was the issue of abortion. In October, 1972, the Congress had expanded the jurisdiction of the Commission on Civil Rights to include sex discrimination.

The Supreme Court, in 1973, in the case of *Roe versus Wade*, had outlawed a Texas law prohibiting abortion except for the purpose of saving the mother's life. The *Roe* decision declared the Texas law to be in violation of the due process clause of the Fourteenth Amendment. The majority of the Court concurred and said that "prior to approximately the end of the first trimester, the abortion decision and its effectuation must be left to the medical judgment of the pregnant woman's attending physician."

The anti-abortion forces raised a great cry at this decision, and, helped along by the Catholic church, began a crusade to outlaw all abortions by promoting a constitutional amendment to achieve this result. Attitudes toward abortion became a prime factor in assessing the qualifications for office for members of Congress, and especially for nominations to various judgeships.

The commission authorized and issued an indepth study of the whole abortion problem which analyzed the impact that a possible constitutional amendment, designed to nullify the *Roe* decision of the Supreme Court on the right to limit childbearing, would have on the First, Ninth, and Fourteenth Amendments to the Constitution. The study also described the threat to enforcement of other civil rights measures in the Constitution that would be posed by a successful effort to include in the Constitution an amendment which would nullify the Supreme Court decisions on the right to limit childbearing. The commission's report concluded that this right cannot be infringed or eliminated without weakening the foundation of all rights.

Meanwhile, the American conscience was at work in another related area, in which thousands of American citizens were summarily denied their civil rights as a part of the war hysteria that swept the country after the bombing of Pearl Harbor. Arthur became a part of this belated attempt to remedy past wrongs.

This happened in the last year of President Carter's administration when the Congress decided to look into the matter of the internment of some 120,000 Japanese-Americans who, under Executive Order 9066 signed by President Roosevelt on February 19, 1942, were herded into relocation centers spread throughout the western states. No one was tried for any crime, but nearly all of them lost their homes, jobs, businesses, and farms. Congress approved the mass evacuation, and the Supreme Court in *Korematsu versus United States* upheld the president's right to issue the order as a war emergency power.

A bill was duly passed and signed by President Carter on July 16, 1980, setting up the Commission on Wartime Relocation and Internment of Civilians. It provided for an objective, unbiased study of the whole internment affair by a commission to:

> Review the facts and circumstances surrounding Executive Order 9066 and the impact of such Executive Order on American citizens and permanent resident aliens.
>
> Review directives of the United States military forces requiring the relocation and, in some cases, detention in internment camps of American citizens and recommend appropriate remedies.

The bill further provided for a commission of nine members to be appointed, three by the president, three by the Speaker of the House of Representatives, and three by the president *pro tempore* of the Senate. Arthur became a member of this commission as one of President Carter's appointees. And he found it a very sobering experience indeed to listen to the testimony of surviving internees as they told of their harrowing sufferings thirty-nine years earlier.

As Senator Matsunaga put it, "Although historians and many Americans have long recognized the internment of Japanese-Americans as a black page in American history, the federal government itself has yet to acknowledge the wrong which was committed in complete disregard of due process of law."

Very little publicity has been given to the work of the Wartime

Relocation and Internment Commission. In fact, most Americans have forgotten about the internment of this group of citizens during World War II.

But it happened, and the commission sought to uncover the actual facts by holding hearings on the West Coast, as far north as Alaska, and in Chicago, Washington, and New York. The victims of the internment thus had an opportunity to tell their story. The commission then made its report to the Congress, including a recommendation for reparations. Subsequently the Congress approved the recommendation of the commission, including reparations to each of the interns who are still living.

Arthur began to speak out about what he conceived to be a discernible retreat on the part of the Reagan administration in many areas of progress in civil rights. He felt that there was official abandonment of the role of the federal government as the advocate on behalf of unprotected citizens. The immense political power of the New Right forces was making itself felt, and the Reagan administration was responding to these pressures by advocating watering down the Voting Rights Act, retreating on affirmative action, on busing as a tool to desegregate public schools, getting solidly behind legal prohibition of abortion for any reason, and so on.

The announcement of the Reagan administration's revoking the Internal Revenue Service policy denying tax exemptions to private schools that deny admission to Blacks was another example of the government's relinquishing its role of protecting the unprotected. Arthur felt there was a noticeable "turning back of the clock" as far as progress in protecting the traditionally unprotected was concerned.

Naturally, this highly vocal activist position Arthur took was noticed by the new administration, and he knew it was only a matter of time until he would be replaced as chairman of the United States Commission on Civil Rights.

The Washington Post, September 12, 1981, had a story about the matter that came out of Los Angeles. It said that a Black fundamentalist preacher, the Reverend Hill, had turned down the offer to head the commission. Hill was a Republican and a member of Reverend Jerry Falwell's Moral Majority. Mr. Hill reportedly felt he wanted to spend his full time on being a minister and on his work as president of the Step Foundation, a privately funded poverty program backed by the Moral Majority and several conservative religious groups.

On November 4, a story appeared in *The San Diego Tribune*, which said: "The Reagan administration appears intent on weakening the influence of the U. S. Commission on Civil Rights by appointing a new chairman—expected to be San Diegan Clarence Pendleton—and a staff director supportive of the administration's philosophy of less federal enforcement in areas of American life .... The administration also intends to reduce the commission's budget, partly to save money and partly to diminish the panel's effectiveness, sources said."

The story also identified Alfred Balitzer, a professor of government at Claremont Men's College in California, as the administration's proposed new staff director. Mr. Balitzer confirmed this report.

The intention to dilute the influence of the commission, or even to abolish it, was also apparent on Capitol Hill. But Arthur refused to be stilled. "I am not going to tailor my recommendations to the climate that may exist at some time. Even though we are going through a period of fiscal difficulty there are some values that remain constant," he said.

Monday, November 16, was the day the White House chose to make the official press release about Arthur's successor. The weeks of speculation were over.

Arthur was told that the White House was announcing that morning the selection of Clarence Pendleton, of San Diego,

California, to be chairman of the Commission on Civil Rights. He was then told that the president hoped that he would continue to serve until Senate confirmation of Mr. Pendleton. He was further informed that Mary Louise Smith, a former chairman of the Republican party, had been selected to be a member of the commission in Doctor Stephen Horne's place.

That ended the conversation. The speculation about Arthur's successor was over.

The White House press release did not even mention Arthur's name. It was a simple statement that the White House was nominating Clarence Pendleton to be chairman of the United States Commission on Civil Rights. I thought it a really insulting way for the administration to handle the matter.

This was Arthur's first official contact signaling the end of his service with the commission. Not mentioning Arthur's name in the White House announcement guaranteed that it would not be regarded as a routine announcement, and it resulted in an avalanche of press coverage which it certainly would not have had if it had been handled in a more sensitive manner.

I didn't know anything about the firing of Arthur until late in the afternoon of that Monday. I had gone to my yoga class in the morning and then went out to luncheon with friends, and didn't return home until about four o'clock. Arthur telephoned me soon after that to get me up to date on the day's happenings. He left soon thereafter for Baltimore, where the commission was conducting two days of hearings on "Urban Minority Economic Development."

As a result, I was home alone when the reactions began to come in. I was watching John Chancellor on the NBC news and heard him say that President Reagan had fired Arthur from the commission. Our grandson Ed called to say that he had heard Dan Rather's much more complete coverage of it on CBS news.

The telephone began ringing in the late afternoon. The news had been on the radio all day. Our children and several of our grandchildren were among the first callers, all of them expressing in volatile language their indignation about the firing. An old friend from ODM days, Fletcher Waller, called from Florida to express his feelings, and they weren't very complimentary to the president. That evening I had calls from many friends in the Washington area, and also long distance calls from New York, Florida, Illinois, Ohio, and so on. Some of those who called had not been heard from in years—old college friends and other associates.

Some asked, "How is Arthur taking it?" Well, the answer to that was that Arthur was busy doing his job in Baltimore and was certainly not, as the saying goes, "falling apart."

Nor was I. The fact is that I was having an absolutely wonderful time at home answering the telephone. Too bad Arthur missed all of that fun.

The next morning Arthur was on the "Good Morning, America" show. And, in a very short time, he was actually besieged with requests to go on television news shows and to give radio interviews. From all over the country the requests kept coming. This went on for weeks. He was on the "Saturday Magazine" program in Washington, and on "Meet the Editors," a weekly program. The story was also covered on Paul Duke's "Washington Week in Review," and on Agronsky's program.

The daily press kept the story alive for weeks. There were editorials in many newspapers, and a number of regular commentators wrote stories about it. The incident also furnished material for some cartoonists.

Time magazine gave two columns to it, complete with pictures of Arthur and Mr. Pendleton. The *Time* headline was "Firing a Fighter," with subheading: "A set-back for civil rights?" The story began: "His credentials are impeccable, his party loyalties unassailable. A lifelong Republican, Arthur S. Flemming, 76, was appointed secretary of Health, Education, and Welfare in 1958 by Dwight Eisenhower. In 1974, Richard Nixon named him chairman of the U. S. Commission on Civil Rights, a bipartisan advisory committee whose purpose is to monitor enforcement of civil rights laws. Flemming turned out to be an especially unflinching warrior in the struggle for civil rights. In recent months, after having concluded that Reagan and company lacked commitment to the cause, he began attacking the administration. Last week he found himself out of a job. Nominated as his successor is Clarence M. Pendleton, Jr., 52, a black Republican, president of the Urban League of San Diego and a friend of White House Counselor Edwin Meese III." The rest of the story was background material about the commission and Mr. Pendleton. *The Chronicle of Higher Education* for November 25, 1981, carried a two-page story. *Newsweek* carried a story built chiefly around Mr. Pendleton.

On the floor of Congress, too, the firing of Arthur was noticed. Two members of the Senate, Lowell Weicker (R-CT) and Charles Mathias (R-MD) rose to deplore the action of the president; and Representative Corliss Collins (D-IL) said she "felt a real sense of outrage" when she heard the news.

Congressman Don Edwards (D-CA) issued a public statement strongly critical of the president. It is worth noting that Arthur was never a constituent of any of these members of Congress. Also, they represented the East, Midwest, and Far West.

Senator Weicker was the first to react, and he took the floor the day the newspapers appeared with the announcement of Arthur's removal from the commission. He began by reciting in full and complete detail Arthur's long record of responsibilities in government, in education, and in the church. His appraisal of his career was praiseworthy in the highest terms. Then he shifted to the political aspects of the president's action. In Senator Weicker's words:

> I do not know what party he [i.e., Arthur] is registered in, Mr. President, I assume, since he was a member of the Eisenhower

cabinet, he is a Republican. Believe me, there are few Republicans that have distinguished themselves in the area of civil rights. Mr. Flemming is one of them. This country is better off for his efforts. . . .

It escapes me how this administration, which is not exactly perceived as being activist in the area of civil rights, would want to let go one of the few Republicans who is so perceived. By means of these few words on the Senate floor, I just want to let Doctor Flemming know that I think he is one of the great Americans of these times, and he has never been needed more than he is today.

Senator Mathias's tribute came on November 29, and he was equally enthusiastic in his praise of Arthur's record of service. He, too, recited at length Arthur's various positions of responsibility. Speaking particularly of the Commission on Civil Rights, he said:

When Arthur Flemming became chairman of the Commission on Civil Rights in 1974, he brought to this new office the same enthusiasm and intelligence that had marked all his previous work. Under his tutelage, the commission left no civil rights issue unexamined.

It has produced insightful and penetrating reports on the progress Blacks, women, ethnic minorities, Native Americans, the handicapped, and the elderly have made toward true equality in our society. No issue has been too controversial for the commission to explore, no allegation of discrimination too insignificant for it to consider.

Mr. Flemming has been tireless in the struggle to protect our cherished civil rights. His testament to us is that the struggle is unending, that we must always be vigilant against encroachment on our most basic rights and privileges.

It was nearly three months after he fired Arthur that the president finally got around to sending the name of Clarence Pendleton up to the Senate Judiciary Committee for confirmation as chairman of the United States Commission on Civil Rights. On March 15, 1982, Mr.

Pendleton was confirmed and subsequently sworn into office as the first Black chairman of the commission.

The president was not so successful with one of his other nominees for the commission. The White House announced that the president intended to send the Senate the name of the Reverend B. Sam Hart, a conservative Black radio evangelist. This announcement touched off an immediate clamor when Mr. Hart held a news conference and said he was opposed to the Equal Rights Amendment, busing to achieve racial balance in public schools, and that homosexuals had no civil rights. Senator Heinz and Senator Spector, both of Pennsylvania, opposed the nomination and, in fact, said they had not even been told of the president's choice of Mr. Hart. Eventually, the White House withdrew the nomination.

The nation was beginning to get the message. For twenty-five years one president after another had not changed the membership of the commission in order to preserve its integrity as a bipartisan, independent body.

President Reagan had decided to break with this precedent and "pack" the commission with members who would "rubber stamp" his efforts to undermine school desegregation and affirmative action in the field of employment.

At the first meeting of the commission at which the two new members were present (Clarence Pendleton and Mary Louise Smith) the following resolution was passed:

> The United States Commission on Civil Rights at its monthly meeting of April, 1982, sets aside its agenda and pauses in its deliberations to offer and record our abiding gratitude, our professional respect, and our personal regard for

ARTHUR S. FLEMMING

The Nation is indebted and the Commission is grateful to him

- For his recognition that in every person there is a spark of the divine and that therefore, all are endowed by their creator with certain unalienable rights;

• For his unswerving commitment to the Constitution of the United States and his long-standing insistence that its protections, as well as well as its obligations, apply to all persons without regard to status;

• For his persistence in demanding that the laws of the land and the decisions of the courts be defended and enforced; and

• For eight years of untiring efforts and informed, creative, courageous, and inspiring leadership as Chairman of the United States Commission on Civil Rights.

Now, therefore be it resolved that this 12th day of April, 1982, that this statement be adopted, that it be made a part of the official record of this meeting, and that a suitable copy be presented to Dr. Flemming.

/s/Penny
Clarence M. Pendleton, Jr.

/s/Mary Louise Smith
Mary Louise Smith

/s/Mary Frances Berry
Mary Frances Berry

/s/Blandine C. Ramirez
Blandine C. Ramirez

/s/Jill S. Ruckelshaus
Jill S. Ruckelshaus

/s/Maury Saltzman
Maury Saltzman

/s/John Hope, III
John Hope, III
Acting Staff Director

I thought the manner in which Mr. Pendleton signed this formal document, that is, by using his nickname "Penny," rather interesting, especially since he had a bare nodding acquaintance with Arthur.

In the spring following the firing of Arthur, awards and honors were received from civil rights organizations through the country. All were accompanied by generous appraisals of his contribution to civil rights. Among them were:

- The National Education Association Friend of Education Award
- The National Education Committee on Human Relations Special Award for dedicated service and advocacy on behalf of   human and civil rights
- North Philadelphia Action Branch of the National Association for the Advancement of Colored People presentation of its "One Nation" Award
- The John F. Kennedy Lodge of B'Nai Brith "Profiles in Courage" Award
- The National Pacific-Asian Resources Center on Aging Honor for leadership and outstanding accomplishment in civil rights
- Washington Urban League, Inc., Whitney M. Young, Jr., Memorial Award
- Conference of Minority Public Administrations Distinguished Public Service Award
- The Leadership Conference on Civil Rights Hubert Humphrey Civil Rights Award
- The National Urban Coalition on Civil Rights Hubert Humphrey Humanitarian Award

In April, 1982, he was elected to a two-year term as president of the National Council on Aging. And, in May, 1982, Wayne State University in Detroit conferred on Arthur his forty-sixth honorary doctorate degree.

16

AND THEN . . . QUO VADIS?

I sometimes wonder if President Reagan really thought that removing Arthur from the Civil Rights Commission would silence him. If he did, he badly miscalculated the nature of the man that Richard Nixon—in appointing him commissioner on aging—described as "the most tenacious person he knew in pursuing the goals he set for improving the lot of those [i.e., older] people."

Right off, he made speech after speech explaining his view that the policies of the Reagan administration constituted a regressive movement in the area of civil rights. At a fundraising dinner of the Leadership Conference on Civil Rights on February 22, 1982, Arthur said: "So far the positions taken by the Reagan administration, if enforced, represent to us a backward step in the area of civil rights. They are determined to do everything in their power to weaken or eliminate civil rights laws."

Elaborating on this theme in an interview in *The Public Administration Times*, published by the American Society for Public Administration, March 1, 1982, Arthur answered the questions put to him thus:

Question: The ASPA National Council has expressed deep concern over cutbacks in civil rights enforcement by the Reagan administration and Congress. These cutbacks represent a dramatic deemphasis in the efforts to achieve equal employment opportunity. Based on your efforts on civil rights enforcement, what do you see as its future?
Flemming: The nation is at a very significant crossroads. We are operating under reasonably good civil rights laws and under very

good court decisions. We have reached a point where the emphasis is on the implementation of those laws and those court decisions. Whenever you move in the direction of implementing civil rights laws and court decisions you are sure to disturb the status quo. When you disturb the status quo you are sure to create opposition to the laws and court decisions.

Today, the strategy of those who are opposed to the implementation of civil rights laws and court decisions has become clear. The opposition has concluded that the best thing to do is to either eliminate or to weaken the methods which need to be employed in order to implement the civil rights laws and court decisions. For example, in the area of education, it is clear that under *Brown vs. Board of Education*, the task that confronts the nation is to break up segregated school systems. If you are going to break up a segregated school system, it is going to be necessary to reassign students. In connection with the assignment of students, some of them will need transportation assistance. The opposition to desegregation, therefore, has been focusing over a period of the last three years on Congress to enact riders to appropriation bills, which prohibit the executive branch from using money for the purpose of implementing desegregation plans which call for pupil transportation beyond the immediate neighborhood. These are usually referred to as anti-busing riders. The Civil Rights Commission has opposed these riders. Up until the beginning of the Reagan administration, the executive branch has opposed these riders. The Reagan administration, however, favors the objectives that are embodied in the anti-busing riders.

Question: Does that mean that the Reagan administration opposes desegregation?
Flemming: They are opposed to using the methods which you need to implement a desegregation plan. Some people who favor these anti-busing riders will say that they do favor desegregation or favor providing equal opportunities in the field of education. But saying that they favor it, and then at the same time opposing the methods that you have to use in order to implement a desegregation plan means that in reality they are taking a position which results in

blocking the desegregation of the schools. Let's take another example in another area, the area of equal employment opportunity. It's clear that if public or private employers are going to make progress in the direction of opening up opportunities for minorities and women they must develop and implement affirmative action plans. Recently, however, the House of Representatives passed a rider to the Labor Department appropriations bill which has the effect of pulling the rug out from under the use of affirmative action plans in the enforcement of equal opportunity laws. The Reagan administration has also indicated that they are opposed to affirmative action plans. In fact, they have indicated that they are going to try to get the Supreme Court to reverse a position that it took a number of years ago upholding an affirmative action plan that had been worked out voluntarily by labor and management. The Commission has consistently supported and advocated the use of affirmative action plans in the field of equal employment. So one can see that in these two major areas—namely, the areas of desegregation and equal employment—the commission has taken the positions which are in opposition to the positions taken by the President and the administration.

These quotations indicate very clearly that Arthur did not intend to "fold his tents like the Arabs and silently steal away." And there was no certainly dearth of crusades to keep his adrenalin flowing.

Even before the president replaced him as chairman of the Commission on Civil Rights, Arthur had been approached and asked to become director of a National Coalition for Quality Integrated Education, and he decided to accept this opportunity. Among his reasons for accepting the coalition post, he stated publicly, was to test the positive influence of school integration. The coalition was made up of civil rights organizations, including the National Education Association, where Arthur was to have an office. He was not, however, confining his activities to promoting excellence in desegregated schools.

He got right to work on an idea that he had been mulling over for some time, and he persuaded a group of former federal officials to form an organization to monitor civil rights activities in Congress and the administration. This became the new "Citizens' Commission on Civil Rights" and was a privately financed bipartisan group whose purpose was to oversee the government's enforcement of laws barring discrimination on the basis of race, sex, religion, ethnic background, age, or handicap. In the group were three former secretaries of Health, Education, and Welfare (Elliot Richardson, Wilbur Cohen, and Arthur); a former secretary of Labor, Ray Marshall; and five former members of the United States Commission on Civil Rights (Theodore Hesburgh, former chairman of the commission, Erwin Griswold, Frankie Freeman, Manuel Ruiz, and Rabbi Murray Saltzman).

Word of the organization of this so-called "shadow" commission reached the president's ears. His response was to make one of his famous phone calls to Arthur at his office.

The president began the conversation by telling Arthur that the new commission had been called to his attention, and he was happy to know that Arthur was continuing his interest in matters concerning civil rights.

That the Citizens' Commission on Civil Rights was not just a showcase was obvious from the beginning. Several indepth reports have been issued by the commission under the direction of William L. Taylor, the vice-chairman of the commission, former director of the Center for National Policy Review at the Catholic University Law School, and himself a former executive director of the United States Civil Rights Commission.

The first of these reports was on *Congressional Efforts to Curb the Federal Courts and to Undermine the Brown Decision* (*Brown versus Board of Education, 1954*) and came out in October of 1982.

The second was entitled, *A Decent Home—A Report on the*

Continuing Failure of the Federal Government to Provide Equal Housing Opportunity, published in April, 1983.

Then followed a report on *Affirmative Action to Open the Doors of Job Opportunity: A Policy of Fairness and Compassion That Has Worked*, June, 1984.

More recently the commission issued a 650-page report called, *One Nation Indivisible: The Civil Rights Challenge for the 1990s*. This report takes note of the fact that during the 1980s the thrust and direction of civil rights policy has been the subject of ongoing debate, conducted in many forums, including the courts, the halls of Congress and the executive agencies, scholarly journals, and the media.

Noting that during the eight years of the Reagan presidency major policy changes in civil rights had been made, the Citizens' Commission reported on handling of civil rights policy issues during the Reagan years. The investigation covered not just the most publicized issues but all aspects of federal law and policy that deal with equal opportunity for racial and ethnic minorities, women, the elderly, and disabled persons.

The commission's latest report is an evaluation of the Bush administration record in the area of civil rights on balance; it makes clear that a good deal that should be done is not being done.

Arthur knows exactly where he stands, and is not at all shy about making his attitudes public. Many examples come to mind.

One steamy day in August, 1983, with the temperature soaring toward the 100° mark, Arthur went over to St. Elizabeth's Hospital to speak at a rally to protest the president's plan to cut approximately seven hundred employees from the staff of the hospital, most of them in programs designed to help minority patients. His presence there was noticed by some newsmen covering the rally, and he was asked just why he was involved in that particular protest. These were young men who had no way of knowing that Arthur had supported, while president of the

Washington Federation of Churches nearly forty years earlier, a movement that led to the appointment of a full-time chaplain on the staff of St. Elizabeth's Hospital. Later, as secretary of Health, Education, and Welfare, he was actively involved in budget and administrative matters there. The present involvement was a "natural" for him.

Later that same week came the Twentieth Anniversary March commemorating the 1963 Poor Peoples' March on Washington, the setting for Martin Luther King's famous "I have a dream" speech, and the forerunner of important civil rights legislation. This commemorative march had as its theme "Jobs, Peace, and Freedom."

Arthur was in on the plans from the beginning as co-chairman of the religious division and attended speeches and rallies in Washington. All of this activity led eventually to the big day of the actual march, August 27.

I took an exceedingly dim view of Arthur's participation in the march itself, as the weather was predicted to be a hot, humid 95° Washington kind of day. I had been listening to warnings that people with allergies and older people should stay indoors. At seventy-eight years, I thought Arthur could miss that march, and I urged him not to go.

"Why not?" he asked.

"Because you're too old," I replied, knowing full well that I was waving the red flag in front of the bull.

So he insisted on going to the march, too. At 9 AM I drove him across the Fourteenth Street bridge and let him out to make his way alone, as policemen barred automobile traffic beyond that point. Then I returned home to do what I do very well—that is, worry.

He arrived back home around seven-thirty in the evening, having listened to some fifty speeches at the Lincoln Memorial. He was absolutely delighted to have been with the three hundred thousand fellow crusaders who jammed the parade area on that memorable day. No sign of fatigue was apparent. The only wear and tear I could observe was a bit of sunburn.

More recently, on August 29, 1989, he was down at the Supreme Court building joining the silent protest march organized by Benjamin Hooks, chief executive officer of the National Association for the Advancement of Colored People, to let the Court know that there are many dissenters outside of the Court to the erosion of the rights of minorities and women. Arthur was just one of many thousands of people of all races circling the Court building that day. Afterward he participated in the program on the west side of the U.S. Capital building, joining those who were urging the passage of legislation designed to reverse the Supreme Court decisions.

Another area that occupied a lot of his time was Social Security. After leaving the United States Commission on Civil Rights he accepted the invitation from another former secretary of Health, Education, and Welfare, the late Wilbur Cohen, to join him as co-chairman of Save Our Security (SOS), a group of 120 organizations, with a combined membership of 40 million, protecting the integrity of the Social Security System. These people come from many walks of life—senior citizens, the disabled, trade unionists, teachers, veterans, social workers, religious organizations, women's groups, civil rights groups, and minority groups. Their efforts on behalf of Social Security are vital to the work of the coalition, which is a nonpartisian, educational, and advocacy organization.

Wilbur Cohen and Arthur were two kindred spirits. Wilbur had been appointed secretary of HEW by President Johnson after a long period as a career civil servant in the Social Security Administration. Though of different political parties, Arthur and Wilbur were soulmates, believing passionately that the federal government should help the have-nots in our society, and both worked tirelessly to bring about improvement whenever they felt injustice existed. Arthur felt a deep sense of loss when Wilbur died suddenly in 1987.

Arthur was happy to become involved in any battle over the rights of older persons or minorities. One interesting occasion occurred when he telephoned me one evening at six-fifteen (the time he usually leaves his office for home) to say that he had to meet Elliot Richardson to help him to prepare for an appearance in the United States District Court later that evening for the purpose of trying to obtain a temporary restraining order to prevent the Treasury Department from using Social Security funds to meet current government bills. Word had gotten out earlier that this was exactly what the Treasury Department intended to do. Arthur and Wilbur Cohen, as co-chairs of the Save Our Security Coalition, along with the American Association of Retired Persons, were among the plaintiffs in the case, and Elliot Richardson was their counsel.

Arthur telephoned again at about eight-thirty to say that he didn't know just when he would be home.

From then on, the hours passed slowly. At eleven-thirty I heard his key in the door.

"This is as worrisome as waiting for teenagers to come home," I greeted him.

His excitement was apparent. The temporary restraining order had been denied but "without prejudice," which meant that the case was still alive. Again, he had been actively involved in activity concerning one of his favorite crusades: helping the old folks and protecting their security.

He gave me a brief run-down on what he had been doing, and I got him something to eat. "I *am* hungry," he said, "and I do have a seven-thirty breakfast engagement in the morning."

That breakfast meeting turned out to be a planning session for another crusade: a "Call to Action" to emphasize the fact that poverty is a growing problem in the United States. An analysis, by the Center on Budget and Policy Priorities, revealed that about 14 percent of Americans are entrenched in poverty. Arthur led a news conference at which the report was released, and he was joined by leaders of the National Council of Churches, the Union of the American Hebrew Congregations, The Center on Budget and Policy Priorities, and the National Political Congress of Black Women.

The purpose was to promote public awareness of the problems of poverty and was called "Thanksgiving Action on Poverty." Protests were planned in five cities: Atlanta, Des Moines, New York, Chicago, and Los Angeles.

Arthur was asked to speak at the Los Angeles protest, and of course he went.

When the fiftieth anniversary of the signing of the Social Security Act by President Franklin Delano Roosevelt was observed in Hyde Park, New York, in mid-August of 1985, Arthur journeyed up to Hyde Park on a hot Sunday afternoon to participate in a ceremony at the graveside of President Roosevelt. Again, on the following Wednesday, he returned to Hyde Park to speak at a more elaborate celebration with people who came from all over New York State and New England. About five thousand persons gathered to honor the memory of President Roosevelt for his historic promotion of the Social Security legislation. Other speakers were New York's Governor Mario Cuomo and the late Congressman Pepper.

Arthur used this latter occasion to boost the cause of national health insurance. Health care, not only for the aging, but also for the 37 million Americans who are not under any health plan, is a consuming interest of his. He was in frequent communication with Congressman Pepper, chairman of the House of Representatives Committee on Aging and later Congressman Ed Roybal who succeeded to that chairmanship when Congressman Pepper became chairman of the House Rules Committee.

Arthur's deepest involvement now continues to be the promotion of a national health plan for all Americans. He works with many organizations that have just one objective: the enactment of legislation that will provide for universal right of access to adequate health care, including long-term care, and that will make adequate provision for cost containment. He travels the country reiterating his theme song: that we are the only industrialized nation in the world, with the exception of South Africa, that does not recognize and implement the right of access to health care.

He also underlines the importance of gearing our health care system more toward health promotion and disease prevention instead of being concerned only with those who are already ill.

As late as October 24, 1989, Arthur appeared before the Pepper Commission on Health Care, urging that "we pool our resources, as a national community, in order to make it possible for our people, wherever they may live, to have access to adequate health care." Quoting further from his testimony:

> We welcome the establishment of the Pepper Commission. We welcome especially the fact that this commission will make "specific recommendations to the Congress respecting federal programs, policies, and financing needed to assure the availability of comprehensive health care services for all individuals in the United States."
>
> We are confident that your recommendations on programs, policies, and financing will add up to an action program designed to make it possible for us to join all the other industrialized nations of the world, except South Africa, in recognizing and implementing the right of access to health care.

In fact, there are frequent occasions when Arthur appears before congressional committees to plead for legislation pertaining to civil rights or the rights of older person. Democrats and

Republicans alike give him a respectful hearing. In one six-day period in 1990 he testified before four different committees on Social Security and civil rights proposals before the Congress.

The presidential campaign of 1988 between the Democratic candidate, Massachusetts Governor Michael Dukakis, and the Republican candidate Vice-President George Bush, did not find Arthur sitting quietly on the sidelines either.

He was convinced that legislation calling for universal right of access to health care,the inviolability of the Social Security system, and vigorous implementation of civil rights were the really important issues of the campaign, and that Michael Dukakis was the only candidate who addressed these issues candidly and forthrightly. As a result, Arthur decided to support the Democratic candidate. He became, along with Congressman Pepper, the co-chairman of Seniors for Dukakis.

One particularly enjoyable community involvement in the Washington area was his service as chairman of the board of the Greater Washington Community Foundation. He was given an original copy of the King James Version of the Bible in appreciation of this service, and this is certainly one of his most cherished possessions. He served as a member of that board for two two-year terms.

His membership and chairmanship of various boards, both local and national, boggles the mind. He chairs four local organizations and is a member of six others. On the national level, he chairs seven organizations, and is a board member of twenty-four others. Just counting them up makes me tired.

Arthur continues to receive awards in appreciation for his various activities. In the past years these have included the Leadership Conference on Civil Rights Hubert Humphrey Award, the Ollie Randall Award of the National Council on Aging, and The Caring Award presented to him by The Caring Institute as one of the most caring Americans for his "lifetime of public service and his constant crusade for social justice through service to seven presidents, concern for government employees, and example of being a public servant."

On September 28, 1989, at a dinner in downtown Washington honoring the memory of Congressman Claude Pepper, who died May 30, he was presented the first Pepper Distinguished Service Award by the Mildred and Claude Pepper Foundation. In identifying Arthur as the recipient, the program stated:

> Dr. Arthur Flemming is truly a man of the people, having devoted his life to serving humanity. All his endeavors have been marked by the same noble, dedicated spirit which characterized Claude Pepper's life, and his service has resulted in better lives for millions of Americans. The Mildred and Claude Pepper Foundation is honored to recognize the outstanding public service rendered by Dr. Flemming and to present to him the first Pepper Distinguished Service Award.

It was truly a night to remember, with Geraldine Ferraro as the master of ceremonies, Congressman Dick Gephardt the speaker, and Bob Hope as the entertainer. And I was seated next to Bob Hope at the dinner. What a thrill!

The occasion was a particularly memorable one for us as the planning committee had generously invited our children to attend. So Sue and John, Harry and Nancy, and Tom and Maria were there, too. Seated at the table with them were Marguerite Thomas, who for twenty years has managed Arthur's life at the office and has been able to see that he gets where he is supposed to be when he is supposed to be there, and Roberta and Jim Havel. Roberta is the executive director of SOS.

California State University at Los Angeles has established The Roybal Center for Applied Gerontology. In gratitude for Congressman Roybal's leadership in the field of aging funds were contributed to endow a chair at the center, which will also carry his name. To help in working out a program for the center the officials at Cal State, at the suggestion of Congressman

Roybal, sought the advice of Arthur. His years as a college president and teacher, plus his experience in the field of aging, made him a natural to help in planning this program. So several trips were made to Los Angeles for this purpose.

Sandwiched among speeches, meetings, and travels, there are frequent occasions for family celebrations. In a family the size of ours—five children and spouses, twelve grandchildren and eight spouses, and eleven great-grandchildren (at last count), life tends to be a fairly continuous round of special events. Birthdays, weddings, graduations, and christenings are all part of the pattern of our life. We manage to participate in virtually all of these events.

Throughout these pages much has been made of Arthur's exceptional physical stamina. In the fifty-five years of our marriage, I can remember only three times when he stayed at home because of illness. Each time he would stay in bed a day or two—never longer—and each time laid low by some kind of flu. At no time did he agree to my calling the doctor.

But an accident occurred right at home a little over a year ago that really grounded him. He fell over a stool in our living room one Friday night after he had turned all of the lights out, and he had to pay attention to the pain that followed the fall. Since I have been the victim of rib fractures at least five times myself, I diagnosed the injury as a rib fracture. So I gave him some Tylenol, and he went to bed. My own experience had taught me that there isn't much to do with a rib fracture except to wear a rib belt (to ease the pain a bit), rest, and remember to breathe deeply.

The next morning, Saturday, he got up and dressed and announced that he intended to keep a speaking engagement he had with a group of health care people at Sibley Hospital in Northwest Washington.

"You are not going to keep that engagement," I said. "You can get Sue to go in your place." Sue is a graduate oncology nurse with her own home oncology therapy business. She was amply qualified to take over this speaking chore.

He agreed to call Sue, and she readily agreed to rearrange her schedule and take over his engagement. That she was a most acceptable substitute was shown by the reaction he later had to her speech on that occasion.

After that he remained home for an entire week. Each morning, however, he got up and completely dressed as if going to his office. Sue came to see him every day to check his temperature, lungs, and blood pressure and called the doctor herself to report what had happened and what she was doing for him.

"I don't need to see him," the doctor said. "You are doing all of the right things, so just keep on with your routine."

Arthur didn't, of course, stay in bed, but spent his time in his den watching games, the news reports, and reading. After the first couple of days, when word got around about what had happened to him, he began receiving bouquets, fruit, books, and piles of "get well" cards. I think he really enjoyed this experience, even concluding that being confined at home wasn't too onerous after all.

Then it was back to work as usual.

Whenever he finishes one assignment, there is always something to replace it. The past year another new responsibility was undertaken when the Social Security administrator, Gwendolyn King, asked him to chair a group of persons from outside of government to make recommendations for modernizing the Supplemental Security Income Program for the Aged, Blind, and Disabled. Trips to all Social Security regional offices have been made, and hearings have been held in New York, Baltimore, Washington, Chicago, Montgomery, Alabama, Los Angeles, and Atlanta prior to recommendations being made to the president and to Congress.

At eighty-six, his shoulders are a bit stooped, his gait a bit slower, but when he opens his mouth to speak, his voice is clear and strong as he continues to crusade for the things he believes in.

ACKNOWLEDGMENTS

This book, begun in 1953, was originally undertaken to provide an account of Arthur's life for our children. It was completed in its original version in 1972, and was registered with the Library of Congress Copyright Office later. I had no intention at that time of EVER picking it up again.

Nearly ten years later, a guest in our home, Doctor Charles Duncan, retired Dean of the School of Journalism at the University of Oregon, asked if he could read it. I agreed, and he reacted with so much enthusiasm about it that for the first time it entered my consciousness that I might have done something worthwhile. Moreover, he insisted that I must take it up again and update it to include Arthur's public activities since 1972.

At that time, I really wasn't interested in adding to the book. But, in November, 1981, when President Reagan fired Arthur from the chairmanship of the United States Commission on Civil Rights, I was suddenly motivated and on fire to add the events of the years since then.

So, I am immensely grateful to "Chuck" Duncan for getting me back to work on the project.

A chance encounter with another academic professional, Professor Astere Claeyssens of the George Washington University, provided additional impetus. He, too, asked to read the book and subsequently added his voice in praise of it. He offered to help me find a publisher, but did not live to see this accomplished. Thank you, Astere, for encouragement and assistance.

Some of the nicest things that have happened to me in my long life have resulted from accidental seating arrangements at dinner parties. On one such occasion I chanced to be seated next to Bill Halamandaris, of Caring Publishing. Val Halamandaris, the publisher at Caring Publishing, was also present. Bill told me he was looking for a particular kind of book to publish, so I told him about mine. He came out to our house the following Monday to pick up the manuscript, and the outcome of that social encounter is that publication is set for late October, 1991. Thank you, Bill. Every single meeting with you over this project has been sheer pleasure.

This is also true of my association with Christopher Laxton, who has provided the editorial expertise. Thank you, Chris.

My grateful thanks are also herewith expressed to Rebecca Staebler, for editing and proofreading; to Tracy David, for help in transferring the manuscript to the computer; to Audrey Cowgill, for design and layout; to J. Andrew Simmons, for design of the dust jacket and design direction; and to the other members of the staff at Caring Publishing.

B.F.
September 9, 1991
Alexandria, Va.

A P P E N D I X

Honorary Degrees

The following institutions have conferred
honorary degrees on Arthur:

Doctor of Law

Ohio Wesleyan University, Delaware, OH, 1941
The American University, Washington, DC, 1942
Temple University, Philadelphia, PA, 1948
Connecticut Wesleyan University, Middletown, CT, 1949
Oberlin College, Oberlin, OH, 1950
Alfred University, Alfred, NY, 1954
Indiana Central College, Indianapolis, IN, 1955
University of Chattanooga, Chattanooga, TN, 1955
Albright College, Reading, PA, 1956
Davidson College, Davidson, NC, 1956
Illinois Wesleyan University, Bloomington, IL, 1956
Otterbein College, Westerville, OH, 1956
Tufts University, Medford, MA, 1956
Miami University, Oxford, OH, 1958
St. Louis University, St. Louis, MO, 1958
Georgetown University, Washington, DC, 1959
Adelphi College, Garden City, NY, 1959
Lehigh University, Bethlehem, PA, 1959
Gettysburg College, Gettysburg, PA, 1959
Albany Medical College of Union University, Albany, NY, 1959
Elizabethtown College, Elizabethtown, PA, 1959
University of Illinois, Urbana, IL, 1959
Dakota Wesleyan University, Mitchell, SD, 1960

Springfield College, Springfield, MA, 1960
Macalester College, St. Paul, MN, 1965
Rockhurst College, Kansas City, MO, 1967
University of Portland, Portland, OR, 1967
Moravian College, Bethlehem, PA, 1970
St. Michael's College, Winneski Park,VT, 1971
Atlanta University, Atlanta, GA, 1979
University of Massachusetts, Boston, MA, 1991

Doctor of Humane Letters

Case Institute of Technology, Cleveland, OH, 1954
College of Wooster, Wooster, OH, 1959
Kentucky Wesleyan University, Owensboro, KY, 1959
Yeshiva University, New York, NY, 1960
North Carolina College, Durham, NC, 1960
Simpson College, Indianola, IO, 1960
Morningside College, Sioux City, IO, 1961
College of Osteopathic Medicine and Surgery, Des Moines, IO, 1961
Monmouth College, Monmouth, IL, 1968
Detroit Institute of Technology, Detroit, MI, 1959

Doctor of Civil Law

Ohio Northern University, Ada, OH, 1954

Doctor of Public Service

Denison University, Granville, OH, 1956

Doctor of Public Affairs

Baldwin Wallace College, Berea, OH, 1959
Whitman College, Walla Walla, WA, 1962

Doctor of Humanities

Hunter College, NY, 1978
Wayne State University, Detroit, MI, 1982

Honors and Awards

Following is a partial list of the many honors and awards that have been conferred on Arthur:

Public Affairs

The United States Department of the Navy's Distinguished Civilian Service Award, August 1, 1944.

Society for Advancement of Management Award—in recognition of signal contributions to advancement of management in government, August 23, 1948.

Warner W. Stockberger Award of the Society for Personnel Administration for outstanding leadership in adapting federal personnel administration to the critical needs of the country during the recent war and post-war period, 1948.

Certificate of Achievement of the Chamber of Commerce of Kingston, NY, in recognition of unselfish service on behalf of his fellowman through outstanding national contributions to the general welfare of the country, February 2, 1950.

The Presidential Medal of Freedom, highest civilian award, presented by President Eisenhower, February, 1958.

The President's Committee on Employment of Physically Handicapped Commendation in grateful appreciation for service in behalf of our physically handicapped fellow citizens, January 5, 1961.

National Geriatrics Society Man-of-the-Year Award, May 13, 1972.

National Association of Retired Federal Employees Award for tireless work to secure a better life for America's older citizens, September, 1972.

Department of Health, Education, and Welfare Arthur J. Altmeyer Award for outstanding contributions to economic security, April 11, 1974.

The National Black Caucus on the Black Aged, Inc., Award for outstanding service to the aged and profound appreciation of his stalwart efforts on behalf of all elderly and his courageous and consistent support of us and his sincere care and concern about people of all races, creeds, and ages, May 7, 1974

American Association of Retired Persons Andrus Award, June, 1980.

Alice M. Brophy Award for unremitting dedication and commitment to the field of aging by Urban Elderly Coalition, November 5, 1980.

John F. Kennedy Lodge of B'Nai B'Rith "Profiles in Courage" Award, 1982.

Washington Urban League, Inc., Whitney M. Young, Jr. Memorial Award, March,1982.

Leadership Conference on Civil Rights Hubert Humphrey Civil Rights Award, 1982.

The National Urban Coalition Hubert H. Humphrey Humanitarian Award, 1982.

B'Nai B'Rith International Chai Award for outstanding contributions in area of community service, citizenship, and humanitarianism, April, 1983.

Common Cause Public Service Achievement Award for work in civil rights field, 1983.

Pacesetter in Public Administration in recognition of the outstanding contributions made to public administration profession, by the National Capital Area Chapter, American Society for Public Administration.

Government Accounting Office Public Service Award, November 28, 1984.

Public Employees Round Table Public Service Award, September 9, 1984.

National Consumers League Trumpeteer Award conferred on people who have not been afraid to raise their voices in support of social justice, a fairer marketplace, and a safer work place, 1987.

The Caring Institute of America selected Arthur Flemming as one of the most caring Americans and presented to him a Caring Award for his "lifetime of public service and his constant crusade for social justice through service to seven presidents, concern for government employees, and example of being a public servant." He was one of twelve selected from nominations by members of Congress, mayors of cities over twenty-five thousand, and eighteen thousand other leaders in business, media, and the arts to nominate the "most caring person they know," December, 1988.

The Mildred and Claude Pepper Foundation First Distinguished Public Service Award, September 1989.

The Allied Signal, Inc., Distinguished Achievement Award in Aging, November, 1990

Education

The American University Alumni Recognition Award for outstanding achievement in education and public affairs, May 28, 1948.

The George Washington University Alumni Achievement Award for notable achievement in the field of education and government and for conspicuous service to the university, June 3, 1958.

The Fairbanks Award of the American Collegiate Public Relations Association for distinguished service in higher education, 1960.

The Alexander Meikeljohn Award for the outstanding contribution to academic freedom in 1962, given by the American Association of University Professors.

The University of Oregon Department of Political Science Department conferred honorary lifetime membership in the department and Distinguished Service Award for duty above and beyond the call of students, faculty, and alumni and for service to the department, May 28, 1968.

National Education Association Special Award for civil rights and education, 1982.

National Education Association Friend of Education Award, 1983.

Church

The Washington Federation of Churches Annual Laymen's Award, 1949.

Membership in the Methodist Hall of Fame in Philanthropy.

Citation from the Council on World Service and Finance, in grateful recognition and sincere appreciation of outstanding work and meritorious service as a member of the Council of World Service and Finance of the Methodist Church during the years 1953–56.

Shepherd's Award by the National Council of Churches for Christ in America, October 7, 1961.

Annual Brotherhood Award of B'Nai B'Rith Portland Lodge #65, February 25, 1963.

Oregon Council of Churches Award for inspiring leadership, wise counsel, and generous giving of time and resources, December, 1966.

Annual Brotherhood Award of the National Conference of Christians and Jews, March 13, 1967.

The Russell Colgate Distinguished Service Citation for distinguished service to Christian education by the Division of Christian Education, National Council of Churches, November 29, 1969.

Century Club Award of Appreciation for friendship and generous support and service to young people through the Young Men's Christian Association.

Benjamin Mays Award for Christian Leadership in the Political Order, by the Center for Theology and Public Service, October 18, 1981.

General

Governor's Award for the Advancement and Prestige of Ohio, presented by C. William O'Neill, Governor

University of Oregon Distinguished Citizen Award, June, 1984.

Ohio Wesleyan University, Distinguished Achievement Award, June, 1982.

Ohio Senior Citizens Hall of Fame.

National Institute for Employment Equity "Milestone Recognition Award" for distinguished service in field of civil rights and equal employment opportunity, May, 1987.

National Association for the Advancement of Colored People Board of Directors Award, in recognition for exceptional service to older Americans, July, 1988.